Language and Class in
Victorian England

THE LANGUAGE LIBRARY

EDITED BY DAVID CRYSTAL

Language and Class in Victorian England

K. C. PHILLIPPS

Basil Blackwell
in association with
André Deutsch

© K. C. Phillipps 1984

First published 1984

Basil Blackwell Publisher Limited
108 Cowley Road, Oxford OX4 1JF, England

Basil Blackwell Inc.
432 Park Avenue South, Suite 1505
New York, NY 10016, USA

in association with André Deutsch Limited
105 Great Russell Street, London WC1B 3LJ, England

British Library Cataloguing in Publication Data

Phillipps, K. C.
    Language and class in Victorian England.—
    (Language library)
    1. English language—Social aspects—Great
    Britain   2. English language—Great Britain
    —Usage—History—19th century   3. Speech
    and social status—Great Britain—History—
    19th century
    I. Title   II. Series
    428   PE1073
ISBN 0–631–13689–4

*Also included in the Library of Congress Cataloging in Publication
lists*

Typeset by Thomson Press (India) Limited, New Delhi
Printed in Great Britain by The Pitman Press, Bath

For Jenifer

Contents

Acknowledgements

I wish to record my gratitude to my wife, whose wide reading in Victorian literature, and instinct for finding out the amusing anecdote, have been of great service in the compilation of this book; and to Dr Ian Fisher, who studied for a doctorate on a related topic under my direction, and whose conversation I found very stimulating. I should also like to thank Professor David Crystal, Editor of the Language Library, for his patience with my queries, and for the soundness of his advice.

Phonetic Symbols

The following letters are used as phonetic symbols with their usual English values: p, b, t, d, k, g, f, v, s, z, h, w, l, r, m, n. Other symbols are used with the values indicated by the italicized letters in the key-words below.

Consonants

ʃ	*sh*ip		θ	*th*in
ʒ	plea*s*ure		ð	*th*en
tj	*ch*in		j	*y*es
dʒ	*jud*ge		ç	German i*ch*
ŋ	si*ng*		ʍ	voiceless /w/

Vowels

i	s*i*t		ə:	b*ir*d
i:	s*ee*		*a*:	*fa*ther
y:	French s*û*r		ɔ	h*o*t
e	g*e*t		ɔ:	s*aw*
ε:	French f*ai*re		u	p*u*t
a	f*a*t		u:	s*oo*n
ə	fath*er*		ʌ	b*u*t

Diphthongs

ei	d*ay*		ɔi	b*oy*
ou	g*o*		iə	h*ere*
ai	fl*y*		εə	th*ere*
au	n*ow*		uə	g*our*d

Square brackets are used to enclose phonetic symbols. A colon after a phonetic symbol indicates length.

Introduction

The Victorians would not have known what was meant by U and non-U English. These convenient, if rather brash, terms for the language used by the upper and lower classes first appeared in 1954 in an article by Professor A. S. C. Ross in a Finnish periodical.[1] In the quarter of a century since then, partly owing to further publicity by Ross himself and by Nancy Mitford, these phrases acquired some currency and favour, though doubtless the phenomena they describe have been in retreat.

A curious anticipation of the Ross/Mitford commentaries is *The Social Fetich*, by Lady Agnes Grove which appeared in 1907. The book is dedicated to Thomas Hardy who, according to Robert Gittings (*The Older Hardy*, p. 128), probably helped with its production, though he does not seem to have curbed the whimsical and kittenish tone. Nancy Mitford's debt to Lady Grove (to whom she was related, incidentally) was considerable, particularly in matters of U and non-U behaviour and possessions. Lady Grove's strictures on language are spread abroad in the slim volume in random profusion. To write or say *a hotel* is as bad as styling a baronet's daughter *Lady* Araminta, and those who are guilty of inviting you to *take* food and drink would be quite capable of *taking* your umbrella (*or 'umberella'*, as they would doubtless pronounce it). *Blouse* and *envelope* should be pronounced in the French way; it is better to call a *piano* a *pianoforte*·and *port*, *port wine*.[2] But as an abbreviation *photo*, she says, is worse than *port*, and to be *photoed*, worse still. We may speculate here on the somewhat arbitrary limits of linguistic permissiveness; for popular usage, in fact, stopped short of *photoed* for *photographed* or, more usually, *having had one's photograph taken*. In much the same way, of two abbreviated words condemned by Victorian etiquette books, *thanks* for *thank you*, and *invite* for

---

[1] A. S. C. Ross, 'Linguistic Class-indicators in Present-day English', *Neuphilologische Mitteilungen*, 55 (1974), pp. 20–56; hereafter referred to as 'Ross'.

[2] 'It is the only wine to which the word itself is tacked on,' she writes, though earlier in the century Uncle Pumblechook, in Dickens's *Great Expectations* (ch. 4), somewhat punctiliously says: 'I have brought you, Mum, a bottle of sherry wine – and I have brought you, Mum, a bottle of port wine.'

invitation, the first is now acceptable everywhere, whereas the second has retained its vulgarity unscathed. The action of the U-speaker in insisting upon traditional usage is mostly a rearguard action, but sometimes the line holds.

Lady Grove's book is a late development, and probably a sign that a high society is in decline. To generalize and theorize about customs and shibboleths that should be inbred and taken for granted encourages self-consciousness and undermines confidence. She herself seems to have felt this when she writes of the forbidden word *gentlemanly*: 'If the expression is used at all, *gentlemanlike* is the word to use.'[3] More typical of the high Victorian way of dealing with these things is that of the irascible Johnny Stanley (of the same family), writing from Calcutta in 1860: 'Beale and Hills...are snobs – they talk of Lord Hay for Lord W. Hay, wear net neckcloths, they talk about gentlemen and say dresses for gowns' (*The Stanleys of Alderley*, p. 241). When we read this, we may reflect, not only that there are snobs and snobs (p. 45), but also that we are in the special territory that Nancy Mitford was to make peculiarly her own.

A glance at the table of contents will reveal that the information in this present book is weighted towards upper-class usage. This is due to the preponderant concern, not only in Victorian books of etiquette, but also in letters, memoirs and novels of the period, with the usage of high society. Writers all tend to be of the school of Mrs Elton in Jane Austen's *Emma*: 'One is apt', said Mrs Elton, 'to speak only of those who lead.' Manuals of etiquette, especially, tend to be written by anonymous members 'of the Aristocracy', and none, predictably, by a member 'of the Commercial Classes'. As long as the poor are regarded – as they often are in early Victorian novels – as picturesque individuals rather than members of a class, it is difficult to generalize about their speech. Moreover, the further down the scale we go, the greater the likelihood of a multiplicity of different provincial dialects, with which it would be unprofitable to tangle in an undertaking of this kind. Ross singles out the dialectal sentence 'That be worse nor Dunkirk's fall', said of the fall of Tobruk in a small Buckinghamshire town by a speaker aged about sixty, as certainly not U, but also as something quite outside the scope of a discussion on U and non-U class indicators (p. 24). It is not until the 1880s, with novelists like Besant, Rice and Gissing, that the poor are seen with the generalizing eye of the sociologist.

Queen Victoria's was not only the longest reign by any British monarch; it was also a time of unprecedented change, which included the gradual break-up of a rigid class-system. This last was felt as a matter for congratulation by

---

[3] Throughout the book, words in italics in quotations highlight the particular word or phrase under consideration.

many – by Charles Kingsley, for example, in the preface to *Alton Locke* (1850):

> The whole creed of our young gentlemen is becoming more liberal, their demeanour more courteous, their language more temperate. They inquire after the welfare or at least mingle in the sports of the labouring man, with a simple cordiality which was unknown thirty years ago . . . and that it is in any way degrading to 'associate with low fellows' is an opinion utterly obsolete.

The appeal by those who would break down the barriers was mostly to a common humanity. Even with the highest in the land, this solvent might work, as Mrs Carlyle noted in 1853:

> When I was paying a bill at Wain's on Monday, he asked with an attempted solemnity, 'had I heard the news?' 'No, I had heard nothing; what was it?' 'The Queen!' 'Well?' 'Premature labour.' 'Well; what of that?' 'But – accompanied with death!' 'The child you mean?' 'No, the Queen! – very distressing isn't it, ma'am – so young a woman? Is there anything I can have the pleasure of sending you today?' I hardly believed the thing, and by going a little further satisfied myself it was 'a false report.' But was not that way of looking at it, 'so young a woman,' noteworthy? Mr Wain being a model of respectable shopkeepers. What a difference since the time of the Princess Charlotte! (*Letters*, p. 240).

When it came to such matters of life and death, the extremes met, as that favourite subject of early Victorian balladmongers, the Royal couple seen as a working–class husband and wife in time of childbirth, demonstrates. Mrs Gaskell reflects the theme in *Mary Barton* (1848) when the question arises, in workaday Manchester, of whether married women should be employed in factories:

> 'I wish our Jem could speak a word to th'Queen, about factory work for married women' . . .
> 'I say it's Prince Albert as ought to be asked how he'd like his missis to be from home when he comes in, tired and worn . . . and maybe, her to come in by-and-by, just as tired and down in th' mouth.' (chapter 10)

But such confusion of rank, and consequently of language, was rare in the early Victorian period. In *Middlemarch*, for example, set at the time of the 1832 Reform Bill, George Eliot speaks of certain old families in the town who were 'conscious of an inherent social superiority which was defined with great nicety in practice, though hardly expressible theoretically' (chapter 23). What was true of *Middlemarch* was true of Victorian society generally, and language was a principal, precise, pragmatic, and subtle way of defining one's position, or of having it defined by others. It is the aim of this book to illustrate these distinctions and definitions.

I

The Upper Classes

THE LANDED GENTRY

The question of refinement in speech was a matter of far more importance in nineteenth-century England than it is today. If asked, our grandfathers and great-grandfathers would have said that the best speech was that of the court and of the gentry, or of the nobility and the gentry; perhaps even, if the question had been put to our more rural and bucolic ancestors, of the 'quality'. The further question raised here, of what constitutes a gentleman or a lady, brings us to one of the central issues of many novels of the early and mid-Victorian period. In practice, for the nineteenth-century reader there were various moral, social, cultural and financial considerations, and these were variously invoked. There were, to start with, as they would have said, both meritorious and traditionary considerations:

> And then came to her mind those curious questions: what makes a gentleman? what makes a gentlewoman? ... And she answered the question. Absolute, intrinsic, acknowledged, individual merit must give it to its possessor .... So far the spirit of democracy was strong within her. Beyond this it could be had but by inheritance, received as it were second-hand, or twenty-second hand. And so far the spirit of aristocracy was strong within her. (Anthony Trollope, *Dr Thorne*, chapter 6)

We may trust the Victorians to put moral considerations first, but this is not the etymological priority. C. S. Lewis (*Studies in Words*, p. 21) speaks of the 'moralization of status words', whereby those words implying superior status can become terms of praise, those implying inferior status, terms of disapproval: as for example, *chivalrous* and *gentle* compared to *ignoble* and *villain*. However, it is thus that Trollope's base-born Mary Thorne meditates on a proposal of marriage from the squire's son Frank Gresham. Indeed the conflicting claims of an established aristocracy and a rising meritocracy, within an existing social framework, forms one of the commonest themes of mid-Victorian novels.

To Robert P. Ward, writing in 1827, there had seemed in effect to be little problem in the distinction that Mary Thorne here attempts to make. In practice he thought the man of merit was likely to be the man of high birth:

> By a gentleman, we mean not to draw a line that would be invidious between high and low, rank and subordination, riches and poverty. The distinction is in the mind. Whoever is open, loyal and true; whoever is of humane and affable demeanour, whoever is honourable in himself, and candid in his judgement of others, and requires no law but his word to make him fulfil his engagement; such a one is a gentleman, and such a man may be found among the tillers of the earth. But high birth and distinction for the most part insure the high sentiment which is denied to poverty and the lower professions.

This passage, from Ward's *De Vere; or the Man of Independence*, is quoted as a footnote to a lively discussion of the subject of gentlemen in a volume of 'Sketches of a Country Town' by Mary Russell Mitford, published in 1835 under the title *Belford Regis* (III, chapter 1). Fine though this definition is in Miss Mitford's opinion, she observes that English country practice is grounded more pragmatically on the answer of Mr Dubster in Fanny Burney's *Camilla*: when asked what made him a gentleman he gravely replied, 'Leaving off business'. Yet the subject of gentility, as Miss Mitford realizes, is much more problematical than this, and it is particularly difficult in 'the midland counties close to London'. In London itself, the question is easily settled. A man 'falls insensibly into that class to which his rank, his fortune, his habits, and his inclinations are best adapted'. In the distant provinces class division is also easy, because traditional. 'There, the inhabitants may almost be comprised in the peasantry, the yeomanry, the clergy, and the nobility and gentry.' But in the 'small midland counties close to London', where 'persons of undoubted fortune but uncertain station are as plenty as blackberries', the 'provincial lord chamberlain' is hard put to it 'to grant or refuse the privilege of entrée'. Incidentally, it is worth noting that both 'the provincial lord chamberlain' and Miss Mitford seem to have been spared, or to have conveniently ignored, the further confusion that was to arise from the claims of all the prosperous would-be gentlemen from the industrial north.

As to the cultural and educational implications of the word, these are evoked with his usual quick-wittedness by Archdeacon Grantly at the end of Trollope's *The Last Chronicle of Barset*, when Grace Crawley, daughter of the eccentric and indigent curate of Hogglestock, Josiah Crawley, is to marry the Archdeacon's son, Major Grantly. Clearly some adjustment is called for on both sides. Both Grantly's snobbery and Crawley's inverted snobbery must be kept in check. Crawley must wear a black dress coat, and Archdeacon Grantly must recognize that Crawley is that most dangerous of parsons, the parson who will not fill his after-dinner glass. But on one point there proves to be complete agreement between the two men. When

Crawley laments his inability to provide a dowry for his daughter, and expresses a wish that he and the Archdeacon 'stood on more equal grounds', the Archdeacon rises from his chair:

> 'We stand,' said he, 'on the only perfect level on which such men can meet each other. We are both gentlemen.'
> 'Sir,' said [Crawley], rising also, 'from the bottom of my heart I agree with you. I could not have spoken such words; but coming from you who are rich to me who am poor, they are honourable to the one and comfortable to the other.' (chapter 83)

Crawley here would see their common education and vocation as qualifications for the title. Archdeacon Grantly is chiefly using the word *gentleman*, one suspects, to relieve an embarrassing situation. Indeed, with speakers possessed of less presence of mind than the Archdeacon, the processes of selection and definition are often a cause of embarrassment, as in this second instance from the same novel:

> Mr Walker ... had explained, in a manner intended to be half earnest and half jocose, that though Mr Toogood was an attorney like himself... still he wasn't quite – not quite, you know – 'not quite so much of a gentleman as I am' – Mr Walker would have said, had he spoken out freely that which he insinuated. (chapter 42)

Trollope proceeds to justify Mr Walker's distinction here, and to justify it on more worldly grounds than the perpetual curate of Hogglestock would have liked:

> As regards the two attorneys, I will not venture to say that either of them was not 'a perfect gentleman'. A perfect gentleman is a thing I cannot define. But undoubtedly Mr Walker was a bigger man in his way than was Toogood in his, and did habitually consort in the county of Barchester with men of higher standing that those with whom Mr Toogood associated in London.

Over and above such pragmatic considerations, were considerations of heredity. Writing of the 1840s, Augustus Hare (*The Story of My Life*, I, p. 137) notes that there was still a decided preference for what was sometimes called a 'gentleman born':

> The curates always came to luncheon at the Rectory on Sundays. They were always compelled to come in unceremoniously at the back door, lest they should dirty the entrance; only Mr Egerton was allowed to come in at the front door, because he was a 'gentleman born'.

Gentleman, nevertheless, was not a word to be too much insisted on. In chapter 14 of Thomas Hardy's *A Pair of Blue Eyes* (1873), Mrs Swancourt and her protegée Elfride Swancourt are out in their carriage in Hyde Park, when Elfride artlessly says, 'I have noticed several ladies and gentlemen looking at me.' To which Mrs Swancourt replies:

> 'My dear, you mustn't say "gentlemen" nowadays.... We have handed over "gentlemen" to the lower classes, where the word is still to be heard at tradesmen's balls and provincial tea-parties, I believe. It is done with here.'
> 'What must I say then?'
> '"Ladies and men" always.'

Grace Crawley has some difficulty on this point, when she writes to Major Grantly refusing his offer of marriage in the circumstances of her father's trial for theft: 'I know [she writes] that a gentleman ought not to marry any girl to do himself and his family an injury by it' (*The Last Chronicle of Barset*, chapter 36). But Grace, unlike Elfride, is aware of the solecism. Discussing the letter afterwards with her mother, she says:

> 'It was such a bad letter.'
> 'I daresay it was very nice.'
> 'It was terribly stiff, and all about a gentleman.'
> 'All about a gentleman! What do you mean, my dear?'
> 'Gentleman is such a frightful word to have to use to a gentleman; but I did not know what else to say.' (chapter 41)

If Grace Crawley and Elfride Swancourt can make such errors, what chance has poor Ruby Ruggles, from the lower orders, in Trollope's *The Way We Live Now*, (chapter 48)?

> Ruby was glib enough with her pen, though what she wrote will hardly bear repeating. She underscored all her loves to him. She underscored the expressions of regret if she had vexed him. She did not want to hurry *a gentleman*. But she did want to have another dance at the Music Hall.

The truth was that the word *gentleman* was heavy with moral overtones, and this tended to make it objectionable in everyday contexts. However, it could be used with devastating effect in rebuke, as when Tennyson's wife, Emily, wrote to Lewis Carroll refusing him permission to keep a manuscript copy of one of the Laureate's poems: 'A *gentleman* should understand that when an author does not give his works to the public he has his own reasons for it' (R. B. Martin, *Tennyson: The Unquiet Heart*, p. 487).

A sociolinguistic point parallel to the use of *gentleman* occurs with *lady* in Henry Kingsley's *Ravenshoe* (1862). This rather underrated novel turns on the hero, Charles Ravenshoe, a well-educated member of the upper classes, being ousted from his position and deliberately (and, it seems, perversely) sinking himself into anonymity as a groom. Here his employer asks about a lady of his acquaintance, and Charles replies: '"Handsome?" "Remarkably so. Possibly the handsomest (he was going to say 'girl' but said 'lady') I ever saw in my life"' (chapter 36). Obviously, Ravenshoe nearly forgets that he is a groom, and is about to refer to the female in question on terms of equality, as a *girl*. To quote Trollope on this point (*Framley Parsonage*, chapter 10): 'Girls are girls from the age of three up to forty-three, if not previously married.' However, as a servant, it is Charles Ravenshoe's place, as he realizes, to refer to a lady as a *lady*. Incidentally, the two quotations, from *A Pair of Blue Eyes* and from *Ravenshoe*, tend to give the lie to Ross's statement (p. 21n): 'Forty years ago [i.e. in 1914] U-speakers made use of *lady* and *gentleman* without self-consciousness.' Ross goes on to say: 'Today [i.e. in 1954] the use of these words in the sense "man" and "woman" between U-speakers has almost entirely vanished save when prefixed with *old*.' My reading of Victorian literature suggests, to the contrary, that these upper-class inhibitions about referring to an individual as *a lady* or *a gentleman* are at least a century old.

Confirmation of this is found in an anonymously published book, *Society Small Talk, or What to Say and When to Say It* (1879). This has a valuable chapter on 'Vulgarisms of Speech', in which priority is given to what was clearly a vexed question: when to use the words *man, woman, gentleman* and *lady*:

> In common parlance a man is always a man to a man and never a gentleman; to a woman he is occasionally a man and occasionally a gentleman; but a man would far oftener term a woman 'a woman' than he would term her 'a lady'. When a man makes use of an adjective in speaking of a lady, he almost invariably calls her a woman; thus he would say, 'I met a rather agreeable woman at dinner last night;' but he would not say, 'I met an agreeable lady;' but he might say, 'A lady, a friend of mine, told me,' etc., when he would not say, 'A woman, a friend of mine, told me,' etc. Again, a man would say, 'Which of the ladies did you take in to dinner?' He would certainly not say, 'Which of the women' etc.

When both the sexes are to be considered together, *Society Small Talk* recommends, not *men and women*, which is 'very advanced', nor *ladies and gentlemen* which is 'all but vulgar', but a compromise: *ladies and men*. As we see by comparing this with the quotation from *A Pair of Blue Eyes* above, Thomas Hardy had done his homework! One consideration here is that the words *lady* and *gentleman* are used so much more freely by the lower ranks of society, that an impression of unctuousness or ingratiation can be suggested by their uninhibited use among equals. Clearly it was with relief that upper-class people proceeded as quickly as possible to such a state of informality as made the two words *lady* and *gentleman* more or less unnecessary:

> When people are on ceremony with each other, they might perhaps in speaking of a man call him 'a gentleman', but otherwise it would be more usual to speak of him as 'a man'. Ladies, when speaking of each other, usually employ the term 'woman' in preference to that of 'lady'. Thus, in speaking of

each other they would say, 'She is a very good-natured woman', 'What sort of a woman is she?' the term 'lady' being entirely out of place in such circumstances. Again, the term 'young lady' gives place as far as possible to the term 'girl', although it greatly depends upon the amount of intimacy existing as to which term is employed.

As early as 1834, a manual of *Hints on Etiquette* had warned against 'the fear of being thought vulgar' which drives 'meritorious people, who have risen by their own exertions' to make excessive effort to be 'superlatively delicate'. 'Such people are shocked at the word *breeches*, will substitute *inebriated* for "very drunk", and cannot be brought to allow that there are such animals as *women* in the world.'

There was a further fear that the appellations *lady* and *gentleman* (titles, after all) had become too common. Hence the affected pseudo-tolerance of the snobbish Lady Agnes Grove, writing at the beginning of this century in *The Social Fetich* (p. 116):

> I never think of disputing the coveted title of 'young lady' to the 'young persons' who serve one in shops, and I hold that a person is a fool who does. Whereas the male servers are perhaps the only individuals about whom I use the word 'gentleman'. The story is told of the beautiful Duchess of Somerset that when someone asked her in a shop, 'Was this the gentleman who served you?' she replied, 'No, it was that nobleman with the bald head.' But nowadays we are less high-handed and more democratic; perhaps also less witty.

When Mrs Trollope, mother of Anthony Trollope, went to America (*Domestic Manners of the Americans*, chapter 10), she may well have felt that these fears about the variable status of *lady* and *gentleman* were realized:

> My general appellation amongst my neighbours was 'the English old woman', but in mentioning each other they constantly employed the term 'lady'... as 'the lady over the way, what takes in washing' or as 'that there lady out by the gulley, what is making dip-candles'. Mr Trollope was as constantly called 'the old man', while draymen, butchers' boys, and the labourers on the canal were invariably denominated 'them gentlemen'.

Yet our own world shows signs of being as topsy-turvy as Mrs Trollope's America. Female scientists rescued from South Georgia during the Falklands crisis were referred to as 'women scientists', while in the same news bulletins of spring 1982 school dinner servers were described as 'dinner ladies'.

With *lady* as with *gentleman*, a comparable amount of embarrassment about eligibility can occur. Here a minor character, Mr Oriel, in *The Last Chronicle of Barset* (chapter 55), is asking Mark Robarts for information about Grace Crawley:

> 'Is she—what you call—?'
> 'You mean, is she a lady?'
> 'Of course she is by birth, and all that,' said Mr Oriel, apologising for his inquiry.
> 'I don't think there is another girl in the county so well educated,' said Mr Robarts.

The path to the social position of lady was not an easy one. Besant writes, in 1882 (*All Sorts and Conditions of Men*, chapter 17): 'many men have fallen in love with dressmakers; some dressmakers have acquired partially the manners of a lady.' The essential attributes of a lady, according to George Eliot (*Silas Marner*, chapter 11), are 'high veracity, delicate honour in her dealings, deference to others, and refined personal habits'.

Clearly, up to the mid-century and beyond, how acceptable the courtesy titles of *lady* and *gentleman* were depended on the outlook, democratic or otherwise, of the speaker. Lady Harriet Cumnor, in Mrs Gaskell's *Wives and Daughters* (1865), explains that she has a relative who is too exclusive in this matter:

> Any one who earns his livelihood by any exercise of head or hands, from professional people and rich merchants down to labourers, she calls 'persons'. She would never in her most slip-slop talk accord them even the conventional title of 'gentlemen'.

The phrase *young person*, used by Lady Grove above, was especially useful to describe young ladies when there was some doubt concerning their status: 'They are not young ladies, they are young persons' says Pooh-Ba in *The Mikado* (Act I). A short story entitled 'A Genteel Establishment', in *Household Words* (1852, IV, p. 561), makes some gradations clear:

> I have frequently seen this gardener in conversation with a young – no, not a lady; and yet she was scarcely so low as what we understand by an 'individual' or a 'party'. A *young person* is the word.

The phrase was dismissive, however. Surtees, in *Handley Cross* (1843), tells of a Miss Menlove, who felt that though her acquaintance, Mrs Flummocks, 'Miss Menloved' her to her face, she '*young person'd* her behind her back' (chapter 62). The status of the *person* makes an ideal subject for the pen of Henry James:

> The functionary whom in America we know and dread as an hotel-clerk belongs in England to the sex which, at need, is able to look over your head to a still further point. Large hotels here are almost always owned and carried on by companies, and the company is represented by a well-shaped female figure belonging to the class ... known as 'persons'. The chamber-maid is a young woman, and the female tourist is a lady; but the occupant of the glass cage,

who hands you your key and assigns you your apartment, is designated in the
manner I have mentioned. The 'person' has various methods of revenging
herself for her shadowy position in the social scale, and I think it was from a
vague recollection of having on a former occasion felt the weight of her
embittered spirit that I determined to seek the hospitality of the humbler inn.
(*English Hours*, 1879, p. 268)

These gradations were important, and the distinction, or lack of
distinction, which they imparted was deeply felt, particularly in the earlier
years of Victoria's reign. Augustus Hare, for example, looked back wryly
from the 1890s on the strongly demarcated class-system of his youth:

Then Uncle Julius turned round, and in a voice of thunder, audible to every
one on the road, exclaimed, 'Ignorant and presumptuous young woman!' He
had never seen her till that day. As she said to me years after, when she was a
wife and mother, 'That the Archdeacon should call me ignorant and
presumptuous was trying, still I could bear that very well; but that he should
call me a *young woman* was not to be endured!' (*The Story of My Life*, I,
p. 110)

In this important matter of what constitutes a lady or gentleman, it is
possible to declare oneself out of court by the very phraseology with which
one discusses the issue:

'Quite the gentleman,' was the Captain, according to the waiter, and 'one of
the handsomest gents as ever he'd set his eyes upon'. (Trollope, *The Vicar of
Bullhampton*, chapter 29)

Phoebe ... who looked, in her pink wreath and white muslin dress, 'quite the
lady', at least in her mother's eyes. (Mrs Oliphant, *Salem Chapel*, chapter 34)

Mrs Oliphant's inverted commas are very significant. At the beginning of
the century a similar phrase could be used by Jane Austen with no sense of
irony. Colonel Fitzwilliam, in *Pride and Prejudice* (chapter 30), was 'not
handsome, but in person and address most truly *the gentleman*'; while Jane
Fairfax had, according to Frank Churchill, 'a most distinguishing
complexion – so peculiarly *the lady* in it!' (*Emma*, chapter 64).

The abbreviation *gent* occurs in the quotation from *The Vicar of
Bullhampton* above, and the following item from the 1854 volume of *Punch*
(p. 39) illuminates its status:

Railway Guard to Third Class: Where's the man that has been smoking? He
had better not let me catch him. I'll soon put his pipe out.
To Second Class: Now, gents, smoking isn't allowed – it's a fine of forty
shillings.
To First Class: If you please, gentlemen, smoking is against the rules. I
must require you to put your cigars out.

There were many who qualified but imperfectly for the title of gentleman, though they probably considered themselves eligible. Such people had their uses, to make up a whist club in a small place like Jane Austen's Highbury, for example: 'a whist club established among the gentlemen and *half-gentlemen* of the place' (*Emma*, chapter 24). Forty years later, the type was still extant: 'He was only what may be called an *intermediate gentleman*, that is to say, he could act the gentleman up to a pint of wine or so, after which quantity nature gradually asserted her supremacy, and he became himself again' (Surtees, *Ask Mamma*, chapter 31). No-one was ever much deceived by spurious gentility, least of all the servants, whose intonation might reveal much: 'We all know the tone in which servants announce gentleman when they know that the gentleman is not a gentleman,' writes Trollope (*Can You Forgive Her?*, chapter 60). For the opposite sex, too, there were disqualifications. Mrs Brattle, a miller's wife in *The Vicar of Bullhampton* (chapter 7), was 'a modest, pure, high-minded woman, – whom we will not call a lady, because of her position in life, and because she darned stockings in a kitchen.'[1] It follows that the adjective *ladylike* must not be too lightly bestowed. Mary Graham questions her Uncle, Dr Thorne, about his possible marriage to the rich, but rather raucous Miss Dunstable:

> 'I'm sure she's clever.'
> 'Yes, I think she's clever.'
> 'And, and – and *womanly* in her feelings.' Mrs Gresham felt that she could not say *ladylike*, though she would fain have done so had she dared. (*Framley Parsonage*, chapter 28)

The masculine equivalent of *ladylike* is perhaps *gentlemanly*, though this word had been under some proscription from the earliest part of the century. H. C. Wyld, in his *A History of Modern Colloquial English* (p. 17), quotes one of Macaulay's letters (28 May 1831), in which he records that Lady Holland objected to certain words, saying: 'Then there is *talented*, *influential* and *gentlemanly*. I never could break Sheridan of saying "gentlemanly" though he allowed it was wrong.' There is an amusing short story by Meredith, 'The Case of General Ople and Lady Camper', which

---

[1] A particularly heinous misdemeanour throughout the century, it would seem. Jane Austen called, in September 1804, on a Miss Armstrong: 'Like other young ladies she is considerably genteeler than her parents. Mrs Armstrong sat darning a pair of stockings the whole of my visit. But I do not mention this at home, lest a warning should act as an example.' *Letters*, p. 142. Paradoxically, the kind of ornamental needlework that ladies employed themselves in was often called, throughout the century, by those who engaged in it, *work*. 'Will you ring the bell for some *working* candles?' asks Lady Middleton in *Sense and Sensibility* (ch. 23). Bulwer Lytton, in *A Strange Story* (1862), writes of a character as taking pleasure neither 'in music, nor books, nor that tranquil pastime which women call *work*' (ch. 48).

first appeared in 1877, and which turns on the assertion of superiority by a
member of the landed gentry over a man from the City. What is important
for our purpose is that this assertion takes a largely linguistic form. Lady
Camper, niece of an Earl, asserts with confidence her social ascendancy over
General Ople, a man 'with many City friends', to obtain a husband 'tuneable
so as not to offend her ears'. *Gentlemanly* is one of several words she
proscribes:

> 'I say, I am no longer young, but I call the place a *gentlemanly* residence. I was
> saying, I . . . .'
> 'Yes, yes!' Lady Camper tossed her head, half closing her eyes with a
> contraction of the brows, as if in pain.
> He perceived a similar expression whenever he spoke of his residence.
> (chapter 2)

At the end of the century, Lady Agnes Grove, in *The Social Fetich* (p. 11),
also forbids *gentlemanly*: 'If the expression is used at all, "gentlemanlike" is
the word to use.' But clearly she thinks it is not desirable to use such
expressions, perhaps from an aristocratic belief that to become self-
conscious on what should be taken for granted undermines confidence.

Incidentally, Lady Camper prohibits the word *female*, even as an
adjective. Discussing her Christian name of Angela, the General ventures
that 'there is not a more beautiful female name', and receives the reply:
'Spare me that word "female" as long as you live' (chapter 4). This word
does indeed deteriorate in the course of the century. While Jane Austen
could write, 'He and the *females* of the family were sitting together' (*Pride
and Prejudice*, chapter 56), *female* as a synonym for 'woman' (though not
necessarily in General Ople's adjectival use), is now, according to the *OED*,
'commonly avoided by good writers, except with contemptuous
implication'.

As always in English society, old-fashioned ideals and revolutionary
aspirations can exist side by side. By the 1880s, partly owing to the vast
extension in the number of 'gentlemen' foreseen fifty years before by Miss
Mitford (p. 5), the very idea of a gentleman is being repudiated by, for
instance, some of the characters in Gissing's *Demos* (chapter 1):[2]

> Gentleman . . . Upon my word, that is the vulgarest of denominations! Who
> doesn't call himself so nowadays! A man's a man, I take it, and what need is
> there to lengthen the name? Thank the powers, we don't live in feudal ages.

The hero of this novel, the revolutionary Richard Mutimer, considers the
term *lady* in the same light (chapter 8):

[2] It is amusing, from more than one viewpoint, to find that as late (or as early) as 1891, one of
Gissing's characters inquires: 'But is an advertising agent a gentleman?' (*New Grub Street*,
ch. 22).

How often he had spoken scornfully of that word 'lady'! Were not all of the sex women? What need for that hateful distinction? Richard tried another experiment with his imagination. 'I had dinner with some people called Waltham last Sunday. The old woman I didn't much care about; but there was a young woman'... Well, why not?

Why not indeed? Yet even the young Marxist of the 1980s might still hesitate, as did the young socialist of the 1880s, before using the words *lady* and *woman* interchangeably on all occasions, especially, as Ross points out (p. 21n), for elderly members of the species. Nor was this depreciation of the concept of the gentleman entirely new with Gissing. Already in *North and South* (1854) Mrs Gaskell, through that robust northerner John Thornton, had upheld the cause of *man* as against *gentleman*:

> 'I take it that "gentleman" is a term that only describes a person in his relation to others: but when we speak of him as "a man", we consider him not merely with regard to his fellow-men, but in relation to himself – to life – to time – to eternity.... I am rather weary of this word "gentlemanly", which seems to me to be often inappropriately used, and often, too, with such exaggerated distortion of meaning, while the full simplicity of the noun "man", and the adjective "manly", is unacknowledged – that I am induced to class it with the cant of the day.' (chapter 20)

The collective noun *gentry* was one that some gentlefolk[3] seem to have had reservations about. For one thing, it had long been possible to use the word in a dismissive and ironic way, as when a character in Peacock's *Crotchet Castle* observes sarcastically, of journalists, 'Truly, the praise of such *gentry* must be a feather in any one's cap' (chapter 5); or when Lady Stanley uses the word of middle-class excursionists from Manchester, trespassing on Alderley Edge: 'The Manchester *gentry* are much more annoying to one's comfort and enjoyment than operatives as one can neither hand cuff nor great dog them if they are intrusive' (*The Ladies of Alderley*, p. 62). Wilkie Collins, in *The Woman in White* (1860), calls *gentry* a 'detestable word': 'I wish I could say the same of the *gentry* – detestable word, but I suppose I must use it – of the gentry in the neighbourhood' (chapter 7). The word might be detestable, but as a subject for novel-writers, the gentry had their appeal. In May 1886 *The Mayor of Casterbridge* completed publication serially, but Thomas Hardy had it published in volume form only with some difficulty. The publisher's reader for Smith, Elder complained that the lack of gentry among the characters made the novel uninteresting (Florence Emily Hardy, *The Life of Thomas Hardy*, I, p. 236).

Still more dubious was the word *genteel*. It could be used without irony by

---

[3] *Gentlefolk*: '"They're *gentlefolk*" meaning "they're U" is an expression once used by the U. It can hardly be heard today' (Ross, *Don't Say It*, p. 55).

Jane Austen but, to quote the *OED*: 'a few years before the middle of the nineteenth century this word was much ridiculed as being characteristic of those who are possessed with a dread of being taken for "common people", or who attach exaggerated importance to supposed marks of social superiority.' From that time on, it was hardly possible to use *genteel* for serious effects. We find Trollope, for example, resorting to the older word *gentle*, where *genteel* would have come naturally to Jane Austen: 'There were also other visitors [at a squire's coming-of-age party] of the *gentle* sort, to do honour to the occasion' (*Dr Thorne*, chapter 1). In Trollope's novels the word is chiefly used by, and of, those who have no claim, to say the least, to the status of hero or heroine. In language that betrays her limitations, Mary Snow (*Orley Farm*, chapter 48) writes to Felix Graham, to whom she is engaged to be married but whom she is not destined to marry, about a third person: 'He is quite a *genteel* young man, and very respectable in the medical line.' Still more interesting is Mrs Gaskell, describing the young Dr Gibson: 'Rather handsome than otherwise; thin enough to be called "a very *genteel* figure" in those days, before muscular Christianity had come into vogue' (*Wives and Daughters*, chapter 3). Obviously, by 1865 the slim and perhaps slightly dandified figure that formed an ideal of masculine good looks in the first forty years of the century had given way to the Broad Church *machismo* of the muscular Christian; and it is equally clear that the word *genteel*, compared to its earliest use, had acquired a suggestion of effeteness which it has never entirely lost. *Society Small Talk* (p. 115) couples *genteel* with *stylish* as 'tabooed' words among the 'vulgarisms of speech':

> 'Stylish' and 'genteel' are relegated to the show-room, where they are very much at home in each other's company.... 'Stylish' being bred in the show-room is the right word in the right place, but it is hard upon unfortunate 'genteel', that, conveying in itself so much, it should have met with such a fate.[4]

There is evidence that *genteel* had been demoted in status even earlier than the *OED* suggests, in a passage from *Pelham*, by Bulwer Lytton, published in 1828. In this novel a conversation takes place between Henry Pelham, of impeccable ancestry and upbringing, and a middle-aged, obviously less well-bred, citizen of Cheltenham (not so refined a town in

---

[4] Further evidence of the unacceptability of *stylish* is found in the *OED*, which quotes Lady Frances Verney (1884): 'But *stylish* is of the shop, shoppy, and belongs to the dialect of milliners' apprentices and waiting-maids alone... in England.' Yet the first quotation for *stylish* is from *Sense and Sensibility*, and for *stylishness*, from *Northanger Abbey*. *Stylish* is one of many words that deteriorated as the century progressed. The word which replaced it, to a great extent, was *smart*, which, far from being taboo, was a vogue word, at least in the 1880s. The word had long been in use, yet the *OED* (*smart*, sense 13) talks of the 'reappearance of the word in this sense' from about 1882, with phrases like *smart people*, *smart set* etc.

1828 as it was later to become). I have followed Lytton in italicizing the 'vulgarisms':

> 'The society is very good still, is it not?'
> 'Oh, very *genteel*,' replied the man, 'but not so *dashing* as it used to be. (Oh! these two horrid words! low enough to suit even the author of "————").'
> 'Pray,' asked I, glancing at Messrs Ritson and Smith, 'do you know who those gentlemen are?'
> 'Extremely well,' replied my neighbour; 'the tall young man is Mr Ritson; his mother has a house in Baker Street, and gives quite *elegant* parties. He's a most *genteel* young man; but such an insufferable coxcomb!'
> 'And the other?' said I.
> 'Oh! he's a Mr Smith! His father was an eminent brewer..... The young Smith is a very *knowing hand*, and wants to spend his money with spirit. He has a great passion for "high life" and therefore attaches himself to Mr Ritson, who is *quite that way inclined*.' ...
> 'I shall die,' said I to myself, 'if I talk with this fellow any longer.' (chapter 40)

Apart from *genteel*, some other italicized words may call for comment here. *Dashing* is defined by the *OED* as the action of 'cutting a dash', and this word, like the phrase *high life*, perhaps carries a suggestion of self-consciousness and self-congratulation that is not thought typical of the best society, members of which are expected to take to their life-style with a certain nonchalance. As George Eliot puts it in *Daniel Deronda* (chapter 14), in the best society 'the advantages of the world are taken with that high-bred depreciation which follows from being accustomed to them.' It is surprising to see the word *elegant*, so often and so precisely used by Jane Austen, also consciously italicized by Lytton. Yet there are, as the *OED* points out, vulgar and indiscriminate applications of this word (*elegant*, sense 8, 'vulgarly used for "excellent, first-rate", in humorous literature sometimes as an "Irishism" with spelling *iligant*'). The anonymous author of *The Vulgarities of Speech Corrected* (1826) warns against the wholesale use of the word:

> I once knew a tradesman at a fashionable watering-place, who had picked up the word 'elegant', which he applied without distinction to every thing, and talked of 'elegant weather', 'an elegant morning' or 'an elegant day' ... to the no small amazement of many of his customers, who laughed heartily at his affectation. (p. 18)

If some Regency expressions had lost status, there were other words and turns of phrase which, though old-fashioned, carried prestige, and marked the speaker as the kind of person designated by Ross as 'old-fashioned U'. The elderly Lady Lufton, in Trollope's *Framley Parsonage*, a refined yet self-willed Tory of the old school, might well have been, when young, a spirited heroine of one of Jane Austen's novels. Her use, for example, of the word *country* recalls that of Jane Austen. *Country* for both ladies is a word with strong proprietary and localized overtones.[5] To quote R. W. Chapman's appendix to his edition of *Sense and Sensibility*, in Jane Austen's novels 'except when opposed to town, *country* means a district.' Similarly with Lady Lufton:

> She liked cheerful, quiet, well-to-do people, who loved their Church, their country, and their Queen. . . . She desired that all farmers round her should be able to pay their rents without trouble... that the working men should be saved from rheumatism by healthy food and dry houses; that they should all be obedient to their pastors and masters. . . . That was her idea of loving her country. She desired also that the copses should be full of pheasants, the stubble-fields of partridges, and the gorse covers of foxes; in that way, also, she loved her country. (chapter 2)

Country in these limited and localized senses became less common as the century continued. Perhaps not even Lady Lufton would have talked, as Jane Austen did, of 'a proper unobjectionable *country* family' (*Emma*, chapter 26), in a sense of the word which is nowadays borne by the word *county*.

County, in the sense of 'county gentry and county families collectively' was, accordingly, somewhat new in Victorian times. Mrs Gaskell evidently thinks that Mrs Gibson (*Wives and Daughters*, chapter 16) insists upon it rather too much: 'Amongst the "county people" (as Mrs Gibson termed them) who called upon her as a bride, were the two young Mr Hamleys.' The younger of these two men did not appeal to her: 'a clumsier, more common, awkward stupid fellow, I never saw – to be called "*county*", I mean[6] (chapter 35). By extension, the word came to be not merely a matter of territory, but also of personalities. Squire Brown writes to his undergraduate son: 'It will give me the opportunity of introducing you to my brother magnates from other parts of the county. . . . It is a good thing for a young man to know his own *county* well' (Thomas Hughes, *Tom Brown at Oxford*, chapter 29).

The cardinal significance of land in all this is obvious; and we may trust Archdeacon Grantly to have seen its importance: 'Land is the only thing that can't fly away. And then, you see, land gives so much more than the rent. It gives position and influence and political power, to say nothing about the game' (*The Last Chronicle of Barset*, chapter 68). Compared to

---

[5] A localized sense of the word is still retained in hunting contexts. Henry Kingsley, in *Leighton Court* (1866) writes: 'The *country* was a difficult, nay dangerous *country*, but then, with its continually recurring copses, it was a very slow *country* . . . a better *country* for a lady, perhaps, than faster *countries* nearer London (chapter 5).

[6] This use of a sort of conditional infinitive is probably another instance of Mrs Gibson's lack of refinement, in such contexts. Cf. Mrs Oliphant, in *Salem Chapel* (chapter 21): '*To be only tradespeople* they do dress more than I approve of.'

land, everything else in the early Victorian period seemed unstable: 'A banker's profession is so insecure,' writes Lady Stanley in 1844, as she confidently contemplates her Cheshire acres (*The Ladies of Alderley*, p. 84). Land, and plenty of it, was a method of asserting one's position among the landed. Hence a recurring emphasis on the word *park*, without which a house might have to be called something as ignominious as a *grange* (p. 86). A character in Miss Braddon's *Lady Audley's Secret* (1862) lived in a 'prim, square, red-brick mansion... in the centre of prim, square grounds, scarcely large enough to be called a park, too large to be called anything else – so neither the house nor the grounds had any name' (chapter 23). With a spacious park one might aspire, by a notable understatement, to a *place*; something about which already, in *Mansfield Park*, Henry Crawford has definite ideas:

> The air of a gentleman's residence... you cannot but give it.... But it is capable of much more.... You may raise it into a *place*. From being the mere gentleman's residence, it becomes, by judicious improvement, the residence of a man of education, taste, modern manners, good connections. (chapter 25)

It undoubtedly sounded well to say, of an acquaintance: 'Sir Charles Buckhurst... a Berkshire man: Shirley Park is his *place*' (Disraeli, *Coningsby*, I, chapter 6). As Trollope put it: 'I don't know that there is any kind of life better than that of an English country gentleman in his own *place*' (*Can You Forgive Her?*, chapter 5).

In a small country like England there can be only a few large landowners, who will tend to be aristocratic in outlook. We are not surprised, then, that, speaking as he does in favour of land, Archdeacon Grantly is one of those who uses the word *democratic*, as it could be used in the last century, with very unfavourable overtones of mob-rule. In his eyes, Trollope tells us, there was something '*democratic* and parvenue' about a round dining-table (*Barchester Towers*, chapter 21). With an equally unfavourable use of the word, Mrs Gibson (*Wives and Daughters*, chapter 58) warns her step-daughter: 'Now, Molly, I can't have you democratic. Rank is a great distinction. It is quite enough to have dear papa with *democratic* tendencies.' The combined elements of birth, money and position that are summed up in the word *interest* make themselves felt, though the word itself becomes rarer as the century proceeds. Archdeacon Grantly felt that 'the church was beautiful... because one man by *interest* might have a thousand a year, while another man, equally good, but without *interest*, might only have a hundred' (*The Last Chronicle of Barset*, chapter 83).

It is against this solid background of rank, land, and property that the customs and usage of upper-class society must be seen. Marriage, clearly, was of vital importance in the transfer of such property, and again the language, particularly the language of the elderly, is often conservative.

When, for example, Mrs Grantly, wife of Archdeacon Grantly, wishes to see her daughter married, she uses a word which suggests this territorial stability, and Trollope makes a significant comment:

> Mrs Grantly, however, had been heard to say, that she was in no hurry to see her daughter established in the world – ordinary young ladies are merely married, but those of real importance are *established*. (*Framley Parsonage*, chapter 11)

Griselda Grantly eventually makes a prestigious match with the Whig magnate Lord Dumbello, and Lady Lufton magnanimously congratulates Mrs Grantly on her match-making, using the word *alliance* which, with its dynastic overtones, is especially gratifying:

> 'I am sure I hope she will be very happy,' said Lady Lufton, 'and I trust that the *alliance*,' – the word was very agreeable to Mrs Grantly's ear – 'will give unalloyed gratification to you and her father.' (chapter 30)

Lady Bracknell, in Wilde's play *The Importance of Being Earnest* (1895), uses the same word when turning down Jack Worthing's application for her daughter's hand, refusing to let her 'marry into a cloak-room, and form an *alliance* with a parcel!' When matches are seen in a less favourable light, the word *alliance* tends not to occur. Mrs Gowan, in *Little Dorrit* (I, chapter 26) feels that her son has not prospered by marrying Minnie Meagles: 'Henry might have done much better; there is scarcely anything to compensate for the *connection*'. She realises, however, that the Meagles family would be pleased: 'I know such people will do anything for the honour of such an *alliance*.' The choice of words here depends on the point of view. It is interesting too that Jane Austen speaks of an *establishment* being formed for wealthy daughters on marriage; and of *alliances* or *connections* according to the advantageousness, or otherwise, of a match.

In the changing world of nineteenth-century England, however, more uneven, and less prestigious 'alliances' were becoming common, even in the best society. The main plot of *Framley Parsonage* turns on this point. Should Lord Lufton stoop to Lucy Robarts, a doctor's daughter? For his part, Lord Lufton asserts that he would be a Radical, only that it would break his mother's heart. It is clear too that the appeal that he and Lucy have for each other is all the greater because of their differences in rank. But Lucy draws back: 'What will *the world* say of me as to such an alliance?' (chapter 16). *World* is used here in a sense corresponding to the *OED* sense 17: 'Human society considered in relation to its activities, difficulties, temptations and the like; hence, contextually, the ways, practices, or customs of the people among whom one lives; the occupations and interests of society at large'. In the game of Consequences, which is first illustrated in the *OED* from Jane

Austen, the final question, after the match-making, is always what the world said, with *world* used in just such a way.

The impression of universality in this use of *world* is an illusion. The habit of limiting oneself to certain acquaintances, excluding others, and calling the result 'the world' is not a peculiarly English habit of mind, as expressions like *tout le monde* and *demi-monde* indicate. Indeed, C. S. Lewis (*Studies in Words*, p. 266) thinks that *world* in some contexts is an attempt to render the French *le beau monde* or *le monde*. At all events, there were those, even in the nineteenth century, who found this use of the word constricting: '"My dear, he knows the world!" "He knows the peerage!" said Laura peevishly.' This is Laura Seckerton, heroine of Henry Kingsley's *Leighton Court* (chapter 5). Kingsley goes on to explain: 'Laura, you see, did not believe in the grand monde. She believed that the real great world was the wide world the sailors and soldiers told her of!' Nevertheless, 'the world' could be a *grand monde* indeed, as when Disraeli writes with relish of an entertainment of June, 1879: 'The Wiltons gave... a dinner to the Prince of Wales... and afterwards, the principal saloon turned into a charming theatre received *the world* to witness the heroine of the hour, Sarah Bernhardt' (*Letters to Lady Bradford and Lady Chesterfield*, II, p. 224).

A phrase that occurs quite often in Trollope is *before the world*, that is, in the public eye. The assumption is that by living in, and being seen by, the best society, one learns to cultivate *sang froid* and *savoir faire*. Thus, though Johnny Eames arrives late at a party, it does not signify:

> They were a little later than they should have been had they considered that Eames was to be introduced to his new acquaintance. But he had already lived long enough *before the world* to be quite at his ease in such circumstances. (*Last Chronicle of Barset*, chapter 24)

Mark Robarts, in *Framley Parsonage*, 'had not so full a command of his feelings as his brother-in-law, who had been so much more *before the world*, (chapter 10). Presumably the converse of this is *out of the world*, meaning not moving in fashionable society. Thus Squire Dale is scandalized by Crosbie's jilting of his niece, Lily Dale, but wonders whether he should be: 'I have lived a good deal *out of the world*, and am, therefore, perhaps, more astonished than I ought to be' (Trollope, *The Small House at Allington*, chapter 29). Amusingly, this recalls the use of the same phrase by Mr Woodhouse in *Emma* (chapter 29), when he reacts to the rather less serious misdemeanour of leaving windows open at public dances: 'Bless me! I never would have supposed it. But I live *out of the world*, and am often astonished at what I hear.'

A parallel exclusiveness, suggested paradoxically by a word that connotes universality, is noted by Disraeli in *Endymion* (chapter 47):

'I will send to Lord Willesden and Henry Grantley immediately, and perhaps you will send a card, which I will write here, for me to the new man.'
And in this way Mr Ferrars soon found that he was what is called *'everywhere'*.

The pronouns *somebody* and *nobody* had long been used in a socially exclusive way with an indefinite article, meaning 'a person of consequence' or the reverse. When there was no article, the usage could be ambiguous:

London, *June (in the Park)*,
Fine Lady: How strange it is to see all these smart carriages driving about and
   nobody in them.
My simple self: Nobody in them! why, they are quite full of people.
Fine Lady: Ah, ye-es – people, but nobody all the same. *We* never drive in
   the Park now. It was only to show you this mob that I came....
   They drove us out of the Row long ago. (Augustus Hare, *The
   Story of My Life*, 1874, IV, p. 199)

In much the same way, Disraeli writes in a letter: 'London quite *empty*, only ... a million of vulgar' (*Letters*, II, p. 164).

Disraeli was one of the last fashionable writers to refer to London as *town*, as Jane Austen and Thackeray had done. Queen Victoria quotes Lord Melbourne: 'My mother used always to have her chair, and it was the usual mode of conveyance; *the Town* is grown too large for it now!' (*Girlhood of Queen Victoria*, II, p. 95). This had been common usage since 1700, according to the *OED*, but by the end of the nineteenth century it had ceased to be fashionable, doubtless because the expression was being taken over by an increasing army of commuters. Lady Grove, in *The Social Fetich* (p. 11), manages a neat side-blow at England's second city in her condemnation of the expression:

[Vulgar people] are pretty nearly certain to go up 'town' or leave 'town', as the case may be, the town in question, the existence of which is thus uniquely recognized, not being, as one might suppose it to be, Birmingham, but London.

Town for London has continued to be non-U usage in England throughout this century. Ross confirms Lady Grove's condemnation.

As the seat of government and the home of the monarch, the site of their town houses and the venue of the Season, London had a firm place in the affections of upper-class English men and women; but still stronger was their attachment to the countryside. The first Lady Stanley writes, in 1849: 'I would not exchange with anybody in London now I have smelt and looked at the country' (*The Ladies of Alderley*, p. 201). H. C. Wyld, in his *A History of Modern Colloquial English* (p. 167), sees a strong link with the country estate as an important traditional influence in upper-class speech:

All of the fine ladies and gentlemen of the Court, from the days of Charles II to those of Anne, spent some portion at least of each year on their estates; they might affect to jeer at rustic speech, but they were not unfamiliar with it, and its accents doubtless often mingled with their own, as they lapsed in unguarded moments into the speech of their native county. It is just this constant touch with country pursuits and rustic dialects which distinguished, and still distinguishes, the upper classes from the middle classes in towns . . . . It was possible to speak with a rustic accent and still be a gentleman; it was not allowable to speak like a 'Sunday citizen' or a 'comfit-maker's wife' . . .

Wyld is writing here mainly of the Restoration period, but as he implies, there is continuity in the attitudes revealed. A good deal of prejudice still existed in Victorian times among the landed classes against the language of middle-class townsmen with no roots in the country – the townsmen who took to the countryside for occasional recreation. The word *cockney* could be used with the meaning 'a townsman, as the type of effeminacy, in contrast to the hardier inhabitants of the country' (*OED* sense 3). Disraeli, in *Coningsby* (1844), describes a badly furnished mansion with 'large tasteless lamps and tawdry chandeliers, evidently true *cockneys*, and only taking the air by way of change' (IV, chapter 9). 'The modes and manners of the house', he continues, 'were not rural; there was nothing of the sweet order of a country life' – he means, of course, upper-class country life. It is the message, too, of *Mansfield Park*. *Cockney* was also a word frequently on the lips of the Poet Laureate (from deepest Lincolnshire after all), to describe urban intruders into his peace at Farringford. The story is told that on one occasion, when reading *Maud* aloud, he came to the well-known passage, 'Birds in the high Hall-Garden', calling 'Maud, Maud, Maud, Maud', and turned to a nervous hearer, asking her what birds they were: 'Nightingales, Mr Tennyson'. 'Pooh', he thundered, 'you *Cockney*! They were rooks!' (See Joanna Richardson, *The Pre-eminent Victorian* p. 141).

Thus it came about that, while every care was to be taken not to acquire a cockney or other city accent, it was permissible even in the nineteenth century, when the old and new public schools were spreading much more uniformity in upper-class speech, for a country squire to give some indication of his rural origin. Squire Hamley of Hamley, in *Wives and Daughters* (chapter 22), could both converse with his fellow gentry and speak to his farm labourers 'from time to time in their own strong nervous country dialect'. He favours idioms in dialectal syntax, as: 'It's a very dangerous thing to shut two young men of one and three and twenty up. . . with a girl of seventeen – *choose what* her gowns may be like, or her hair, or her eyes' (chapter 7). John Clark, in his *The Language and Style of Anthony Trollope* (p. 87), draws attention to the point in Trollope's *John Caldigate* (chapter 23) where Caldigate, the squire, adjusts his speech 'with delicate courtesy' to that of his tenant:

'I can tell from their very walk what sort of mothers they'll be . . . . But it ain't only that, squoire.'

'The *young 'un* will do well too, I hope.'

'In course he will.'

Again, when the patrician hero, Charles Ravenshoe, in Henry Kingsley's novel, meets a fellow Westcountryman in Oxford, the following dialogue ensues:

'Where be gwine? Charles Ravenshoe, where be gwine?'

'We'm gwine for a ride on the watter, Jan Lee.'

'Be gwine in the 'Varsity eight, Charles Ravenshoe?'

'Iss, sure.' (chapter 22)

So they continue, 'to the great astonishment of the surrounding dandies'.

In this way country vigour and freedom from inhibition are extolled over town-bred dandyism. Even in the country, however, there were signs of change, and of a more fluid society in Victorian times than earlier. Conflict between tradition and change is well illustrated by Trollope in *Barchester Towers* (chapter 35), with his account of Miss Monica Thorne's *fête champêtre* and the problems that ensue. Miss Thorne's arrangements were orderly and traditional:

> The quality, as the upper classes in rural districts are designated by the lower with so much true discrimination, were to eat a breakfast, and the non-quality were to eat a dinner. Two marquees had been erected for these two banquets: that for the quality on the esoteric or garden side of a certain deep ha-ha; and that for the non-quality on the exoteric or paddock side of the same.

The phrase *the quality* for 'the nobility and gentry', which had been in regular use in Jane Austen's day, generally occurs in mid-Victorian novels in inverted commas, or with some indication, such as Trollope gives here, that it is a bucolic and obsolescent usage. Interestingly, and rather exceptionally, the Miss Brownings, in *Wives and Daughters* (chapter 21), had in their youth followed the earlier usage of separating the nobility as the quality, from the gentry:

> I don't mean but what the gentry took their daughters to York, or to Matlock, or Bath, to give them a taste of gay society when they were growing up; and the quality went up to London, and their young ladies were presented to Queen Charlotte, and went to a birthday ball perhaps.

There is a further, and rather amusing distinction, made by Trollope in *The Vicar of Bullhampton* (chapter 17), between the nobility, or at least landed magnates, and lesser landowners. A small squire, Mr Gilmore, is described by the Marquis of Trowbridge as 'a man not big enough to have his tenants called *his people*'.

NAMES FOR MEALS

Looking again at the *Barchester Towers* quotation above, we can see already
a distinction that Ross was to make a hundred years later: the quality are to
eat a breakfast, no doubt because they have dinner in the evening. Ross
(p. 43) is quite categorical on this point: 'U-speakers eat lunch in the middle
of the day...and dinner in the evening.... Non-U speakers (also U-
children[7] and U-dogs), on the other hand, have their dinner in the middle of
the day.'

There still is a great divide over names of meals, though no doubt less so
than a hundred years ago. Occasionally a compromise was possible, by
giving the same meal different names: 'The testimonial...should be
presented at a half-a-crown six o'clock meal, which would serve the
aristocracy for a dinner, and the democracy for a supper' (Surtees, *Handley
Cross*, chapter 55).

Ross's formula is an easy one, but the question of meal-times is more
problematic the further back into the nineteenth century we go. In the
appendix to the Oxford edition of Jane Austen's *Emma*, R.W. Chapman
points out that at the beginning of the century the best people breakfasted at
about ten o'clock (sometimes taking a walk before breakfast), and dinner
seems to have been at various times between four o'clock and six-thirty, or
in fashionable circles even later. Sometimes, in Jane Austen's novels,
mention is made of an informal midday meal, a *luncheon* or a *nuncheon*, but
the two main occasions for food were breakfast and dinner. The differentiation of two rooms, in most substantial houses, as *dining-room* and *breakfast-
room* (the latter dating, the *OED* quotations suggest, from the early
nineteenth century), indicates the preponderance of these two meals in
'Society'.

Charlotte M. Yonge, like Jane Austen, occasionally corresponded with
aspiring young authors, and in a letter of 1864 she provides a historical
novelist with interesting details of the meal-times of her own youth (she was
born in 1823). Perhaps because there were children in the Yonge household,
dinner was what we should call a late midday meal:

> I do not think luncheon was a regular meal, and high teas were never heard of.
> Indeed I think a 'noon-cheon' as even my grandmother used to call it was only
> a refection of bread and fruit or bread and cheese when dinner was as late as
> three o'clock, and that the chief meal was at two or three in all but the grandest

---

[7] William Brookfield, in 1844, notes this distinction about Marlborough: I dined in Hall,
almost as at Cambridge, a dinner being provided for the Masters at a table separate from and
placed a foot higher than those at which the youngsters dine at one (when the Masters
lunch)' (*Mrs Brookfield and her Circle*, I, p. 134).

houses keeping London hours. (Georgina Battiscombe, *Charlotte Mary Yonge*, p. 114)

A midday dinner was also routine for that family man, the Vicar of Bullhampton. On Sundays, at least, they had a *late dinner* at the Vicarage at half-past two, and there is mention elsewhere in the novel of going for a walk after tea in an August dusk. This suggests a sort of high tea: late, final and substantial (*The Vicar of Bullhampton* chapters 2, 50). Ladies, at least, might dress for such a tea (*North and South*, chapter 4), but then some ladies dressed and re-dressed frequently as a way of proving their refinement. The punctilious Miss Marrable in *The Vicar of Bullhampton* 'dressed with the greatest care, always wearing silk at and after luncheon. She dressed three times a day, and in the morning would come down in what she called a merino gown' (chapter 9). Miss Marrable, be it noted, spoke of *luncheon*. The abbreviation *lunch*, though it is the usage of good speakers in the novels, was frowned on in some circles. Even as late as 1903, the editors of the *OED* describe *lunch* as 'a more colloquial synonym of *luncheon*; now the usual word except in specially formal use, though many persons object to it as vulgar'.

The tradition of a very light luncheon, in expectation of an early dinner, died hard. It seemed to represent a primordial rural abstemiousness. Writing of the 1850s, Dean Hole recalls (*Then and Now*, p. 176): 'Luncheon consisted of a glass of sherry and a biscuit (dinner being at five or six o'clock).' By the time of *Can You Forgive Her?* (1864–5), this was thought inconveniently early. At Vavasor Hall in the Lake District, home of Alice Vavasor's grandfather, it was 'at the vexatious hour of five' (chapter 31).

As luncheons became more substantial, anxiety about the danger of over-eating was voiced. Trollope, who was always happy to see the middle classes reconciling themselves to their station in life, approved of the action of the wife of a well-to-do and aspiring tradesman in *Ralph the Heir* (chapter 5):

> When the villa at Hendon had been first taken, Mrs Neefit had started late dinners; but that vigilant and intelligent lady had soon perceived that this simply meant, in regard to her husband, two dinners a day, and apoplexy. She had, therefore, returned to the old ways, – an early dinner for herself and daughter, and a little bit of supper at night.

There might be seasonal variation in the time of the evening meal:

> His Lordship, who always ate a hearty lunch, was generally very easy about the matter [of dining hours], sometimes dining at seven, sometimes at eight, sometimes in summer even at nine o'clock. (Surtees, *Ask Mamma*, chapter 77)

The earlier pattern of meal-times, which Jane Austen would have found normal, can alternate, for special purposes, with the more fashionable late dinner. In Clough's poem *The Bothie of Tober-na-Vuorlich* (1848), a reading-party of young Oxford students in Scotland have an earlier dinner-time in high summer with the chance of an evening walk:

> Reading nine hours a day with the Tutor, Hobbes and Airlie;
> One between bathing and breakfast, and six before it was dinner
> (Breakfast at eight, at four, after bathing again, the dinner)
> Finally, two after walking and tea, from nine to eleven.

When the days are shorter, in September, the reading-party have a late dinner to allow as much daylight as possible to view the Scottish scenery in the afternoon:

> Breakfast at eight, and now, for brief September daylight,
> Luncheon at two, and dinner at seven, or even later.
> Five Full hours between for the loch and the glen and the mountain.

The fact that Clough devotes so many of his hexameters to the subject suggests what a live issue the hours of dining were in the mid-century. They represented a focus of anxiety at a time when new wealth was sharply questioning old social values. Innumerable instances point to the ubiquity of this topic, but we might finally consider *Wives and Daughters* (1865). In this novel Mrs Gibson, a rather foolish and socially insecure person, is invited to the house of Lord and Lady Cummor for lunch, and to meet the Duchess of Menteith. She is annoyed when Lord Cumnor, possibly not without malice, refers to the meal as her dinner:

> In vain she piped out in her soft, high voice, 'Oh, my lord! I never eat meat in the middle of the day; I can hardly eat anything at lunch!' Her voice was lost, and the duchess might go away with the idea that the Hollingford doctor's wife dined early. (chapter 25)

Though 'desperately hungry', Mrs Gibson sends away most of her lunch to prove her social status. Some time later, Lady Harriet, daughter of the Cumnor family, pays a call on Mrs Gibson, and asks at midday if she may have lunch with the Gibson household:

> Oh, I only want a little bread-and-butter, and perhaps a slice of cold meat – you must not give yourself any trouble, Clare – perhaps you dine now? Let me sit down just like one of your family. (chapter 32)

Mrs Gibson agrees willingly, but scotches any suggestion of a midday 'dinner': 'Yes, you shall; I won't make any alteration . . . But we dine late; we only lunch now.' This strenuous refinement is something of an imposition on the rest of Mrs Gibson's household. When she goes to stay in London for a week her husband and her step-daughter Molly look forward to returning to their former unregenerate condition. Molly thinks:

We'll have bread-and-cheese for dinner, and eat it on our knees; we'll make up for having to eat sloppy puddings with a fork instead of a spoon all this time, by putting our knives in our mouths till we cut ourselves. Papa shall pour his tea into his saucer if he's in a hurry; and, if I'm thirsty, I'll take the slop-basin. (chapter 40)

Mrs Gibson, as Mrs Gaskell makes clear in this chapter, wishes to 'squeeze herself into "county society"', and two of her methods are to dine late in emulation of the gentry, and to discourage 'tea-drinkings' with the townsfolk of Hollingford. Here, as in some other contexts, dinner and tea act as social distinctions. At least since the time of the founder of Methodism, John Wesley, the Nonconformists have been associated with tea. '[An invitation] to dinner, Arthur?' says Mrs Vincent wryly to her son, the Nonconformist minister at Salem Chapel. 'I thought your people only gave teas.'[8] But Arthur is delighted to tell his mother that he has not been invited by any of the Salem people, but by 'one of the great people in Carlingford, Lady Western' (Mrs Oliphant, *Salem Chapel*, chapter 12).

THE REGENCY LEGACY

It is intriguing to observe the continuance of Regency vocabulary well into the Victorian period in society novels. It is vocabulary that a Ross of the time, had there been such a person, would probably have classified as 'old-fashioned U'. To some extent there was a tradition of appropriate language handed down, for novel-writing purposes, from Richardson and Fanny Burney and Jane Austen, to writers as different as Mrs Gaskell and Thackeray. Certain themes, such as courtship, had their own terminology, and since courtship happened in life as well as in novels, there was no doubt a linguistic interaction between the two. A novel like Mrs Gaskell's *Wives and Daughters*, which Norman Page, in *The Language of Jane Austen* (pp. 191–2), rightly sees as very Austenian, makes use of language that had grown customary with the best people over at least a century, though one suspects that some usage was consciously archaic by 1865. When Mrs Gibson in this novel (chapter 26) allows that her daughter may speak to the nobility if spoken to with the words 'I'm *candid* about that, at any rate', using *candid* in the sense 'liberal, generous', rather than 'frank'; when Sir

---

[8] Probably *teas*, the plural of the word, was in itself not refined. The early and mid-Victorian phrase, since *dish of tea* had become archaic and dialectal, was *to take tea*, though the later Victorian etiquette books condemn this also as sounding too predatory. The unrefined Mrs Goodenough invites people to 'come and drink tea' (*Wives and Daughters*, chapter 40). This, along with the aforementioned *tea-drinkings* of Hollingford townspeople, is clearly non-U. The ultimate grammatical corollary of *teas* and *coffees* is their use in the singular with the indefinite article, as 'Would you like a tea or a coffee?' Most speakers with any claim to refinement still avoid this.

Charles Morton *notices* Molly Gibson's better health to Lady Harriet, or, as we might say (in a non-U way), passes a remark about it (chapter 58); when the woman who is soon to be Mrs Gibson shows a 'becoming *consciousness*' in the company of Dr Gibson, that is an awareness tending to warmth of feeling to the point of embarrassment (chapter 10); when the same Mrs Gibson finds the company of a certain young man 'a very pleasant *variety*', or as we should say 'a change' (chapter 29); when Mrs Gaskell, as narrator, writes of 'the *stretch* of restraint' that her heroine is living in (chapter 48), or of her hero writing 'a manly *feeling*, sensible letter' (chapter 33) – in all these and many other instances there is a quiet assertion through language that this is a refined, old-fashioned tale in an upper-class idiom that has been tried and tested for its purpose.

The last example, 'a feeling, sensible letter', embodies that favourite idiom of the first quarter of the century, the present participle used adjectivally. In her *Letters* (p. 229), Jane Austen writes of 'a very kind and *feeling* letter'. When he came to write his last novel, *Endymion* (1880), Disraeli described his young hero of the 1820s as 'Under-Secretary of State, and "very *rising*"' (chapter 3), quoting in inverted commas the idiom of sixty years before, the present participle being used adjectivally to the extent of being modified by an adverb of degree. Disraeli began as an outsider, but made himself pre-eminently at home in the best society of mid-Victorian England. A considerable novelist as well as a statesman who was twice Prime Minister, he published no novels in the middle years of his political life, from *Tancred* (1847), to *Lothair* (1870). But he did note down a few reminiscences in the 1860s which are in a relaxed tone that brings us very near to his speaking voice. We may be sure that a man of his great intelligence, equipped with the linguistic skill of his race, and one so assiduous to impress the best society of his day, would have completely mastered the idioms and turns of phrase of the upper classes. What becomes clear, in reading the *Reminiscences*, is the extent to which they recall the language of the earlier novels, such as *Vivian Grey* (1826), and *Henrietta Temple* (1836). The impression gained from these *Reminiscences* is similar to that gained from *Wives and Daughters*: the upper classes tended, much more than the other classes, to favour, not antiquated, but old-fashioned idioms and vocabulary. Thus he describes a family as '*expensive* and embarrassed' (*Reminiscences*, p. 134), with *expensive* in the 'now rare' sense of 'extravagant'. A *position*, for him, can still be something that one posits, what we should call a proposition: 'But this does not affect my *position* that it is difficult if not impossible to ruin a family well rooted in the land' (p. 135). He is particularly fond of traditional terminology to sum up the character of politicians. Thus he tends to use the word *organization* in a sense which has been ousted by predominantly bureaucratic usage, of a person's temperament or 'make-up': 'Louis Napoleon was a very goodnatured man . . . . The first Emperor was not so . . . . There was no similarity in their *organization'* (p. 18). In *Endymion* (1880), he writes of 'Waldershore . . . one of those vivid and brilliant *organizations* which exercise a peculiarly attractive influence on youth' (chapter 22). Jane Austen's phrase 'a man of information' often recurs: 'the greatest bore in the House and perhaps in society, but . . . a man of great *information'* (*Reminiscences*, p. 87). 'Molé was a grandseigneur of the very highest breeding . . . . Excellent talents, very general *information*, a complete political culture' (p. 23), – the last word being used as something derived from the *OED* sense 3 (obsolete), 'the training of the human body'.

In his letters, Disraeli uses *curious* in the older sense of 'showing the interest of a connoisseur': 'a first-rate dinner which even Prince Hal [the future Edward VII], very *curious* in such matters, noticed with much praise' (1879, *Letters*, II, p. 260). Jane Austen, at the beginning of the century, had noted that Lord Bolton was 'particularly *curious* in his pigs, has had pigstyes of a most elegant construction built for them' (*Letters*, p. 36). It must also have been old-fashioned, by the 1870s, to *direct* a letter and to refer to the address as the *direction*: 'I'm glad to *direct* this to Melbury . . . . If Monty sees the *direction* he will begin to sigh' (*Letters*, II, p. 156).

Lest my examples be thought too literary, it is profitable to turn to an elderly letter-writer such as Maria Josepha, first Lady Stanley. She too keeps up certain usages. She has *promiscuously* in the sense of 'summarily, without ceremony': 'Here comes Nightingale [the doctor] *promiscuously*, not sent for' (*The Ladies of Alderley*, p. 158); and Jane Austen's word *blamable* meaning 'to blame': 'I shall make a close enquiry to find out who could have been so *blamable'* (p. 162); as well as the intransitive use of the verb *to fix* in the sense of 'to settle (to marriage)': 'This summer she hopes to dedicate to a little English tour not to be in a hurry to *fix'* (p. 77). When she encounters a new race of satirical critics at a ball in 1847, she has a word from her youth to describe them: 'She . . . had the amusement of seeing many *quizzes* as to dress among the Yeomanry wives and daughters' (p. 145). She too has the verb *to notice* meaning 'to mention': 'E. was the first to have a suspicion, and *noticed* to you that Albert always shook hands with Emmy at night, when the party separated' (p. 76). It might be pointed out, of course, that all elderly speakers use old-fashioned expressions. My contention is, however, that in a highly conservative society like Victorian upper-class England, these expressions carried more weight and were retained longer, being less readily dropped even by the younger generation. One notices also that, if there are two meanings for the same word, the older will quite often be upper-class. A good example occurs with the word *abroad* in Trollope's novel *Mr Scarborough's Family* (chapter 44). For Jane Austen this word usually meant 'out of the house', and Peter Prosper, an old-fashioned squire, maintains this meaning against Miss Thoroughbung, of the brewing trade, whose commercial interest leads her to accept recent developments in meaning more readily:

> 'I think you are inclined to be – gay .... While I am sober, and perhaps a little
> grave .... I fear that you would look for your bliss *abroad.*'
> 'In France and Germany?'
> 'When I say abroad, I mean out of your own house.'

It is not fashionable to criticize the novels of Jane Austen, but one way of characterizing them is to say that they are cool: cool, but relatively colourless – elegantly colourless, like Miss Tilney in *Northanger Abbey*, who always wore white. A reason for this is that she is much concerned with judging her characters, and therefore with abstract ideas – or, as she calls them, with typical lack of pretension, *notions*: 'Like my dear Dr Johnson, I beleive [*sic*] I have dealt more in notions than facts' she writes (*Letters*, p. 181). It is a playful reference, but one capable of a wider interpretation. To the Victorian, such a concentration on the abstract in a letter was less acceptable. We are reminded of Miss Matty's reading aloud of the letters of her elder sister, Miss Jenkyns, which were much influenced in style by Mrs Chapone, and more typical of the eighteenth century, doubtless, than any of Jane Austen's. 'Oh dear,' says the narrator, 'how I wanted facts instead of reflections, before those letters were concluded!' (Mrs Gaskell, *Cranford*, chapter 5). When Dickens, in 1854, came to write *Little Dorrit*, he saw the social arbitress, Mrs General, as embodying a negative, proscriptive and colourless tradition that was the adverse side of this coolness in Regency writing, the legacy of the eighteenth century. Mrs General corrects Fanny Dorrit's speech by substituting abstract rectitude for random vitality:

> 'I should think so,' observed Miss Fanny ... 'But they would not have been
> recalled to our remembrance, I suspect, if Uncle hadn't tumbled over the
> subject.'
> 'My dear, what a curious phrase,' said Mrs General. 'Would not inadvert-
> ently lighted upon, or accidentally referred to be better? (II, chapter 5)

'Up then would come Mrs General', writes Dickens (II, chapter 15), 'taking all the colour out of everything, as Nature and Art had taken it out of herself.' The prismatic art of Dickens gave licence to a more colourful language, but the patrician coolness of Regency English still made its influence felt amongst the writers of the time. To take one small example, Jane Austen is fond of framing sentences with the impersonal *there is* instead of a personal subject. A dentist in his surgery might still favour the phrase '*There was* a tooth amiss' (*Emma*, chapter 52). However, in Jane Austen the same clinical rectitude is extended to moral blemishes: 'She saw that *there had been* bad habits; that Sunday-travelling had been a common thing' (*Persuasion* chapter 17). We can observe this rather censorious formula continuing in the correspondence of the woman who was in some ways a lineal descendant of Jane Austen, Mary Russell Mitford:

John Ruskin, the Oxford Undergraduate, is a very elegant and distinguished-looking young man, tall, fair and slender – too slender, for *there is* a consumptive look. (*Life and Friendships of M. R. Mitford*, p. 374)

And in Mrs Gaskell:

Margaret thought him colder, if more brilliant than formerly; but *there were* strong intellectual tastes. (*North and South*, chapter 47)

And in Lord Stanley, writing to Lady Stanley in 1862:

I do not think Lady Bath is beautiful, *there is* a thinness of lip and pinched mouth. (*The Stanleys of Alderley*, p. 280).

Inheritor of these and other traditional formulas, the young Victorian of the upper classes, like all young people, would yet be learning to deride many features of the speech of the elderly whose archaisms might, to use Jane Austen's word, be 'too staring'. For this reason, because he was 'so quaint in his manners and so eccentric in his mode of speech', Archdeacon Grantly had at first hesitated to support the Reverend Josiah Crawley's promotion to the living of St. Ewold's (*The Last Chronicle of Barset*, chapter 82). Crawley favours words like *thereanent* (chapter 83) and *nathless* (chapter 74). He also uses the archaic construction, perhaps derived from his reading of older works of theology, of following the conjunction *as* with a present participle: 'On the lowest step of the throne of the Church no woman has been allowed to sit *as bearing* authority' (chapter 62); 'I say not this at all *as praising* myself' (chapter 68). He retains occasional third person singular endings in -*eth* ('It *seemeth* to me', chapter 68), and the Prayer Book usage of the auxiliary *do* in unemphatic positive sentences. Thus in a typical lament, he complains that Archdeacon Grantly has addressed him as '"My dear Crawley" – for of late there seems to have grown up in the world a habit of greater familiarity than that which I think *did* prevail when last I moved among men' (chapter 83). A similar character, created forty years before *The Last Chronicle of Barset*, is another old-fashioned clergyman, Christopher Clutterbuck, the unworldy and scholarly friend of the worldly Henry Pelham in Bulwer Lytton's novel *Pelham* (chapter 63). He frequently reads aloud to Pelham a Greek ode of his own composition, while treating his friend to a 'dish of tea' (the phrase in author's quotes indicates its obsolescence as early as 1828).[9] It is interesting to note the archaisms Clutterbuck shares with Crawley. He orders a barrel of oysters to be

[9] By the time of the publication of Thomas Hughes' *Tom Brown's Schooldays* (1857), the phrase was the usage of 'our grandmothers': 'The unfortunate bachelor their master, whose one enjoyment in the shape of meals was his "dish of tea" (as our grandmothers called it) in the evening; and the phrase was apt in his case, for he always poured his out into the saucer before drinking' (II, Ch. 8). This last can never have been a U habit, but schoolmasters, like Henry V and his Kate, have always been 'the makers of manners' within their little realms.

'dressed in the fashion that *seemeth* best' and uses phrases like 'In this I *do* strangely err,' and 'The boy is my nephew, a goodly child, and a painstaking,' where the absence of the prop-word *one* is abnormally archaic. Typically old-fashioned is the use of *grateful* for *gratifying*: 'I own that there is much that is *grateful* to the temper of my mind in this retired spot' (chapter 63).[10] A third clergyman with an old-fashioned turn of phrase is the Reverend Henry Fitzackerley Chamberlaine, bachelor uncle of Harry Gilmore, the hero of Trollope's *The Vicar of Bullhampton*. He specializes in a somewhat stale language of love: language traditional in old-fashioned dramas and novels, but felt as demeaning to an up-to-date love-affair of the mid-Victorian period:

> 'By the bye,' said he, 'what has become of that *flame* of yours, Harry?' Harry Gilmore became black and glum. He did not like to hear Mary spoken of as a flame.... 'Do you mean to say that you did not ask her, after all?' asked the uncle. 'If there be any *scrape*,[11] Harry, you had better let me hear it.'
> 'I don't know what you call a scrape,' said Harry. (chapter 24)

Such people are ridiculed for their old-fashioned expressions; as are Miss Monica Thorne, who still calls a drawing-room a *withdrawing-room*; and her brother, the bachelor Squire Thorne of Ullathorne, who, when in love, appears 'with antediluvian grimaces and compliments' which he has 'picked up from Sir Charles Grandison' (*Barchester Towers*, chapter 22, 46). Here, too, we might include a character like the ancient Dowager Viscountess Bellair, in Disraeli's *Henrietta Temple*, who has known 'the first macaroni and the last dandy', with her archaic figurative use of the verb *to taste*, meaning 'to appreciate', and her antiquated verb *to beau*, meaning to escort': 'She is charming, she will *taste* you, she will be your friend' (IV, chapter 5); 'The girls must *beau* themselves, for I have no young men today for them' (VI, chapter 3). Clearly the language of the upper classes should avoid, at its best, the eccentricity, the tedium, and the over-formality of earlier times.

Yet, if on the one hand Sir Charles Grandison was dead and done for, on the other, colloquial and bantering tones, in the early and mid-Victorian period at least, might be carried too far between ladies and gentlemen:

> 'You are laughing at me, I know.... It's the way of the world just at present that ladies should submit to that sort of thing from gentlemen.'
> 'What sort of thing, Miss Desmolines?'

[10] But at the end of the nineteenth century Epps's cocoa could still be advertised as 'grateful and comforting'. It is indicative of the development of the world's history, however, that these epithets were rumoured to be the names of Epps's two daughters! See W. E. Collinson, *Contemporay English*, p. 65.

[11] There was something immature about this word for 'an embarrassing or awkward predicament, brought about through one's own imprudence'. It comes naturally to Molly Gibson when she considers the goings-on of her step-sister Cynthia: 'The "scrape" (as she called it in her girlish phraseology) was all over' (*Wives and Daughters*, Ch. 46).

'Chaff, as you call it. Courtesy is out of fashion, and gallantry has come to signify quite a different sort of thing from what it used to do.'
'The Sir Charles Grandison business is done and gone. That's what you mean, I suppose.' (*The Last Chronicle of Barset*, chapter 39)

Not only was much 'modern chaff', and perhaps the slang that accompanied it, unacceptable in mixed company; the latest expressions and turns of phrase, those employed by the apparatchiks of the Industrial Revolution, for example, were not immediately welcome. Coningsby, in Disraeli's novel (1844), when visiting northern industrial areas, meets a man who gives him his card with the name Mr G. O. A. Head. He talks freely, as we do today, of train times in timetable usage, such as 7.25, 8.40. Coningsby, and perhaps Disraeli also, appears to find such expressions brash. Next day, Coningsby had to catch a train 'which started, as his friend of the previous night would phrase it, at 9.45' (*Coningsby*, IV, chapter 4). This was 'railroad time', as Mrs Gaskell calls it (*North and South*, chapter 6), and one of many neologisms that had to be accommodated. Sometimes authors used a word under protest, at other times the protest was made by one of their elderly characters. Charles Kingsley, in *Two Years Ago* (1857), blames the ladies for the new development of the word *demonstrative* in the sense of 'given to the outward expression of the feelings': 'Though his feelings were not "demonstrative" as fine ladies say nowadays' (chapter 1). Mr Hale in *North and South* (1859) must allow the new use of *personally*, meaning 'as a matter of personal opinion':[12]

'Papa, I do think Mr Thornton a very remarkable man, but personally I don't like him at all.'
'And I do!' said her father, laughing. 'Personally, as you call it, and all.'
(chapter 11)

When George Eliot, however, writes in *Daniel Deronda* (chapter 11) 'Marriageable men, or what the new English calls *intending bridegrooms*', one feels she is not yet reconciled to the novelty!

If, then, the young man of the 'Upper Ten Thousand' was to distrust neologisms, and at the same time to despise the stiff manners and stagey rhetoric of former times, what sort of language was he to speak? The young Coningsby wonders how he is to address, at a grand public reception, his grandfather Lord Monmouth, whom he has not seen for four years – not since he was a boy, in fact:

To announce himself as Coningsby, as his Lordship's grandson, seemed somewhat ridiculous: to address his grandfather as Lord Monmouth would

---

[12] This sense has to a great extent ousted the meaning 'in personal appearance': 'Mr Poulter . . . was no longer *personally* formidable. He had rather a shrunken appearance' (*The Mill on the Floss*, II, chapter 4).

serve no purpose: to style Lord Monmouth 'grandfather' would make
everyone laugh, and seemed stiff and unnatural. What was he to do? To fall
into an attitude and exclaim 'Behold your grandchild!' or 'Have you forgotten
your Harry?'

Happily, as the novelist goes on to explain, there runs through Coningsby's
character 'a vein of simplicity which was not its least charm'. He therefore
walks up to Lord Monmouth, and says, 'How do you do, grandpapa?'
(*Coningsby*, IV, chapter 6).

The essential simplicity of the life and speech of the upper classes is a
theme that recurs, rather as present-day writers on the Royal family are at
pains to point out that, despite the panoply of state, they are straightforward
English men and women, with simple tastes. Bulwer Lytton advises those
who would write of the *beau monde*:

> There is only one rule ... it is this: let him consider that 'dukes, and lords, and
> noble princes' eat, drink, talk, move, exactly the same as any other class of
> civilized people – nay, the very subjects in conversation are, for the most
> part, the same in all sets – only, perhaps, they are somewhat more familiarly
> and easily treated with us than among the lower orders, who fancy rank is
> distinguished by pomposity, and that state affairs are discussed with the
> solemnity of a tragedy – that we are always my lording and my ladying each
> other – that we ridicule commoners, and curl our hair with 'Debrett's
> Peerage'. (*Pelham*, chapter 67)

The secret of mingling in polite society, then, is to behave naturally (always
provided one is sufficiently well-bred to avoid solecisms). As the hero's
mamma writes to him in Surtees's *Ask Mamma* (chapter 24), quoting a well-
known phrase: 'Remember, well-bred people always take breeding for
granted; "one of us", as they say of others when they find them at good
houses!'

Simplicity was the keynote, though there might be certain clichés which
the well-to-do young man would need to acquire, if he aspired to be a
Member of Parliament, for example. An interesting article by Dickens in
Household Words (III, p. 313), of 1851, entitled 'A Few Conventionalities',
lists some of these. Why, Dickens asks, must an honourable gentleman
'come down' to this House? 'Why can't he sometimes "come up" – like a
horse – or "come in" like a man? Why is an MP always "free to confess"?'[13]
It is well known that Britons never never never will be slaves; then why can't
he say what he has to say, without this superfluous assertion of his freedom?'
Dickens is scathing about the pseudo-emotionalism of some parliamentary
phrases, such as 'to lay one's hand on one's heart', or 'to pin one's faith' on a

[13] Twenty years before this article, W. H. Savage had noted (in *The Vulgarisms and
Improprieties of the English Language*), the use of *free* in the sense of 'willing', as 'a vile
parliamentary jargon', citing 'free to confess' and 'free to admit'.

measure. The peculiar see-saw of parliamentary intonation is pilloried to the extent of setting certain words spoken to a quasi-musical stave. Is Parliament, Dickens asks, to be included in the Prayer Book under the denomination of 'quires and places where they sing'?

INARTICULACY AND LIMITATIONS

Nevertheless, it was not always as easy a matter as acquiring a few clichés, and the plight of the newly-rich making their entry into the best society is wittily considered by Samuel Warren in his once popular novel *Ten Thousand a Year* (1841). Titmouse, a parvenu rich man, formerly a draper's assistant, is advised by his lawyer friend Gammon how to behave when meeting Titmouse's recently acquired aristocratic acquaintance – the Earl of Dreddington and the Earl's daughter, Lady Cecilia:

> He gave Titmouse many minor hints and suggestions. He was to drink but little wine – whereat Titmouse demurred somewhat vehemently, and asked, 'How the d—l he was to get his steam up without it?' . . . to say occasionally, only, 'my lord' in addressing the Earl – and 'Lady Cecilia', in addressing Lady Cecilia; – and, above all, never to appear in a hurry, but to do and say whatever he had to say calmly. (IV chapter 1)

Needless to say, Titmouse, wanting in confidence and composure, jettisons most of this advice in the first encounter. On being congratulated on his punctual arrival, he replies: 'Oh yes, my lord; quite so, your lordship . . . to be sure – wouldn't have been behind time for a minute, my lord; uncommon bad manners, if it please your lordship . . . .' The Earl inquires about Titmouse's property:

> 'I think you said, Mr Titmouse,' quoth the Earl, . . . 'that you had not yet taken possession of Yatton?'
> 'No, my lord; but I go down the day after tomorrow – quite – if I may say it, my lord – quite in style,' answered Titmouse with humble and hesitating jocularity of manner.
> 'Ha, ha!' – exclaimed the Earl gently.

This is the same fatal note of self-congratulation, the same failure to assume one's rights and pleasures casually, which we have noted elsewhere as the mark of the *nouveau-riche*.

When poor Titmouse is asked by the Earl to give Lady Cecilia his arm to lead her in to dinner, he forgets the most important part of his mentor's advice, to preserve his *sang froid*: '[Lady Cecilia] languidly arose . . . and . . . barely touched . . . the proferred arm of Titmouse, extended towards her at an acute angle, and at right angles with his own body – stammering, 'Honour to take your ladyship – uncommon proud – this way, my lady.'

For, though drapers' assistants, and even men-about-town, may favour, as we shall see, a disjointed utterance when among their own kind, in drawing-rooms and dining-rooms when ladies are present, complete sentences are enjoined. (Mr Jingle, Mr Pickwick's henchman, we may reflect, was not a speaker of upper-class English.) In contrast to the Earl, whose sentences are beautifully self-contained, Titmouse has acquired the habit, probably from trade correspondence, of missing out the subject pronoun: 'If ever you should come down to my estate in the country, shall be most uncommon proud to see your ladyship.' Needless to say, he also breaks some crockery, for which he keeps offering to pay. Money is a tricky subject to mention in such circles. The fatal phrases 'Expense is no object' and 'Money is no object' are repeated.

We must beware, however, of imagining that Victorian upper-class speech is necessarily more correct than the speech of the lower classes. George Meredith reminds us that at times the language of the aristocrat is far from being a model of articulation:

> Lord Mountfalcon had never spoken in this way before. He spoke better, too.
> She missed the aristocratic twang in his voice, and the hesitation for words,
> and the fluid lordliness with which he rolled over difficulties in speech. (*The
> Ordeal of Richard Feverel*, 1859 chapter 39)

Of this unfavourable description of upper-class speech, there is amusing confirmation in the language of the debilitated cousin of Sir Leicester Dedlock in *Bleak House*:

> Debilitated cousin thinks – Country's going – DAYVLE – steeple-chase pace. (chapter 40)

> The debilitated cousin only hopes some fler'll be executed – zample. . . .
> Hasn't a doubt – zample – far better hang wrong fler than no fler. (chapter 53)

Trollope makes a sobering observation (one that we can still appreciate), of a certain Belgian, M. Grascour, in *Mr Scarborough's Family* (chapter 46), that 'he would only be known to be a foreigner by the correctness of his language.'

That rather cynical young man, Adrian Harley, who comments in his worldly-wise fashion on events in Meredith's *The Ordeal of Richard Feverel* (chapter 34), was more aware of similarities than of differences in the speech, of the various classes in England:

> I have for the first time in my career a field of lords to study. I think it is not
> without meaning that I am introduced to it by a yeoman's niece. The
> language of the two social extremes is similar. I find it to consist in an
> instinctively lavish use of vowels and adjectives. My lord and Farmer Blaize
> speak the same tongue, only my lord's has lost its backbone, and is limp,

though fluent.... Their ideas seem to have a special relationship in the peculiarity of stopping where they have begun.

There is much here that one would demur at, and even quarrel with, not least the suggestion that a yeoman farmer represents one extreme of the social scale. This is not necessarily Meredith's own considered opinion, of course, though it has all the signs of his great, if at times ill-focused, intelligence. But, as Meredith renders the accents of Farmer Blaize on the one hand, and of the Honourable Peter Blaydon, 'Lord Mountfalcon's parasite', on the other, we can at least observe the similarity he finds in the 'language of social extremes', and also discern the lack of 'backbone' in the speech of the more effete members of the upper class:

> You ain't to be as other young gentlemen. All the better! You're a find bold young gentleman, and your father's a right to be proud of ye. Well, sir – I'm sure I thank him for't – he comes to hear of you and Luce, and of course he don't want nothin' o' that – more do I. I meets him there! What's more I won't have nothin' of it. She be my gal. She were left to my protection. And she's a lady, sir. Let me tell ye, ye won't find many on 'em so well looked to as she be – my Luce! (chapter 23)

> 'No, no; positively you must come,' said the Hon. Peter. 'I've had some trouble to get them together to relieve the dulness of your incarceration. Richmond's within the rules of your prison. You can be back by night. Moonlight on the water – lovely woman. We've engaged a city barge to pull us back. Eight oars – I'm not sure it isn't sixteen. Come – the word!' (chapter 36)

These staccato, short-breathed utterances are, by the very construction of the sentences, guaranteed to prevent the development of ideas any further than their inception, as Meredith says. The niceties of social discrimination, the play of snobbery and inverted snobbery in the first extract, the romantic sensations of the boat trip at night in the second – these things are hinted at, never stated. The staccato mode, often enhanced by the omission of a subject (especially if the subject is a pronoun), has deep roots in the history of upper-class male speech, as this quotation from Disraeli shows:

> 'I say, Jemmy,' said the eldest, a dandy who had dined with the Regent, but who was still a dandy, and who enjoyed life almost as much as in the days when Carlton House occupied the terrace which still bears its name, 'I say, Jemmy, what a load of young fellows there are! Don't know their names at all. Begin to think fellows are younger than they used to be. Amazing load of young fellows indeed!' (*Coningsby*, VIII, chapter 1)

It will be seen that emphasis is gained by repetition. It was a mode of speech that seems to have been *de rigueur* for the fashionable man-about-town. John Eames, with characteristic assiduity, is at pains to acquire it: '"She's a fine girl – a deuced fine girl!" Johnny had said, using a style of language which he had learned since he had left Guestwick and Allington' (*The Small House at Allington*, chapter 4). There was, moreover, a curious accompaniment, at times, to the speech of the dandy or 'fine gentleman'. In *Hard Times* (II, chapter 2), Dickens notes that the 'Gradgrind school' imitated this peculiarity: 'They liked fine gentlemen; they pretended that they did not, but they did. They became exhausted in imitation of them; and they *yaw-yawed* in their speech like them.' This must have been a kind of consonantal laughter (Lord Hawhaw of World War Two propaganda fame is also recalled). At all events there was something foppish about it:

> During breakfast Lord Coleridge told several funny stories. One was of a young dandy army officer. He was asked at the opera if he did not think the prima donna, who had just been singing divinely, had done well, and he replied: 'Verwy – ah – haw – easy is the word'. Lord Coleridge imitated the fop with supreme contempt and with an excellent drawl. (R. H. Dana, *Hospitable England in the Seventies*, p. 317)

The phrasing might be staccato, but the pace of the dialogue was by no means always brisk. Reserve and lack of conversational powers often prevented fluency. Trollope writes of 'the loose little talkings, half flat and half sharp, of men when they meet together in idleness' (*Can You Forgive Her?*, chapter 16). Fluency in speech is generally not a characteristic of the country gentleman: 'There are a class of men ... to whom a power of easy expression by means of spoken words comes naturally. English country gentlemen, highly educated as they are, underrated as they usually are, self-confident as they in truth are at bottom, are clearly not in this section' (Trollope, *Rachel Ray*, chapter 24).

In a series of essays *England and the English* (II, chapter 2), published in 1833, Bulwer Lytton caricatures society conversation of the time with all its incoherence, inconsequence and interruptions. He begins by showing the 'three Graces of our Conversation: Hesitating, Humming and Drawling':

> We are at dinner: – a gentleman, 'a man about town', is informing us of a misfortune that has befallen his friend: 'No – I assure you – now err – err – that – er – it was the most shocking accident possible – er – poor Chester was riding in the Park – er – you know that grey – er – (substantive dropped, hand a little flourished instead) – of his – splendid creature! – er – well, sir, and by Jove – er – the – er – (no substantive, flourish again) – took fright, and – e – er – Here the gentleman throws up his chin and eyes, sinks back exhausted into his chair, and after a pause adds, 'Well they took him into – the shop – there – you know – with the mahogany sashes – just by the Park – er – and the – er – man there – set his – what d'ye call it – er – collar-bone; but he was – er – ter-ri-bly – terribly' – a full stop. The gentleman shakes his head – and the sentence is suspended to eternity.

Another gentleman takes up the wondrous tale thus logically:
'Ah! shocking, shocking, – but poor Chester was a very agreeable – er' – full stop!
'Oh! devilish gentlemanlike fellow! – quite shocking! – quite – did you go to the – er – to-day?'
'No, indeed; the day was so un – may I take some wine with you?'...

Things were not always as bad as this. In one of his fascinating footnotes G. M. Young (*Victorian England: Portrait of an Age*, p. 32n) throws out the remark: 'The Brookfields in the fifties claimed to have introduced the new style of conversation, brisk and allusive. Mrs Carlyle used to torture London parties with the elaboration of her anecdotes.' The Brookfields were great friends of Thackeray. Their descendants, in their edition of *Mrs Brookfield and her Circle*, a collection chiefly of family letters, have much to say about old-style conversationalists who found themselves ill at ease with new-style badinage. Charlotte Brontë could not fall in with it at a party Thackeray gave in her honour (II, p. 356). Macaulay sounded too authoritarian, announcing: 'Mrs Brookfield has asked me if I admire Jane Austen's novels, to which I reply' – and then entering into a lengthy dissertation to which all listened but into which no one else dared intrude (II, p. 377). As for Mrs Carlyle, her instinct:

> was always to take the lead .... In conversion clever and amusing as she often was, Mrs Carlyle had the fatal propensity of telling her stories at extraordinary length. With her Scotch accent and her perseverance in finishing off every detail, those who were merely friendly acquaintances and not devotees sometimes longed for an abridgement, and perhaps also to have their own turn in the conversation. (II, p. 427)

If we are to believe Henry Kingsley, upper-class men had become less boisterous in public by the time of *Geoffrey Hamlyn* (1859), compared to thirty years before, when he describes, by way of 'flash-back', 'three men standing, one of whom was talking and laughing in a tone perhaps a little louder than it is customary to use in the streets nowadays' (chapter 14). Probably we should not make too much of this: upper-class families have always needed to make full use of their vocal chords for such purposes as urging on the hounds and opening bazaars. There is also the phenomenon of outspokenness, which was something of a prerogative of the higher ranks:

> But Mr Vincent turned round hastily as he heard a muttered exclamation, 'By Jove' behind him .... 'By Jove, the fellow will think you are in love with him,' Vincent, with his quickened and suspicious ears, could hear the stranger say, with that delightful indifference to being overheard which characterizes some Englishmen of the exalted classes. (Mrs Oliphant, *Salem Chapel*, chapter 8)

High-ranking ladies, at least in their own homes, tended to speak in quieter tones. In the drawing-room they reigned supreme, and guests were 'stilled' in George Eliot's words, 'by the deep-piled carpet and by the high English breeding that subdues all voices' (*Daniel Deronda*, chapter 35).George Eliot gives a passage of conversation by Mrs Transome in *Felix Holt* (chapter 40), which contrives to characterize such speech: the 'easy phrase, and...refined high-bred tone and accent'. As with the conversation of men, though in a more measured way, there is a studied casualness, exemplified by collocations like *no end of interest*, *that sweet blue-eyed thing* etc.:

> It was entertaining at present to be seated on soft cushions with her netting before her, while Mrs Transome went on with her embroidery, and told in that easy phrase, and with that refined high-bred tone and accent which she possessed in perfection, family stories that to Esther were like so many novelettes: what diamonds were in the Earl's family, own cousins to Mrs Transome; how poor Lady Sara's husband went off into jealous madness only a month after their marriage, and dragged that sweet blue-eyed thing by the hair; and how the brilliant Fanny, having married a country parson, became so niggardly that she had gone about almost begging for fresh eggs from the farmers' wives, though she had done very well with her six sons, as there was a bishop and no end of interest in the family, and two of them got appointments in India.

We may note that the structure of the sentence towards the end here, while never amorphous, becomes rather loose. It was not the part of a high-born lady to sound like a primly grammatical schoolmistress.

Mrs Transome's conversation was obviously family gossip, but it was generally felt that conversation could be improved by reading, by the speaker becoming what Jane Austen called a man, or woman 'of information':

> Cynthia! [says Mrs Gibson] can't you take up a book and improve yourself? I am sure your conversation will never be worth listening to unless you read something better than newspapers. (*Wives and Daughters*, chapter 26)

A manual on *How to Shine in Society*, published in Glasgow in 1860, was explicit on what to read:

> The principal study recommended is history, as more materials for conversation are supplied by this kind of knowledge than by almost any other.... The greater portion of new novels are not worth the time spent on their perusal, but everyone ought to know, and be able to give an opinion of, the one most in vogue, and if he can say something about the author and his literary career, so much the better. If he is in the company of ladies, it is also absolutely necessary to quote at least ten lines from Tennyson's last poem. (p. 23)

Yet, what are we to make of Meredith's statement, quoted above, that upper-class English speech is characterized by 'an instinctively lavish use of vowels and adjectives'? A lavish use of vowels seems a meaningless phrase, but of the lavish use of adjectives there is more to be said. We might turn, for example, to that shrewd observer of the classes, Mrs Oliphant, in *Salem Chapel* (1863). The Nonconformist minister, Arthur Vincent, has made a speech which has found favour with his congregation: 'He was complimented on his speech, and even by some superior people, who had a mind to be fashionable, upon the *delightful evening* they had enjoyed' (*Salem Chapel*, chapter 10). Vincent has every intention himself of aspiring to a higher social position, and he is especially gratified to overhear on a train that the town of Carlingford, to which he has just moved, is thought of as a place with social advantages: 'its *pleasant* parties – its *nice* people – Mr Wodehouse's *capital* dinners, and the *charming* breakfasts – such a *delightful* novelty! – so *easy* and *agreeable* – of the pretty Lady Western' (chapter 1). It is clear from these instances that Mrs Oliphant, too, thinks of 'an instinctively lavish use of adjectives' as characteristic of those who aspire to the best society. Sometimes the adjectives, though plentiful, were not greatly varied: Bulwer Lytton, in *England and the English*, observes: '*Nice* and *dear* are the great *To Prepon* and *To Kalon* ('the good' and 'the beautiful') of feminine conversational moralities' (II, chapter 2). The same point is made by Disraeli in *Lothair*, some decades later, when one of his men of fashion remarks: 'English is an expressive language... but not difficult to master. Its range is limited. It consists, as far as I can observe, of four words: *nice, jolly, charming*, and *bore*; and some grammarians add *fond*' (chapter 28). Tennyson did not like the word *nice*, though he believed it was necessary:

> *Tennyson:* A lady the other day here – a very nice woman (I don't altogether like the word, but I want it), was praising a friend of yours. "Nice" is objectionable, but it is useful – a "nice" person is one that you're satisfied with.
> *William Allingham:* It used to mean fastidious, – discriminative, but there's not much harm in its being turned about and applied to the object.
> *Tennyson:* No; it's something or somebody that satisfies your niceness.
> (Allingham, *Diary*, p. 297)

The best people drew the line at the indiscriminate use of *beautiful*, as used by Milly Costigan, for instance, in Thackeray's *Pendennis* (I, chapter 12). She applies it to a poem Arthur Pendennis has written in her honour, to some filberts she is eating, and to a glass of punch. The Countess of Munster takes up this point in *My Memories and Miscellanies* (p. 176): 'What more grating to one's feelings than to hear of people... calling articles of food "beautiful": "beautiful beef" "beautiful tea", or even a "beautiful cook"!'

The aforementioned article by Dickens, 'A Few Conventionalities' in *Household Words* (p. 315), pokes fun at the 'slang' of Belgravia in terms that suggest the same predominance of the hackneyed epithet:

> Nobody knows who first drawled, languidly, that so and so, or such and such a thing, was 'good fun' or 'capital fun' or 'a – the best fun in the world, I'm told' – but some fine gentleman or lady did so, and accordingly a thousand do. They don't know why. We have the same mysterious authority for inquiring, in our faint way, if Cawberry is a nice person – if he is a superior person – for a romance being so charmingly horrible or a woman so charmingly ugly ... for the glass palace being (do you know) so charming to me that I absolutely bore every creature with it – for those horrid sparrows not having built in the dear gutters, which are so charmingly ingenious – for a great deal more, to the same very charming purpose.

Such stress on adjectives and epithets, often in the superlative degree, or emphasized with an intensive like *so*, lent to conversation generally a quality that stricter observers found quite gushing. Such a one was William Gaskell, husband of the novelist. In a letter of 1854 Mrs Gaskell writes (*Letters*, p. 281):

> I did so like your good long handsome note four or five days ago. I do so thank you for your kindness. There! there are 2 sentences with 'so' in them not followed by 'as', as Mr Gaskell says they ought to be. I will make one grammatical sentence, & have done. I am so much obliged to you as to be incapable of expressing my obligation but by saying that I am always – Yours most truly, E. C. Gaskell.

The young Princess Victoria did not fall behind any of her subjects in this matter of enthusiastic epithets: 'Dearest Ernest and dearest Albert are so grown-up in their manners, so gentle, so kind, so amiable, so agreeable, so very sensible and reasonable, and so really and truly good and kind-hearted' (*Girlhood of Queen Victoria*, I, p. 160). At least one mawkish epithet became socially unacceptable. In Meredith's story, 'The Case of General Ople and Lady Camper', the General's phrase *sweetly pretty* brings him into disfavour:

> 'The park is very pretty in the early morning'.
> 'Sweetly pretty'.
> Lady Camper raised her head, and, with the mildness of assured dictatorship, pronounced: 'Never say that before me.'
> 'I submit, my lady.' said the poor, scourged man. (chapter 5)

SLANG

The desire for liveliness of speech which led to a lavish use of adjectives, also inclined members of the upper classes towards slang. When social climbers imagined that the speech of the upper classes was free from 'low' expressions they were wrong, as G. L. Brook points out (*The Language of Dickens*, p. 59).[14] While the vocabulary of upper-class speech was not as rich as that of the lower-classes in this respect, there were occasional examples of slang words belonging to an upper-class dialect. Brook instances the word *hipped*, meaning melancholy as the kind of word with which the lower orders would have been unfamiliar: Eugene Wrayburn advises his friend Mortimer Lightwood: 'You are a little *hipped*, dear fellow . . . you have been too sedentary' (*Our Mutual Friend*, III, chapter 10). Probably, too, they would not have known the word *dipped*, meaning (of an estate) mortgaged: 'His morals were corrupted by the example of his father, and his estate *dipped*, I thought beyond all hope, by his father's extravagance' (Henry Kingsley, *Leighton Court*, chapter 18). Clearly, with slang, as with other kinds of language, distinctions of class appeared. Mrs Gaskell, the shrewdest of observers, notices this also. When Margaret Hale, in *North and South* (1854), is accused by her mother of having acquired words from the dialect of the industrial town of Milton, the following dialogue ensues:

'But Margaret, don't get to use those horrid Milton words. "Slack of work"; it is a provincialism. What will your Aunt Shaw say if she hears you use it on her return?'
'Oh, mamma! don't try and make a bugbear of Aunt Shaw,' said Margaret, laughing. 'Edith picked up all sorts of military slang from Captain Lennox, and Aunt Shaw never took any notice of it.'
'But yours is factory slang.'
'And if I live in a factory town, I must speak factory language when I want it.'
(chapter 29)

Presumably Florence Nightingale believed that, since she worked with the army, she might use military slang when she wanted to. At all events, in the *Recollections* of Louisa, Countess of Antrim (p. 76) the author's father describes meeting 'Miss Nightingale' in 1856 at Balmoral: 'I was amused to hear her talk in the most natural Regimental slang of the P.M.O. (Principal Medical Officer), of kits etc., etc.'

Meanwhile, there was no doubt that the lowest slang was percolating upwards, and an anonymous reviewer of *David Copperfield* was right to attribute some of this process to the influence of perhaps the greatest Victorian novelist:

Upon our everyday language his influence has been immense – for better or worse. We began by using Wellerisms and Gampisms in fun, till they have got blended insensibly with our stock of conversational phrases; and now in our most serious moments we talk slang unwittingly, to the great disgust of the

[14] At the same time, it was doubtless a high kind of 'lowness' with a supercilious authority in the slang. Of Fred Vincy, his doting mother says: 'Fred is far beyond other people's sons. You may hear it in his speech, that he has kept college company' (*Middlemarch*, Ch. 36).

old school, who complain that, instead of seeking 'the well of English undefiled' at Twickenham, we draw at haphazard from the muddy stream that has washed Mile End. (see *Dickens: The Critical Heritage*, p. 244)

The public schools generated their own slang; and many distinct slang words were associated with the universities. High-spirited and intelligent young men, when they get together in small groups, are great inventors of new language. Such a man is Lindsay, a member of the undergraduate reading-party in Scotland in Clough's The *Bothie of Tober-na-Vuorlich*:

> Lindsay the ready of speech, the Piper, the Dialectician,
> This was his title from Adam because of the words he invented,
> Who in three weeks had created a dialect new for the party.

We learn some of these words later on in the poem:

> And in the chorus joined Lindsay, the Piper, the Dialectician,
> Three weeks hence we return to the *shop* and the *wash-hand-stand basin*
> (These are the Piper's names for the bathing-place and the cottage).

The very process of travelling to Oxford or Cambridge necessitated special usage, as Richard Henry Dana, son of the author of *Two Years Before the Mast*, observes: 'Went "up" to town directly after lunch. London is always "up" except in relation to Oxford or Cambridge, when it is "down" and the Universities are "up"' (*Hospitable England in the Seventies*, p. 56).

Probably the best book to give an impression of Oxford slang is Thomas Hughes's *Tom Brown at Oxford*, sequel to *Tom Brown's Schooldays*. Only the privileged minority educated at Oxford or Cambridge would know words like *sapping* for 'studying hard': 'I never was much of a hand at *sapping*' (chapter 1); or an *aeger* (Latin for 'sick'), meaning a note certifying that a student is sick: 'Put on an *aeger* then' (chapter 6). Only the young student at Oxbridge would refer to the door of his room as his *oak*: 'They found themselves drumming at his *oak*' (chapter 12); only he, or the young scion of the 'quality', would be likely to describe spilt blood as *claret*: 'nothing but a little of his friend's *'claret'* (chapter 12); or would call a man with stamina a *laster*: 'I put him down as a *laster*' (chapter 16); or speak of staying-power as *bottom*, as when a fight with a poacher is described as 'a desperate trial of strength and *bottom*' (chapter 37). The word *cocktail* is used by Hughes, as by Thackeray, of men deficient in genuine breeding; men with 'a good deal of the *cocktail* about them' (chapter 6). The word *hard*, in various combinations, could indicate the possible strenuousness of a student's career: 'The Captain read, as he rode, "*hard* all"' (chapter 12). A *wine*, meaning 'a wine party' and *pluck*, meaning 'to fail, or a failure in examinations': 'Men treated the *pluck* as a real misfortune' (chapter 24) – these were essentially university words. The convenient *to floor* could mean to accomplish an assignment of work or to finish a consignment of drink: 'I've nearly *floored* my little-go work' (chapter 10); 'I have a few bottles of old wine left; we may as well *floor* them' (chapter 24). Catch-phrases, too, were not necessarily a peculiarity of the speech of the lower-classes. Such a phrase as *all serene*, used by the hero of *Ravenshoe* (chapter 7) when he is called before the dean of his Oxford college, was, as Henry Kingsley says, fashionable at the mid-century: '"The dean wishes to see you at once, sir." Charles replied by using an expression then just coming into use among our youth, "*All serene!*"'

Quite often young men – *slang* young men they might be called if they were free of speech and habits, for the adjectival use was frequent–would speak of young women in terms more appropriate to horse-flesh. It is typical of the reductive nature of slang that the word *points*, meaning 'a physical feature in an animal' (*OED* sense 26b), occurs in such discourse:

> I like her form better than anything out this year. Such a clean stepper. You should just dance with her. (*Tom Brown at Oxford*, chapter 38)

> Her figure is elegant, and has the effect of being tall. Not that she is so, but that 'the most is made' as the Honourable Bob Stables has frequently asserted upon oath, 'of all her points'. (*Bleak House*, chapter 2)

> Although he always knew she was the best groomed woman in the stud, he had no idea she was a bolter. (Ibid., chapter 58)

On the other hand, Jane Elton, later Jane Brookfield, complained that certain horsey people talked of their horses 'as if they were rational, I mean human beings' (*Mrs Brookfield and her Circle*, I, p. 71).

Slang often comes to the aid of the embarrassed, in such a difficult matter as distinguishing a gentleman from one who is not, for example. We have just seen that the word *cocktail* could mean 'one deficient in the gentlemanly breeding'; and the word *snob* could be used to the middle of the century and beyond in its pre-Thackerayan sense of one who is socially of no account:

> And here, perhaps, I should remind the reader, that of all the great distinctions in life none perhaps is more important than that which divides mankind into the two great sections of *NOBS* and *SNOBS*. (Disraeli, *Henrietta Temple*, 1836, VI, chapter 18)

> I should be very sorry indeed if you were not to persevere in your hunting; for a red coat and leathers are quite your become, and there is none, in my opinion, in which a gentleman looks so well, or a *snob* so ill. (Surtees, *Ask Mamma*, 1858, chapter 24)

That there were conventions, even within the colloquial language of upper-class men, is proved by the tricky question of the word *fellow*. *Fellow* had inherited some demeaning or contemptuous overtones from an early date, and hence carried suggestions of friendly slang. One may compare Pope's well-known couplet, with a rhyme that suggests a casual unaccented vowel for the second syllable:

Worth makes the man, and want of it the fellow;
The rest is all but leather and prunella.

The word was well established in public schools. The young Arthur Hugh Clough, writing of Rugby in 1837, mentions 'a great improvement in the Chapel service, namely that we have no clerk now ... and the *fellows* respond very well' (I, p. 64). The usage was adopted, to his pupils' surprise, by Arnold himself. To quote Stanley's *The Life and Correspondence of Dr Arnold* (I, p. 157): 'He calls us *"fellows"* was the astonished expression of the boys when ... they heard him speak of them by the familiar name in use among themselves.' Possibly the most idiomatic of these male usages is the habit of referring to one's own activities as those of 'a fellow'. Judging by the *OED* quotations, this seems to have been a Victorian development.[15] The first quotation is from Thomas Hughes's *Tom Brown at Oxford* (chapter 9): 'They don't deny themselves the pleasure of looking at *a fellow* as if he were a Turk.'

These were the ways of men, however. Manuals of the 1870s like *Society Small Talk* (p. 118), deplored the use of the epithet (at least in colloquial contexts) by women:

> The word 'fellow', however much in use it may be between men, sounds very objectionable from the lips of women: and some women are given to the foolish conceit of speaking of every man they may happen to know as a 'Dear fellow', a 'Charming fellow', a 'Handsome fellow' or a 'Clever fellow'.

It is, however, a delusion that books on etiquette regulate behaviour and speech. By the end of the century the word *fellow* seems to have become acceptable for ladies also. 'Mrs Humphry' writes in *Manners for Men* (1897), apologizing for her ineffectual attempts to arbitrate amid the confusion:

> With reference to the word *fellow* a subtle distinction or two must be drawn. In lowly circles a young man is called a *fellow*; young men *fellows*. So it is in good society, but with a distinct difference. It is not very easy to make this difference clear. Young men of good position refer very commonly to others of their acquaintance as 'the fellows', but they would not use the word to describe young men generally. Women, young and old, of the lower classes speak of young men generally as 'fellows', but gentlemen never do so. A lady never uses the expression 'a girl and a fellow'. At the same time she may frequently speak of 'young fellows'. I am aware that there is a want of clearness in all this, but it is a matter among many others that can only be acquired by being accustomed to the usage of good society.

[15] Earlier, probably, is the use of *a man* in this slightly deprecating way. It is a point of character in David Copperfield's acquaintance, Markham. 'I observed that the latter always spoke of himself indefinitely as "a man", and seldom or never in the first person singular.' When he sings a solo, it is 'When the heart of *a man* is depressed with care' from *The Beggars' Opera* (*David Copperfield*, Ch. 24).

'Mrs Humphry' goes on to explain that usage for men and women is different: a women would 'reveal herself as belonging to the uncultured classes if she said "I met a fellow yesterday"; a young man would make an equal mistake if he were to say "My sister's fellow"; but he would be correct enough if he were to say "The fellow my sister's engaged to."' She concludes: 'These little nuances of expression remind one of the old rhyme:

Strange that such differences should be
'Twixt Tweedledum and Tweedledee'.

It is indeed difficult to see a way through these distinctions. Perhaps the best that may be said is that the word *fellow*, used by the upper classes, carried a strong suggestion of casual comradeship. This was true of *the fellows*, and also of the wry self-depreciatory use of *a fellow* as a rough equivalent of the indefinite pronoun *one*: 'What can *a fellow* do?' In contexts where this freedom and casual usage were 'pinned down' by close grammatical limitations, the word tended to lose caste, as with 'My sister's fellow' compared to the more acceptable 'the fellow my sister's engaged to'. One non-U use of *fellow* remains today, according to Ross (*Don't Say It*, p. 52). This is the working-class use to mean 'a male', as in 'That guinea-pig's *a fella!*'

As an appellative, the word *fellow* was not to be bandied about in every assembly, as Elizabeth Barrett relates was the fault of George Borrow:

The story goes that he [Borrow] dined... at Murray's some days ago, and that the conversation turning on Spain he said quietly... 'My good fellows, none of you know anything of Spain except what you learn from romances', – upon which (incredible to be told, – too ludicrous to be credible!) the good company, being far too good in an aristocratic sense, to be addressed as 'good fellows' showed their sense of the insult by rising from table in a body and walking out of the room! (*Elizabeth Barrett to Miss Mitford: Unpublished Letters*, 1843, p. 182)

But of course, the word *fellow* has honourable, precise and uncolloquial university use, for 'the name (corresponding to the Latin *socius*) given to the incorporated members of a college or collegiate foundation (whether in a University or otherwise)' (*OED* sense 7). The contrast between strict and loose uses of the word is marked in Harry Clavering (Trollope, *The Claverings*, chapter 7), who as a fellow of a college objects to excessive familiarity, even complimentary familiarity, in his acquaintance:

There was something in the tone of the other men towards him which did not quite satisfy him. They probably did not know that he was a fellow of a college, and treated him almost as they might have done had he come to them direct from King's College, in the Strand, or from the [*sic*] London

University. Down at Stratton, a certain amount of honour had been paid to him. They had known there who he was, and had felt some deference for him. They had not slapped him on the back, or poked him in the ribs, or even called him old fellow, before some length of acquaintance justified such appellation ... Harry was not disinclined to believe that he was a 'lad of wax', or 'a brick', or 'a trump' or 'no small beer'. But he desired that such complimentary and endearing appellations should be used to him only by those who had known him long enough to be aware that he deserved them. (chapter 7)

Slang and familiarity on the lips of ladies was a more controversial matter. There was greater tolerance as time went on, but in the first quarter of the century, slang was a jealously guarded male prerogative. Probably Lord Melbourne was repeating a common prejudice when he observed: 'Men are less measured in their expressions than women, but when women once take to strong expressions they are much worse' (*Girlhood of Queen Victoria*, II, p. 210). Creevey paid a visit in 1825 to Raby Castle, home of the Earl of Darlington and his parvenue Countess. He found the countess at first 'without a vestige of her former habits'; but said later 'I am compelled to admit that, in the familiarity of a duet and outing, the cloven foot appeared. I don't mean more than that tendency of *slang*, which I conceive it impossible for any person who has been long in the ranks entirely to get over' (*Creevey Papers*, ed. Maxwell, II, p. 86). By the 1860s, Trollope is allowing his heroines more licence than this. The high-spirited Lily Dale in *The Small House at Allington* (1862) enjoys slang expressions, though her elder sister Bell finds them deplorable:

'I don't like those slang words, Lily'
'What slang words?'
'You know what you called Bernard's friend.'
'Oh; a swell. I fancy I do like slang. I think it's awfully jolly to talk about things being jolly. Only that I was afraid of your nerves I should have called him stunning. It's so slow, you know, to use nothing but words out of a dictionary.' (chapter 2)

It is interesting that Lily Dale, with her 'awfully jolly', might have incurred the wrath of the Poet Laureate. When his young visitor Laura Gurney ventured to remark, 'We were awfully late last night,' Tennyson seized her arm: 'Awfully! Don't you know the meaning of that word, damsel? God's wrath is awful' (Richardson, *The Pre-eminent Victorian*, p. 102).

In fact, Trollope takes up a slightly hypocritical attitude towards female slang. At times he seems to disapprove of it in his heroines, but in practice he relies on the occasional lapse to ensure that they will not appear without spirit. In *Can You Forgive Her?* Lady Glencora Palliser is rebuked by a husband who appears to be much less sympathetic:

'And I told you that I liked going with young women, and not with old ones. That's the long and the short of it.'

'Glencora, I wish you would not use such expressions.'

'What! not the long and the short? It is good English. Quite as good as Mr Bott's, when he said in the House the other night that the Government kept their accounts in a higgledy-piggledy way.'

Lady Glencora here is not merely asserting her right to as free a use of slang as her husband's male associates; she is confident that her high position in Society will allow her to use such phrases occasionally with impunity. The same is true of the wealthy heiress Miss Dunstable:

'I shall certainly come and see you turned off' [i.e. married] said Miss Dunstable, taking leave of her new friend. Miss Dunstable, it must be acknowledged, was a little too fond of slang; but then, a lady with her fortune, and of her age, may be fond of almost whatever she pleases. (*Dr Thorne*, chapter 47)

Such were the prerogatives of these fortunate ladies, ladies with the power and the personality to say what they pleased. Lady Harriet Cumnor, in *Wives and Daughters* (chapter 57), could avail herself of similar freedoms; whereas her very proper maid, Parkes (promoted, no doubt, for her propriety), could not:

Parkes had begun to reign by putting Molly on the sofa, and saying 'If you will give me your keys, Miss, I will unpack your things, and let you know when it is time for me to arrange your hair, preparatory to luncheon.' For, if Lady Harriet used familiar colloquialisms from time to time, she certainly had not learnt them from Parkes, who piqued herself on the correctness of her language.

Perhaps we should add that even the greatest of ladies might use slang expressions indirectly, by way of quotation: 'The Queen talked freely of the Prince; he would die; he seemed not to care to live. Then she used these words: "He died from want of what they call pluck" (Disraeli, *Reminiscences*, p. 90).

Mrs Gaskell is in favour of at least a limited freedom of speech for ladies, using in her narrative the colloquialisms that she ridicules Mrs Gibson for despising: 'Mrs Gibson was off, all in her Sunday best (to use the servants' expression, which she herself would so have condemned)' (*Wives and Daughters*, chapter 45). She would not allow Mrs Gibson's view that it is vulgar to bring proverbs into conversation:

'In short, mamma, one may steal a horse, but another must not look over the hedge,' said Cynthia....

'Be quiet, child! All proverbs are vulgar, and I do believe that is the vulgarest of all'. (chapter 28)

On the whole, the anonymous author of *The Vulgarities of Speech Corrected* (1826) would have been on Mrs Gibson's side in this matter. While 'a good proverb, well introduced' might sometimes appear elegant, proverbs often led to 'tiresome sameness and meaningless vulgarity'. Lord Chesterfield, so the author believes, had been correct in his dictum that 'a man of fashion never has recourse to proverbs and vulgar aphorisms' and, the author adds 'they appear to have withered away under the ban of his anathema' (*Vulgarities* p. 104).

This is not, however, a state of affairs that Mrs Gaskell or George Eliot would accept. Increasing acceptance of working folk and their speech ensured proverbs a longer life. It is amusing that when, in 1907, Lady Grove wishes to make the point in *The Social Fetich* (p. 25) that rules of etiquette are made to be broken by those with sufficient position and personality, she uses the same proverb that Mrs Gibson had forbidden her daughter: 'One man may steal a horse, and another not even be allowed to look over the hedge at it.'

One point made by Mrs Gaskell through Mrs Gibson is that to be too censorious about speech is to be oneself vulgar. The same issue is raised by Agnes Grey in Anne Bronte's novel of that name. Miss Murray, the charge of Agnes Grey, at the age of eighteen takes to criticizing her governess for the vulgarity of her connections:

> 'You should tell the good people at home not to bore you with such long letters,' said she; 'and, above all, do bid them write on proper *note-paper*, and not on those great vulgar sheets. You should see the charming little lady-like notes mamma writes to her friends.'
> 'The good people at home,' replied I 'know very well that the longer their letter are, the better I like them . . . and I thought you were too much of a lady yourself, Miss Murray, to talk about the "vulgarity" of writing on a large sheet of paper.' (*Agnes Grey*, chapter 8)[16]

Yet, in this matter of language suitable for ladies, there were lines that had to be drawn. Mrs Gaskell, for instance, does not recommend the way servants heard the gossip of their employers and 'exaggerated the sayings among themselves with the coarse strengthening of expression common with uneducated people' (*Wives and Daughters*, chapter 47). When they talked of matters of courtship such people made use of the heartless catch-phrases and clichés that Marianne Dashwood, earlier in the century, had castigated as 'gross and illiberal' in tendency (*Sense and Sensibility*, chapter 9). Wilkie

---

[16] It is interesting that this reference to *note-paper*, since *Agnes Grey* was published in 1847, antedates the first *OED* quotation, from Mrs Carlyle, by two years. The word, of course, is taboo to strict Mitfordians. The Murrays, in *Agnes Grey* are a 'respectable' (i.e. probably wealthy) but coarse-grained family. A reason for the contempt with which the word is regarded in some quarters is suggested here: the writing of silly notelets with no purpose. The quotation is interesting, but inconclusive.

Collins, writing in 1852, deplored the way women adopted masculine slang, 'unsexing' themselves by 'aping the language and the manners of men – especially in reference to that miserable modern dandyism of demeanour, which aims at repressing all betrayal of warmth of feeling' (*Basil*, I, chapter 5). Wilkie Collins's friend Dickens also found upper-class slang heartless at times. In *Little Dorrit*, Arthur Clennam raises quiet objection to Mrs Gowan's account of her son's acquaintance with the Meagles family:

> 'He picked the people up at Rome, I think?'
> 'Excuse me, I doubt if I understand your expression.'
> 'Picked the people up,' said Mrs Gowan . . . 'Came upon them. Found them out. Stumbled against.'
> 'The people?'
> 'Yes. The Miggles people.'
> 'I really cannot say,' said Clennam, 'where my friend Mr Meagles first presented Mr Henry Gowan to his daughter.' (I, chapter 26)

PROPRIETY IN CONVERSATION

In *Victorian England: Portrait of an Age*, G. M. Young inserts on the title-page the Victorian proverb: 'Servants talk about People: Gentlefolk discuss Things'. It is something that Molly Gibson notes in *Wives and Daughters* (chapter 13), when she returns from a short stay at Hamley Hall to the town of Hollingford and her old friends the Miss Brownings:

> She could not help having a sense of refinement, which had made her appreciate the whole manner of being at the Hall. By her dear old friends the Miss Brownings she was petted and caressed so much that she became ashamed of noticing the coarser and louder tones in which they spoke, the provincialism of their pronunciation, the absence of interest in things, and their greediness of details about persons.

Another point to be borne in mind about good conversation was that the visitor should not be confronted and perplexed by much talk of people with whom he was not familiar. One is reminded here of Mrs Elton's constant reference to 'Mr Suckling', 'Maple Grove' etc. in *Emma* – all meaningless names to the people of Highbury, since they were friends and associations from her native Bristol. The young American Richard Henry Dana was treated very differently when he visited the Lord and Lady Spencer of the day, at Althorp, in 1875:

> The conversation during dinner and in the evening was light and agreeable and such as to put a stranger perfectly at his ease. They did not talk, as people so often do before strangers, about their personal friends, speaking of 'Will' and 'John' and 'Susan' and 'Jane', or using nicknames, which would mean

nothing to a stranger; but if they did speak of friends at all, they spoke in such a way that I was able to understand to whom they referred. (*Hospitable England in the Seventies*, p. 71)

A further habit to be wary of in such society was the paying of compliments, especially, to use a frequent phrase, 'personal compliments'. Even today, we often prefix a compliment with the formula, 'If I may say so', to ward off embarrassment. One does, however, gain the impression that usage relaxed in this matter as the century continued. The *OED* (under *gentlefolk*) quotes the proverb 'Compliments fly when gentlefolk meet.' Nevertheless, the feeling against compliments was strong: 'Must not compliment, I know,' says Miss Bates, 'that would be rude' (*Emma*, chapter 38). The outcome of this restriction was that the verb *to compliment* was often more or less equivalent to 'to flatter': I'll tell you what, Harry, they're deduced well set, these lines of yours, and do you credit. They do; I'm not *complimenting* you' (Hughes, *Tom Brown at Oxford*, chapter 39). Mr Preston, in *Wives and Daughters*, had a stream of compliments 'like turning a tap' (chapter 29): 'he had assumed a tone of gallant familiarity with Lady Harriet, and paid her personal compliments as he would have done to an equal' (chapter 49). To Molly Gibson, the heroine, he delivered speeches in 'that kind of underbred manner', which showed his intention 'to convey a personal compliment' (chapter 20).

The flow of conversation might also be halted by the citing of authors that one had been reading or studying. The young Daniel Deronda is advised: 'Much quotation of any sort, even in English, is bad. It tends to choke ordinary remark' (*Daniel Deronda*, chapter 16). The place for quotations was the House of Commons, though even here, as Disraeli reminds us in *Endymion* (chapter 76), there had formerly been restrictions: 'Charles Fox used to say as to quotations – "No Greek; as much Latin as you like; and never French under any circumstances. No English poet unless he has completed his century."' Foreign phrases in conversation were usually unacceptable. The hero's mother in *Pelham* (chapter 26) writes to her son: 'You will also be careful, on returning to England, to make very little use of French phrases; no vulgarity is more unpleasing.' Mrs Gaskell, through Mrs Gibson and other characters, ridicules the pretentious tendency (found also in Mary Crawford in *Mansfield Park*), to quote French variants of what are often regular English words and phrases:

> The avocations of their daily life prevented their having such little *réunions* except in the vacations. ('Mr Harrison's Confession', chapter 8)

> Little tables, loaded with *objets d'art*, as Mrs Gibson delighted to call them. (*Wives and Daughters*, chapter 39)

As for Latin quotations, George Eliot is extremely sarcastic about these in a review article in *The Westminster Review* entitled 'Silly Novels by Lady

Novelists', October, 1856:

> In 'Laura Gay' ... the heroine [has] a quite playful familiarity with the Latin
> classics – with 'the dear old Virgil', 'the graceful Horace, the humane
> Cicero, and the pleasant Livy'; indeed, it is such a matter of course with her to
> quote Latin that she does it at a pic-nic in a very mixed company of ladies and
> gentlemen.' George Eliot's scathing comment is: 'It is as little the custom of
> well-bred men as of well-bred women to quote Latin to mixed parties; they
> can contain their familiarity with 'the humane Cicero' without allowing it to
> boil over in ordinary conversation; and even references to 'the pleasant Livy'
> are not absolutely irrepressible.

A further, and very vulgar, way of stopping conversation was by elaborate
puns, as Jorrocks finds (*Handley Cross*, chapter 39) in a conversation with
the wife of Marmaduke Muleygrubs, whose name was abbreviated to
'Duke':

> 'The Duke'll come on badly for fish, I'm thinkin'', said Mr Jorrocks, eyeing
> the empty dishes as they were taken off.
> 'Oh, Marmaduke don't eat fish,' replied Mrs M.
> 'Oh, I doesn't mean your duke, but the Duke o' Rutland,' rejoined Mr
> Jorrocks.
> Mrs Muleygrubs didn't take.
> 'Nothing left for *Manners*, I mean, mum,' explained Mr Jorrocks, pointing to
> the empty dish.

Plain English, then, was preferred in the best society, and this also
applied to the choice of individual words. A manual of etiquette, such as *The
Habits of Good Society*, published anonymously in 1859, states this
categorically:

> The best speakers will never use a Latin word where an Anglo-Saxon one will
> do as well: 'buy' is better than 'purchase', 'wish' than 'desire' and so on. The
> small genteel, you will observe, never speak of rich and poor, but of 'those of
> large and those of small means'. Another similar piece of flummery is the
> expression, 'If anything should happen to me,' which everybody knows you
> mean for 'If I should die' (p. 49).

A glance at Ross's article, produced a hundred years later, shows the same
fondness for the plain word, with pairs like *mirror* and *looking-glass*, *mental*
and *mad*, *preserve* and *jam* – each of these pairs being non-U and U
respectively. Mrs Gaskell, in the same tradition, advises against the florid
and the foreign in speech, when there is a choice. In a letter of 1852, she
writes: 'Don't call shifts "chemises". Take the pretty simple *English* word
whenever you can. As Mrs Davenport said the other day, "It is only
washerwomen who call shifts 'chemises' now"' (*Letters*, p. 181). In an essay
on 'Company Manners', Mrs Gaskell mentions people who put on an

unusual fineness of language with their best gowns: 'they say "commence" instead of "begin"; they inquire if they may "assist" instead of asking if they may "help" you to anything'. In addition, the elderly often preferred old-fashioned English expressions. Lady Cumnor (*Wives and Daughters*, chapter 9) has a personal servant called Bradley. Bradley was Lady Cumnor's "own woman" – she disliked the new-fangledness of "lady's maid". Correspondingly, we find *own man*, used instead, presumably, of *valet*: 'And up in the dicky behind was a servant, more arrogant, if possible, than his master – the baronet's *own man*' (*Dr Thorne*, chapter 34).

As to the use of what is sometimes delicately called strong language, there was, in polite circles, rather less of it as the nineteenth century proceeded. Dean Hole, in his book of reminiscences entitled *Then and Now*, (1902) recalls (p. 41): 'Sixty years ago the conventional gentleman was as profuse in his anathemas as . . . a Commination Service. . . . Those were days in which a Primate said to a Premier, "It may save time, my lord, if we assume before we commence our discussion that everybody and everything is damned."' Effective full-toned swearing, according to George Eliot, might confirm a person's status:

'A fine woman, Miss Brooke! an uncommon fine woman, by God!' said Mr Standish, the old lawyer, who had been so long concerned with the landed gentry that he had become landed himself, and used that oath in a deep-mounted manner as a sort of armorial bearings, stamping the speech of a man who held a good position. (*Middlemarch*, chapter 10)

By the time of *Daniel Deronda* (1876) it is seen, at least in George Eliot's eyes, as a sign of Grandcourt's corrupt nature that he swears in the company of his wife (chapter 35): '"I wondered how long you meant to stay in that damned place" – one of the freedoms he had assumed as a husband being the use of his strongest epithets.' Other men contrived to be more considerate before ladies. Mr Loiter, Lady Carbury's publisher, is rather more guarded when giving her advice:

And whatever you do, Lady Carbury, don't be historical. Your historical novel, Lady Carbury, isn't worth a——' Mr Loiter stopping himself suddenly, and remembering that he was addressing himself to a lady, satisfied his energy at last by the use of the word 'straw'. (*The Way We Live Now*, chapter 89)

With a man, the word was not spared. In his *Autobiography* (chapter 6), Trollope tells us that the foreman of the publishers Hurst and Blackett warned him: 'Your historical novel is not worth a damn.' By the 1870s, the young were even over-protected against this offending word. At their preparatory school, the young M. R. James and his coevals were read to on Sundays from books like *Pilgrim's Progress*:

Some of us who knew the text of the *Pilgrim* were agog to see whether in the episode of Doubting Castle the headmaster would give us the author's words and say, 'that lock went damnable hard'. When he came to the point, he checked slightly, and said 'desperate hard'. (*Eton and King's*, p. 10)

As to other kinds of impropriety in language, it is interesting to find the extremes of prudery condemned by several etiquette books. The anonymous author of *The Habits of Good Society* speaks of 'indelicate delicacy':

Perhaps the most delightful instance of this indelicate delicacy of terms was in the case of the elderly spinster – of whom I was told the other day – who kept poultry, but always spoke of the cock as the 'hens' companion'.

He continues, with some frankness for 1859:

If legs are naughty, let us never speak of them; if not naughty why blush to call them legs? The change of name cannot change the idea suggested by it. If legs be a naughty idea, then no recourse to 'limbs' will save you. (p. 48)

At the beginning of our period, in the 1830s, British writers felt a healthy superiority to the mealy-mouthed language they encountered in the Americas:

But I persevered, and named 'The Rape of the Lock' as evincing some little talent... but on the mention of this poem, the serious gentleman became almost as strongly agitated as when he talked of Don Juan... till he muttered, with an indignant shake of the handkerchief, 'The very title!' (Mrs Trollope, *Domestic Manners of the Americans*, chapter 9)

Similarly, Marryat, in *Peter Simple* (1834), had poked fun at the genteel ways encountered in the Barbadoes:

Supper was now announced, and having danced the last country dance with Miss Minerva, I of course had the pleasure of handing her into the supper-room. It was my fate to sit opposite to a fine turkey, and I asked my partner if I should have the pleasure of helping her to a piece of the breast. She looked at me very indignantly, and said, 'Curse your impudence, sar, I wonder where you larn manners. Sar, I take a lilly turkey *bosom*, if you please. Talk of *breast* to a lady, sar; really quite horrid.'

Walter Allen, who quotes this passage in *The English Novel* (p. 150), observes that such a passage could not have been written much later than 1834. 'After that, the joke was on the Victorians quite as much as on the genteel mulattoes of West Indian islands.'

This is an appropriate place to consider the word *delicate* and its antonym *indelicate*. *Delicate*, like *fine* (p. 101), was a somewhat dubious word. It could mean 'finely sensitive to what was proper', but also 'tender or feeble in constitution'. Trollope seems to have felt that there was more bad than good in the word and its associations, as he plays upon the two meanings in this

passage from *Can You Forgive Her?* Lady Glencora Palliser has remained
outside in the cold night air and Alice Vavasor, her companion, is rebuked
for encouraging this:

> 'The frost was so uncommonly severe... that any delicate person like Lady
> Glencora must have suffered in remaining out so long.'
> 'I hope you do not consider Lady Glencora delicate,' said Alice to Mr Palliser.
> 'She is not robust,' said the husband.
> 'By no means', said Mrs Masham.
> 'Indeed, no,' said Mr Bott.
> Alice knew that she was being accused of being robust herself; but she bore it
> in silence. Ploughboys and milkmaids are robust, and the accusation was a
> heavy one. (chapter 28)

What Trollope implies is that, compared to the sheltered and refined
environment Mrs Palliser has devised for Lady Glencora, ploughboys and
milkmaids 'have all the life'. This leads to the further possibility that too
great a fear of the indelicate may be morbid. Yet Alice is doubtless also
remembering an incident in chapter 6 of the novel, where she had herself
wielded the word *indelicate* without much success. The scene occurs at a
large hotel in Basle, below which, men are swimming, naked, in the Rhine.
Alice, despite being promised to a Mr John Grey, is on holiday with her
cousins Kate and George Vavasor. Kate tries to further her rather wild
brother George's suit, when Alice checks her:

> 'You are making me sorry, Kate, that I have ventured to come here in your
> brother's company. It is not only unkind of you to talk to me in this way, but
> worse than that – it is *indelicate*.'
> 'Oh, *indelicate*! How I do hate that word! If any word in the English language
> reminds me of a whited sepulchre it is that; – All clean and polished outside
> with filth and rottenness within. Are your thoughts delicate? that's the thing.
> You are engaged to marry John Grey. That may be delicate enough if you love
> him truly, and feel yourself fitted to be his wife; but it's about the most
> indelicate thing you can do, if you love any one better than him.

As with his cautious treatment of slang among ladies, Trollope hedges his
outspoken comments here with safe remarks about single-mindedness
in courtship and marriage. However, when Kate Vavasor urges Alice to 'lay
aside all delicacy and pretence', one cannot help feeling that this is Trollope
making a muted protest against the powerful sway of this word and its
implications in Society in the high Victorian period. In the end, of course,
Alice marries her cousin and, of course, we can forgive her.

In nineteenth-century England there were certainly many more devia-
tions from anything approaching standard English, even among the upper
classes, than there are today. Apart from the absence of present-day

standardizing influences, those with sufficient power and confidence in themselves (schoolmasters and titled ladies, for example), liked to alter the language arbitrarily:

> Lady William Powlett used to say of a man, that he had fallen into vanity – not that he had fallen in love. She would say 'Mr —— has fallen into vanity with Lady Augusta'. (Disraeli, *Reminiscences*, p. 112)

> The Duchess spoke with an enormous emphasis on every other word, sometimes putting so great a stress on some special syllable, as almost to bring her voice to a whistle.... 'I was telling Lady Glencora...that I never knew a house so warm as this, – or, I'm sorry to say,' and here the emphasis was very strong on the word *sorry*, – 'so cold as Longroyston.' And the tone in which Longroyston was uttered would almost have drawn tears from a critical audience in the pit of a playhouse. (*Can You Forgive Her?*, chapter 22)

No doubt such people had, to use a phrase from Gissing, 'philological crotchets': 'Probably he was a man of philological crotchets; he said, for instance, "pro-spect" (for prospect)' (*Demos*, chapter 1).

UPPER-CLASS EXPRESSIONS

Passing now from general points on what is 'proper' in conversation, it is appropriate to consider particular expressions felt to be signally upper-class in the nineteenth century. By many readers, even today, some of these will still be recognized as shibboleths for the upper-class speaker. So long-established are these small but significant points of distinction in English society.

It is difficult to find early instances for many of the smaller points of distinction made by Ross and Mitford, though Lady Grove has some in her book *The Social Fetich*. She gives rein to her feelings over the cosy clutter of what she calls (p. 11) 'middle-classdom':

> Not only is there an exclusive pronunciation and some distinctive expressions, but there are actual possessions which are reserved solely for the use of middle-classdom. Napkin-rings, fish-knives, tea-cosies, and oh! I shudder as I write the word, 'tidies' and nightgown-cases. The people who use them will, if I may be pardoned for mentioning so intimate a portion of a lady's toilette, substitute the French *chemise* for the homely English *shift*, call that portion of the outer garment that covers the body *a bodice*, talk about a *dress* when they mean *gown* and being *gowned* when they mean *dressed*, and at meals make use of an unnecessary *serviette*, instead of an honest *napkin*. They would no doubt 'ride' in a 'trap', a carriage, a train or a cab. And if the latter were a hansom and one of these were its sole occupant, he or she would possibly betray his or herself by sitting in the middle (or, as they would say, 'the centre') of the seat.

Clearly, Lady Grove's observations are apt to be rather random, but she doubtless would have claimed the right instincts, even when she was by no means sure of her reasoning (p. 28): 'Why, too, does the word *mirror* sound so out of place, when the more cumbrous double-barrelled *looking-glass* sounds quite appropriate?' Much of the clutter of 'middle classdom' that she mentions is Victorian in origin. *Tea-cosy* is first illustrated in the *OED* (under *cosy*) with a quotation from 1863, but there is also a note from Fitzedward Hall, 'known to me about 1848'. The objection to tea-cosies is made clear in *Manners and Rules of Good Society* (1888): 'Tea-cosies should not be used at afternoon tea; a fresh supply of tea should be brought in for new arrivals' (p. 40).

Serviette, the *OED* informs us, was in earlier use a Scottish word for a table-napkin or a towel. In the nineteenth century it was 're-introduced' with the French spelling, at first only as a foreign term. Then the editors add the fatal words: 'It may now be regarded as naturalized, but latterly has come to be considered vulgar.' Their last quote runs: 'I think . . . she was the sort who would call a table napkin a serviette.' It may be noted that there is no recognition here, or in the 1933 Supplement, of the paper serviette.

One of the most longstanding class indicators, it would seem, concerns the question of riding or driving. Matters were fairly simple when there were merely horses to ride on, or to be drawn in vehicles by. Even the convict Magwitch made the distinction naturally: 'My gentleman must have horses, Pip! Horses to ride, and horses to drive, and horses for his servants to ride and drive as well' (*Great Expectations*, chapter 40). As means of locomotion increased, the need to maintain this distinction of a former era was still insisted on. It seems to have obtained on this side of the Atlantic only. R. H. Dana, in *Hospitable England in the Seventies* (p. 77), noted this distinction as something with which he was unfamiliar:[17]

> Lord Spencer at breakfast asked me if I would like to ride with him to visit some farms. 'Riding' in England always means on horseback, and 'driving', in a carriage. He gave me a handsome mount, a really splendid horse.

This distinction between riding and driving had no ultimate justification in etymology or in the former usage of the language, as Dean Alford pointed out in *The Queen's English* (1870):

> There is not necessarily any such limitation of the meaning of the verb *to ride* . . . . *A road* is a broad path on which people may ride on horses and in vehicles; *a road* . . . for ships, is a part of the sea where they may *ride* or be borne at anchor. We have in Jeremiah xvii 25: 'Riding in chariots and on horses'; and such, as may be seen in the dictionaries, is the usage of all English writers. (p. 283)

[17] Dana's *riding on horseback* still strikes a jarring note, as does President Reagan's 'usual Wednesday afternoon *horseback ride*' (ITV News, 5 May 1982).

However, the distinction was maintained with a stubbornness that was sometimes amusing. Gertrude Jekyll, the landscape gardener, an eminent Victorian who survived to 1932, was taken to task by her friend Logan Pearsall Smith on this point. She contended that '*ride* . . . was only used for riding on something with four legs, like a horse or something analogous, like a bicycle':

> 'But Miss Jekyll, '[Logan Pearsall Smith] retorted, 'if you go on a bus, don't you take a ride on it'?
> 'But I never go on a bus!'
> 'But if you were given a lift by a farmer on the road?'
> 'I should call it a lift; a lift, certainly, not a ride.'
> 'But suppose, Miss Jekyll, that you wanted to go home from a hayfield on a loaded hay-cart? Wouldn't you ask if you could have a ride on the cart? Wouldn't you have to say *ride* – not *drive*?' Miss Jekyll looked disconcerted.
> 'Well,' she said at last, 'no, I shouldn't call it a *drive*. No, certainly not a *drive*.'
> 'Would you ask for a *lift* then?'
> 'No, I shouldn't call it a *lift*.'
> 'Now Miss Jekyll,' I insisted. 'What would you ask for?'
> 'I should ask – well I should ask – if you insist on knowing – I suppose I should ask for a *ride* in the hay-cart. But,' she added, 'but then, you know, I should be speaking to quite uneducated people.' (*Reperusals and Recollections*, p. 58)

Miss Jekyll claimed to come of 'armigerous' stock: 'that's my class, the class I belong to', as she put it:

> Armigerous people have certain expressions of their own. They don't, for instance, say *overcoat* – that's an Americanism, but *great-coat*: they *have* tea or coffee or sugar, they never *take* them; they never take anything into their bodies but pills and medicines, and these they don't talk about; armigerous men never say *vest*, they say *waistcoat*, but expect their tailors to use *vest*, in speaking to them and in sending in their bills. It would be an impertinence for a tailor to use the word *waistcoat* to an armigerous person. So, too, an armigerous person staying in a country house would not say: 'May I ask your butler, your footman, your groom, to perform such and such a service,' but would say, 'May I ask your servant.' (p. 63)

Another distinction of long standing was that between *knaves* and *jacks* in playing cards, made famous from the scene in *Great Expectations* where Estella plays cards with Pip: '"He calls the knaves Jacks, this boy!" said Estella with disdain . . . "And what coarse hands he has!"' (chapter 8). Refinement, or lack of it, was apt to be revealed when playing cards: 'As Miss Matty observed, though Mr Hoggins did say "Jack's up", "a fig for his heels", and called Preference "Pref ", she believed he was a very worthy man and a very clever surgeon' (Mrs Gaskell, *Cranford*, chapter 11). Later in the century, Sir Arthur Quiller-Couch touched on the same theme in *The Astonishing History of Troy Town* (1888): 'When Mr Simpson had spoken of the "Jack of Oaks" (meaning the Knave of Clubs) or had said 'fainaiguing" (where others said "revoking") we had pretended not to notice it, until at length we actually did not' (chapter 12).

The word *lounge* which, according to Ross and Mitford, is non-U for *drawing-room*, makes its first appearance in this sense in the *OED* in 1881: 'The *lounge* or drawing-room ... was extremely elegant'. This quotation is taken up by the recent Supplement, with several further instances, including Betjeman's sociologically conscious (and quietly farcical) 'It's ever so close in the *lounge*, dear/But the vestibule's comfy for tea.' The word that, with increasing prosperity and social pretension, was being replaced by *drawing-room* in the nineteenth century was not *lounge* but *parlour*. In *Hodge and his Masters* (1880), Richard Jefferies contrasts the old informality of life on a moderate-sized farm of 200 or 300 acres in his youth with more recent developments: 'None of the family come to the door to meet you. A servant shows you into a *Parlour* – drawing-room is the proper word now – well-carpeted and furnished in the modern style' (chapter 9). So, the Middle English and Anglo-French word *parlur*, with its earlier suggestions of exclusive, tête-à-tête conversations, still to be found in the phrase 'The Mayor's Parlour', has otherwise been quite demoted in class usage, as the late Victorian music-hall song 'When Father Papered the Parlour' suggests. The *OED* indicates this demotion in its definition (*parlour*, sense 2): 'when more spacious and handsomely furnished [the parlour] is usually called the drawing-room.' On the subject of room names, it is, incidentally, suburban usage, and very non-U, to refer to the lobby of the house as a *hall*, unless, as in really large houses, the main door gives on to a room of hall-like dimensions. The point was noticed by Albert Smith in *The Adventures of Mr Ledbury* (1844): 'Mrs Ledbury had requested the man five separate times to rub his shoes as he went through the "hall" – a portion of the mansions of England in the olden time, formerly known as the "passage"' (chapter 15). *Passage* has retained a certain currency in rural England, and in such contexts it has an honourable history. The situation is well summed up by Richard Jefferies in *Amaryllis at the Fair* (chapter 5). He describes the father of Amaryllis going 'into the passage' to get his hat: 'In farmhouses these places are called passages; in the smallest of villas, wretched little villas not fit to be called houses, they are always "halls".'

Sweet, according to Ross (*Don't Say It*, p. 109), 'meaning the after-meat course of lunch or dinner, is a well-known non-Uism. The U still say pudding, but this certainly leads to silliness – can an ice really be described as a pudding?' Nevertheless, in the more lavish meals of Victorian times, the word *sweet* is found and is traditional enough. The *OED* quotes from Hawthorne (*sweet* (noun), sense 1d): 'entremets and "sweets" as the English call them'. As etiquette books and Mrs Beeton make clear, 'sweets', catering for the guest with the sweet tooth, are only one element of a dessert, which could include fruit, nuts and (mostly for men) additional savouries. In Surtees's *Mr Sponge's Sporting Tour* (chapter 35) we find that a certain Lord Scamperdale 'settled to the *sweets*, at which he was a great hand at dessert'; while Jack Spraggon in the same book (chapter 25), 'worked away in his usual carnivorous style, and finished by paying his respects to all the *sweets*, jellies and things in succession.... At length Jack finished; and having discussed cheese, porter and red herrings, the cloth was drawn, and a hard-featured dessert, consisting principally of apples, followed.' These two quotes suggest a certain elasticity in the definition of dessert, but that the word *sweet* had a firm footing in the nomenclature of larger meals cannot be doubted. With more everyday meals, however, the word *pudding* seemed already well established for the after-meat course. Miss Matty in *Cranford* (chapter 14), a staunch supporter of correct usage, is obviously familiar with the term: 'Was that the reason Miss Matty wouldn't order a *pudding* today? She said she had no great fancy for sweet things, and you and she would just have a mutton-chop.' It was also the Queen's English. Writing of one of the less successful Highland expeditions, Queen Victoria says: Unfortunately there was hardly anything to eat... two miserable starved Highland chickens, without any potatoes! No *pudding*, and no fun!' (*Leaves from the Journal of Our Life in the Highlands*, (p. 226).

In one of Disraeli's most fashionable novels, *Lothair* (1870), a very superior picnic takes place. The luncheon baskets, for example, are 'a present from Balmoral'. The conveyance, however, may at first seem odd: 'My Lord has ordered the *char-à-banc*, and is going to drive us all' (chapter 15). A *char-à-banc*, according to the *OED* (letter 'C' was edited in the last century), is 'a kind of long and light vehicle with transverse seats looking forward'. In this century the *char-à-banc* became motorized, popularized, its name often reduced to *chara* and then rendered obsolete by the extension of the word *coach*. The word *chara* would not come under that rather rare designation 'old-fashioned non-U'. For those who remember that *charas* of the inter-war years will know that they attracted a very different clientèle from Disraeli's lords and ladies. The *OEDS* has the quotation: 'A flavour of paper hats and football rattles... clings still about the good old un-English word *chara*. But now the charabancs are all turned into coaches.'

Lothair must vie with Bulwen Lytton's *Pelham* for the title of the most rarefied high society novel of the century. It is interesting that it has, as a naturally correct phrase 'He must be going to be married' (chapter 30). The Countess of Munster objected to the phrase which has to a large extent replaced it:

You meet a happy prospective bride or bridegroom who rushes up to you and informs you with beaming eyes that he or she is 'going to get married' instead of 'going to be married'. These words are a great test, and nothing amazes me so much as the frequent recurrence of the hateful expression in novels written by authors who ought to know better. (*My Memories and Miscellanies*, p. 176)

In the course of the latter half of the nineteenth century, it became unfashionable to refer to the cooked flesh of poultry as *fowl*. Earlier, in *The Adventures of Mr Ledbury* (1844), there is mention of temporarily hired servants, who make off with '*fowls*' legs in their umbrellas' (chapter 22). Gordon Ray, in the second volume of his biography *Thackeray: The Age of Wisdom* (p. 327), depicts, from one of his sources, the novelist carving at a children's party, and calling out in impromptu verse:

Any little child that wants a little *fowl*
Must raise its little hand, and give a little howl.

But by 1907 Lady Grove, in *The Social Fetich* (p. 27), is quite firm on this point: 'If you have on your table no matter what specimen of the genus hen ... it must not be referred to as a *fowl*, it must always be spoken of as a *chicken*.' It is interesting that remote rural usage has caught up with late Victorian society in the last few decades. When I was a child, people in the south-west might have 'a fowl for Sunday dinner'; they now tend to have 'a chicken for Sunday lunch'.

Ross notes (p. 42) the U tendency to be proprietary about baths: 'To take a bath' is non-U against the U 'to have one's bath'. Perhaps not everyone had this sense as strongly developed as Kate Stanley, who at Carlsbad could say 'I am going to my bath now' (*The Stanleys of Alderley*, p. 285).

It is not the thing, of course, to refer to hounds as *dogs*. Hounds are for hunting and dogs are for shooting parties. Surtees makes much play, at various points in his tales, with this solecism:

'Well, I suppose Mr Harkington has a fine set of dogs this season?' 'A fine set of dogs this season!' What an observation! How on earth could any one hope to drive a conversation on the subject with such a commencement! (*Mr Sponge's Sporting Tour*, chapter 35)

In *Manners and Tone of Good Society* (p. 172) there is the warning:

A sportsman would at once dub a man a 'thorough cockney' were he to term the hounds when out hunting 'the dogs' .... It would appear laughable in the eyes of a sportsman were a gentleman or lady to speak of a fox's 'brush' as 'a tail'.

We may trust Kate Stanley to get this last point right: she writes of 'Miss Hope, the pretty girl who used to wear a fox's *brush* in her hat' (*Amberley Papers*, I, p. 112). *Dog* is a word that may be allowed to distinguish sex, however: 'The hounds were a fine lashing-looking lot, chiefly *dogs*' (*Handley Cross*, chapter 14); but Jorrocks adds the caution: 'Beware of callin' 'ounds dogs or sterns tails' (chapter 32).

On this all-important subject of hunting 'unsportsmanlike terms' are to be avoided:

> A man would not ask his friend if he had had 'a good day's hunting', but whether he 'had had a good run'; or he would ask him 'where did you find' and he would use other expressions of a like character. (*Manners and Tone of Good Society*, p. 173)

In an expression like 'Where did you find?' we note the tendency, discussed on p. 71, to use pseudo-transitive verbs, with a strong sense of an omitted object. We can consider, in this context, the absolute use of *to preserve*, meaning 'to keep game undisturbed for personal use in hunting, shooting and fishing'. Thackeray records it in *Pendennis* (I, chapter 26): 'Pendennis don't *preserve* then?'

When shooting, the true sportsman has great power of laconic utterance, which may be contrasted with the garrulity of the inexperienced:

> Thus, the inexperienced sportsman usually exclaims 'Go and find', 'There's a good dog', 'Find it, sir, find it', 'Hie, find', 'There's a good fellow', ... all this in a breath, and with growing excitement, confusing and bewildering the dog, and exasperating his fellow-sportsmen, who, by one word, addressed to the dog, such as 'Hie', 'Seek', or 'Steady' cause him at once to understand his duty. (*Manners and Tone of Good Society*, p. 175)

In addition, there are various words and phrases, not mentioned by Ross, which relate to upper-class customs. For instance, with the drawing-room so often on the first floor in houses of fashion, escorting a lady to dinner often meant 'taking her down' to the dining-room:

> She made a tremendous assault upon Harry Foker, who sat next to her, and to whom she gave all the talk, though I *took* her *down*. (*Pendennis*, II, chapter 2)
> I sat next to Frederica ... and *took down* Lady Alberta Edgcumbe, to the relief of Abercorn who was afraid he would have to *take down* his granddaughter. (Disraeli, *Letters*, II, p. 228)

All the etiquette books deal with the formality of paying calls, leaving cards, and so on. The best cards were thin and without glaze. Hence the vulgarity of a character in Thackeray's *The Book of Snobs* (chapter 12): 'He double-barrelled his name (as many poor snobs do), and instead of T. Sniffle, as formerly, came out, in a porcelain card, as Rev. T. D'Arcy Sniffle.' In *Plain or Ringlets?* (1860) Surtees suggests that the whole process of leaving cards was becoming rather nugatory:

> The science of calling has certainly got into very convenient compass of late, and little now remains to be done save to make a transmission of visiting cards by post a legal tender. As it is, nobody ever expects to get into a house .... If it was not for the drive, the whole calling custom would collapse, and yet people would remain quite as good friends as before. It's the beef and mutton that does the business, not the pasteboard. (chapter 5)

Among the 'good old English customs' that were declining, he lists (chapter 10), 'calling to see instead of *to card*'. The process of leaving cards was one meaning of the verb to *notice*:

> 'Not come yet!' replied Sir Thomas. 'Not come yet!' adding, after a pause, 'Well, I must *notice* him – I must notice him. Tell him when he comes that Major-General Sir Thomas Trout has called upon him – or stay,' added he, 'Jeremiah,' appealing to the coach-horse footman, 'give Miss Constantia a card out of my case.' (*Handley Cross*, chapter 62)

The first *OED* quotation for *out* meaning (of a young woman) 'introduced into society' (*OED* sense 26b), is from *Mansfield Park*, where the question is asked of Fanny Price: 'Pray, is she out or is she not out? I am puzzled. She dined at the Parsonage with the rest of you, which seemed like being out; and yet she says so little, that I can hardly suppose she is' (chapter 5). With the nobility and higher gentry, the issue is complicated by presentation at Court, as a mark of having arrived at a marriageable condition. Writing in 1846, the elderly first Lady Stanley declares her opinion that young ladies should not come out until this presentation has occurred:

> As for Alice ... I daresay it will not at all postpone her marrying, if you were to keep to the old custom and not to take her *out* at all, before she has been presented. (*The Ladies of Alderley*, p. 101)

> When do you wish to *start* Blanche? Is it lawful to do so before being presented. To my mind it is not lawful until the elder sister is disposed of. (p. 142)

Confirmation should come first:

> It would not do to put [confirmation] off for Blanche as then Alice might be in the world and the first year of Society is not generally one of much reflection. (p. 81)

There was at least one phrase which must have been upper-class in nineteenth century England, because it describes an activity that only the very rich could afford. This is the phrase (in context) *by land*, explained by Augustus Hare in *The Story of My Life* (I, p. 151), as he describes early rail travel to London in his youth:

> Long after the railway was made which passed by Whitmore (within a long drive of Stoke), we continued to go in our own carriage, posting, to Shropshire. Gradually my mother consented to go in her own carriage, on a truck, by rail as far as Birmingham .... Later still the whole journey was effected by rail, but in our own chariot. At last we came to use the ordinary railway carriage; but then, for a long time, we used to have post-horses to meet us at some station near London; my mother would not be known to enter London in a railway carriage – 'it was excessively improper' (the sitting opposite strangers in the same carriage); so we entered the metropolis '*by land*', as it was called in those early days of railway travelling.

I append, somewhat at random, certain words and phrases which carry a suggestion of upper-class usage. They are mostly epithets and modifiers, some of the latter being considered under syntax (see the section on upper-class grammar, pp. 67ff.):

1.   *Quantities*, meaning large amounts, has a tone of measured appraisal characteristic of U usage, and works by understatement. Further down the social scale there were slang alternatives (p. 92). Mr Harding in *The Warden* (chapter 16), somewhat naive and out of his element in a London 'cigar divan', meditates with rather aloof patrician phrases on the situation: 'There were *quantities* of books, and long rows of sofas. What on earth could be more luxurious than a sofa, a book, and a cup of coffee?' Earlier, Creevey had written (*Creevey Papers*, ed Gore p. 240) 'there were *quantities* of visitors in the house'; and later Augustus Hare wrote (*The Story of My Life*, IV, p. 430): 'At the end of our séance *quantities* of flowers appeared.'

2.   *Great* in present-day English, if used with reference to physical stature or size, expresses some additional feeling such as surprise, contempt, or admiration. This was the predominant usage of Victorian times also. Augustus Hare's dejection, for example, is indicated by this adjective in the following: 'Here we sat on the boarded floor, with very little food, in a *great* room looking upon some dripping portugal laurels' (*The Story of My Life*, I, p. 153). In contrast, Jane Austen had tended to use *great* with no emotional overtones, where we should now substitute *big*. Mr Elton, she tells us, was 'the adoration of all the teachers and *great girls*' in Mrs Goddard's school (*Emma*, chapter 17). It is interesting to find that Mr Harding retains this usage when talking to his granddaughter: 'When Posy is a *great girl* she can go to the cathedral every day' (*The Last Chronicle of Barset*, chapter 49). Here is the same phenomenon we have noticed elsewhere, of a slightly older usage of a word being called on by linguistically aware novelists, like Trollope and Mrs Gaskell, to indicate old-fashioned refinement. Disraeli also has this use of *great*. Writing in 1878 from Germany at the time of the Congress of Berlin, he says: 'The Empress . . . lives in a very pretty palace, not so gorgeous as the *greater* ones, but furnished with lavish taste' (*Letters*, II, p. 172).

3.   *Capital* is a favoured adjective, in a sense slightly extended from its etymology: 'chief, first-rate'. Paying tribute to Fanny Burney, Jane Austen had written (*Northanger Abbey*, chapter 14) of 'the *capital* pen of a sister author'. *Capital* is used later too between the young Queen Victoria and Lord Melbourne: 'I added I often forgot I was young. "That's a *capital* thing to be reminded of it," he said so kindly' (*The Girlhood of Queen, Victoria*, II, p. 240). The epithet carries a suggestion of accurate yet austere-sounding praise. Disraeli, writing from Berlin in 1878, says 'A *capital* passage and three days' travel brought me here' (*Letters*, II, p. 170). In

Don't Say It (p. 29) Ross notes 'That's capital', meaning 'very good' as 'an old U phrase which is probably obsolete today'.

4.   *Pretty* occurs in what seems a rather old-fashioned way to describe human behaviour, in the sense of 'fine, neat, pleasing, proper'. This survives in such an expression as 'He has a pretty wit', which the *OED* quotes from Sheridan. The word was common in phrases of aristocratic commendation: 'It would be but *pretty* of him to want for you' (*The Ladies of Alderley*, p. 203). *Pretty* has in some contexts come to suggest effeminacy, so that Creevey's 'I had a good walk with him and found him very *pretty* company indeed' (*Creevey Papers*, ed. Maxwell, II, p. 167), sounds less well now than it did in 1828. When Tennyson talked despairingly to the Queen about modern morality, she replied with 'Oh yet we trust that somehow good/Will be the final goal of ill.' 'I thought that was very *pretty*,' said Tennyson, 'to quote my own words in answer to me' (R. B. Martin, *Tennyson: The Unquiet Heart*, p. 539).

5.   The adjective *particular*, in the sense of 'especially attentive to a person; bestowing marked attention' (*OED* sense 9), is obsolete according to the dictionary, being last illustrated from Smollett. But the word still occurs, rather playfully, in contexts of courtship in Trollope, often with a suggestion of mannered, old-fashioned upper-class usage:

> Lord Lufton had met Griselda more than once already.... Lord Lufton had been rather *particular* in his attentions. (*Framley Parsonage*, chapter 11)

> 'Oh, but I'm not going to make a declaration at all,' said Frank. 'Are you not? Now Lady Margaretta, I appeal to you; did you not understand him to say something very *particular*?' (*Dr Thorne*, chapter 6)

6.   The use of the word *thing* instead of a more precise noun, whether to describe a social occasion or something else, lends a studied casualness that is patrician: 'Crabtree Canonicorum is a very nice *thing*; there are only two hundred parishioners; there are four hundred acres of glebe' (*The Warden*, chapter 13); 'I am glad it was a comparatively quiet *thing* on Saturday', (*The Ladies of Alderley*, p. 152). Thackeray implies that this usage can be overdone, as when the inarticulate Marquis of Farintosh, in *The Newcomes*, (II, chapter 4), has *thing* in place of all precise nouns:

> As you weren't there... the Miss Rackstraws came out quite strong. It was quite a quiet *thing*.... Lady Anne, you shirk London society this year... we expected you to give us two or three *things* this season... I said to Tufthunt, only yesterday, why had not Lady Ann Newcome given *anything*?

7.   If, as their critics said, the aristocracy had exempted themselves from the nuisance of work, they often used this word in the sense (*OED* sense 6) of disturbance, disagreeableness: 'He had occasionally been summoned by Dr Keate; that, too, was awful *work*' (*Coningsby*, I, chapter 3); 'I feel very nervous about the large Christmas, party at Alderley – with so many it will

be noisy *work*' (*The Ladies of Alderley*, p. 122). 'It is shy *work* being looked at,' says Blanche Stanley on her engagement to the Earl of Airlie (*The Stanleys of Alderley*, p. 14).

8.   It is always dangerous to oversimplify semantic change, but it is probably true to say that the word *stout* changed its meaning in the nineteenth century from 'robust' to 'corpulent' – the latter meaning being illustrated in the *OED* from 1804. There are several instances in Jane Austen of the older meaning of 'in robust health, especially in reference to recovery from illness', and this old-fashioned meaning continued, perhaps particularly in upper-class circles. Viscountess Palmerston wrote to Lady Stanley in 1864; 'Ld Palm is particularly well after all he has done ... and rode off 13 miles to see one of his racehorses so you may think he is very *stout* not to mind this hot weather and such a ride in the sun' (*The Stanleys of Alderley*, p. 301). The ultra-U cliché *stout fellah*! probably combined this sense of 'robust' (*OED* sense 6) with 'valiant' (*OED* sense 3).

9.   Ross draws attention to the word *civil*, (p. 42) as in 'The guard was certainly very civil,' used 'to approve the behaviour of a non-U person in that the latter has appreciated the difference between U and non-U'. The word in this sense was in full use in the last century. Mr Harding, in Trollope's *The Warden* (chapter 16), on a rare visit to London, enters a 'cigar divan' where the waiter offers him a couple of magazines and an evening paper: 'Was ever anything so *civil*?' thinks Mr Harding. The *OED* maintains a nice distinction between *civil* and *courteous*, the latter being more positive than *civil*: '*Courteous* is more commonly said of superiors, *civil* of inferiors, since it implies or suggests the possibility of incivility or rudeness.' It is a distinction that can hardly be maintained any more. Used in this sense nowadays, the word *civil* seems almost facetious.

UPPER-CLASS GRAMMAR

It would be wrong, as we have seen, to equate upper-class English with grammatical correctness.[18] There were, certainly, many grammars for Victorian ladies and gentleman to read, but young gentlemen, at least, were usually too busy learning Latin. When questioned by a lady about a point of grammar, Lord Ascot, in *Ravenshoe* (chapter 50) replied: "I can't say ... I was at Eton, and hadn't the advantage that you had of learning English

---

[18] One may venture to suggest that it was not gentlemanlike to care too much about grammar. There is an analogy from handwriting: 'At that time [c. 1832] the opinion existed that it was beneath a gentleman to write legibly, or with a hand in the least suitable to a clerk. Fred [Vincy] wrote the lines demanded in a hand as gentlemanly as that of any viscount or bishop of the day: the vowels were all alike and the consonants only distinguishable as turning up or down ...' (*Middlemarch*, chapter 56).

grammar.' Ladies and gentlemen, however, did have the advantage of constantly hearing from each other the most acceptable speech in the land, though they might, as we have seen, condescend to their workmen and inferiors by adopting occasional provincialisms. Even if they read little, they could acquire, free, that means of education for which Mr Tulliver paid for his son at the house of the Rev Walter Stelling: 'Tom's ear and tongue had become accustomed to a great many words and phrases which are understood to be the signs of an educated condition' (*Mill on the Floss*, II, chapter 7). Yet in this condition, in the early part of Victoria's reign, there were still many expressions that a more bookishly educated man might object to. 'Learn to know the House,' the autocratic Lord Monmouth advises the aspiring young politician Coningsby. '*Learn* the House to know you!' (*Coningsby*, VIII, chapter 3). The *OED* includes this sentence and one from Coleridge as evidently among the last instances of *learn* meaning 'teach' with any claim to be standard (*learn*, sense 4b, under a general heading 'now vulgar'). The word uttered in the dogmatic tones of Lord Monmouth, however, would no doubt suggest tradition rather than transgression. It took decades of schoolmasterly nagging to undermine such confidence! To take a further example: in the eighteenth century it had been thought allowable (though many grammarians objected) to follow *you* when it was a singular pronoun with *was*, and *was* instead of *were* had even been found with the subjunctive inversion, as in '*Was* I in your place'. Creevey records some old-fashioned speakers, including William IV, talking to the Lord Derby of the day, with these earlier uses of *was* for *were*:

> Then he said: 'How long have you been Lord Lieutenant of Lancashire, my lord?' and when he told him, the King said: 'I have often heard my father say you *was* the best Lord Lieutenant in England, and so you are now!' (*Creevey Papers*, ed. Maxwell, II, p. 226)

There is no doubt that such usage, though ungrammatical to our ears, was heard from speakers of good standing in the early years of Queen Victoria's reign. The first Lady Stanley, her roots deep in the eighteenth century, writing in the 1840s, has expressions like 'I suppose you *was* the culprit' and 'to see what you *was* doing' (*The Ladies of Alderley*, pp. 54, 62). *Was he* for the subjunctive *were he* might also have been heard. Creevey has: 'Then, *was he* to attempt it, his conduct would be exposed' (*Creevey Papers*, ed. Gore, p. 152).

Perhaps the *locus classicus* in this conflict between bookishness and traditionally acceptable speech is the disputed usage of contractions like *ain't* and *don't*. The anonymous author of *The Vulgarities of Speech Corrected* (1826) laid down the law very tidily (p. 22), overstating the case as grammarians sometimes will:

> The most common example, perhaps, of contractions, is that where the word *not* follows *am, are, is, was, were, do, did, have, had, shall, will, should, would, may, might, can* and *could*. Some of these are much less vulgar than others, but not one of them could be admitted into correct and elegant conversation.

No doubt this was setting the sights of correctness very high, though Susie Tucker points out (*Protean Shape*, p. 89) that the only people in Jane Austen's novels who use contractions (including all the contractions warned against here), are the flighty and the underbred. Even 'Isn't it?' is objected to as 'a bad arrangement of the words "Is it not?"'. Yet, what was more 'offensive to a grammatical ear' was the expression 'a'n't it' – 'decidedly the most vulgar and incorrect expression in common use'. Moreover it was made worse 'by sounding, as is usual, the 'a' long and open, like the word *faint* rather than short like the word *and*'.

The author of *Vulgarities* then turns from *ain't* to *don't*:

> I may remark of the vulgar contraction *don't* that when it follows the words *he, she* or *it* or the name of an individual, it is much worse than any of the others just mentioned, as it involves in that case a grammatical error, and is as bad as the expression *he do, she do, it do,* or *Mr B. do*. In order, therefore, to avoid this gross mistake, it would be well never to use *don't* at all, even after *they* and *we*, when, though it is vulgar, it is not ungrammatical.

The 'gross mistake' of *don't* for *does not* was acceptable colloquially at least down to the 1870s.[19] The following quotation shows the usage of some Oxford undergraduates: 'I put him down as a laster.... However, it *don't* matter now' (*Tom Brown at Oxford*, chapter 16). (But note: 'That girl *doesn't* care a straw for the other men,' chapter 15.) This ties in with the usage of the Vicar of Bullhampton: 'If he *don't* take care, he'll find himself in trouble' (*Vicar of Bullhampton*, chapter 17).

According to John Clark, writing of *The Language and Style of Anthony Trollope* (p. 36), *ain't* was in many respects parallel to *don't*; though *ain't* for *is not* was rarer, and found only with ladies like Lady Glencora Palliser and Miss Dunstable, who prided themselves on their free and easy habits of speech.[20] With men *ain't* in the third person was not common, though Clark found one instance from the normally exact and correct Plantagenet Palliser. I have also found one or two from Thackeray's Barnes Newcome,

[19] It was even acceptable, vestigially, very much later. Harold Macmillan, broadcasting on 19 November 1981, about authors published by the family firm of Macmillan, said he admired Thomas Hardy for his sincerity as a narrator. Many modern novelists, without this deeply felt 'sincerity', 'achieve a certain flashy success; but it *don't* last.' These are the accents of Macmillan's youth, doubtless; and also an excellent, if rather late, illustration of the difference between old-fashioned U English and 'correctness'.

[20] The danger was that of being thought as ignorant as Mrs Hudson, wife of the railway king, who, when visiting Grosvenor House, was shown a bust of Marcus Aurelius and inquired: 'It ain't the present Markis is it?' (Quoted by G. M. Young, *Portrait of an Age*, p. 53n).

who is circumspect enough: 'He *ain't* a prince, you know, any more than I am' (*The Newcomes*, I chapter 8). With other persons of the verb *to be*, *ain't* is fairly common from upper-class speakers:

> And here I come to tell you, and not a word can I get out of you. *Ain't you* pleased? (*Tom Brown at Oxford*, chapter 15)

> '*We ain't* safe in our beds, then,' said his wife.
> '*You ain't* safe in yours, my dear, because you chose to leave it.' (Vicar of Bullhampton and his wife, chapter 3)

It is most interesting to find Lady Grove, in *The Social Fetich* (p. 38) at the late date of 1907, fighting a rearguard action for upper-class colloquial speech, and against the by now considerable forces of strict grammatical correctness: 'If *ain't I* is objected to, surely *aren't I* is very much worse; and which of us can always undertake to keep up to the level of those who invariably say *Am I not?* or *Am not I?*'. For there was no doubt that the schoolmasters had won the battle. *Ain't I*, *he ain't* and *he don't* have ceased to be acceptable British English, though, according to *OEDS*, *he don't* still thrives colloquially in America, as of course in substandard speech it does here. Clark's impression is that these usages were beginning to be frowned on something like a decade before Trollope's death (1882). This would correspond in time roughly to the beginning of compulsory education for children. In fact, as we have just seen, condemnation occurred at least fifty years before. Yet Clark is probably right to think that wholesale opposition was not really organized till the arrival of the ubiquitous primary school teacher, 'a class of people entirely non-U', as Ross calls them (p. 47). Clark sees the outcry against 'dropping the g' in present participles as coming from the same source.

I now add some miscellaneous points of syntax that seem to me characteristic of upper-class writers and speakers. As with points of vocabulary, these are tentative suggestions as to usage rather than dogmatic assertions:

1.   The use of the present tense to express future time is notably characteristic of Jane Austen. The suggestion is often of something pre-ordained, ordered and inevitable: 'You are prepared for the worst, I see ....
Harriet Smith *marries* Robert Martin' (*Emma*, chapter 54). The effect of this tense in many similar contexts in Victorian times is likewise authoritative and dispositional, suggesting the organized life of the upper classes: 'Lady Cork ... *goes* out of town next week to produce her seventh daughter at Marston' (*The Stanleys of Alderley*, p. 267); 'On returning from my drive to Henley I found Arthur here, he had the afternoon to spare and *sleeps* here' (p. 291).

2.   An archaic usage with something of the 'tone' of aristocratic tradition

is that of the past tense where now the perfect (particularly what is sometimes known as the 'perfect of experience') is usual. Thus Mrs Palmer, in *Sense and Sensibility* (chapter 20), using what seems a normal idiom, has 'I never *was* at his house' where we should prefer 'I have never been at his house.' The idiom continues in the nineteenth century, but seems to be in decline: "I don't believe you were ever there before two days ago." "No, I never *was*"' (*Tom Brown at Oxford*, chapter 15). By the time of Browning's poem 'On a Toccata of Galuppi's' (1855), the phrase of the ageing narrator 'I *was* never out of England' is perhaps meant to sound old-fashioned. This is still more true when Carlyle, reported by William Allingham in 1875 (*Diary*, p. 236), says, 'I never *was* at a Royal Academy Exhibition.'

3. One may be more certain, I believe, of an example of traditional upper-class usage, with this third item. This concerns the absolute use of verbs where an object might have been expected. We can, of course, use verbs in this way still, but they are found in society novels of the nineteenth century almost to the extent of being a shibboleth, suggesting as they do an assumed knowledge and a certain exclusiveness. I have already mentioned *to preserve* meaning 'to preserve game' and *to find* meaning 'to find a fox' (see *Upper-class Expressions*). As so often, one can trace the tradition back through the century. When Disraeli writes (*Endymion*, chapter 18): 'There were anecdotes, too, of illustrious persons which always interest,' he recalls the same construction in Jane Austen: 'Any thing *interests* between those who love' (*Emma*, chapter 10). Disraeli, the Queen, and other aristocratic correspondents, are particularly fond of one of these pseudo-transitive verbs which has since, unhappily, fallen into disuse. This is *answer*, the force of which is now taken by expressions like *meet the case, fill the bill*, or simply *do*:

> Spoke of actresses; of their marrying out of their sphere; of its often not *answering*. (*Girlhood of Queen Victoria*, I, p. 256)
>
> Playing at being a hero and not doing it does not *answer*. (Disraeli, *Letters*, II, p. 145)
>
> I should not think, with the difficulty of getting people, that it would *answer* to have Lady Ashburton who cannot exist without amusement. (*The Ladies of Alderley*, p. 209)

In his *Reminiscences* (p. 138), Disraeli writes of a brilliant conversationalist: 'Such a ceaseless flow of contemporary anecdote I never heard. And yet she never *repeats*.' This last is clearly an absolute use of a reflexive verb, and the same is true of the characteristic *to show*, meaning, of a great person, to show oneself in public: '"Which is the Duke?" at last Frank contrived to whisper...." Oh – he's not here," said George; "I suppose he'll be in presently. I believe he never *shows* till just before dinner"' (*Dr Thorne*, chapter 19). Another curtailed reflexive verb is *to paint*, meaning, as we should now say, 'to use make-up': 'I wonder now whether she *paints*. Did you ever see such colour' (*Barchester Towers*, chapter 37). This curtailment occurred with colloquial verbs as well, and such verbs to have been especially common among the young in the best society:

A gentleman will always *lick* in a fair fight. (*Tom Brown at Oxford*, chapter 12)

I don't *take* [i.e. take you, understand]. (chapter 41)

Send us a card 'to *remind*'. (chapter 10)

'Is it settled', she asked...'has he *popped*?' [i.e. popped the question, proposed marriage]. (*Last Chronicle of Barset*, chapter 7)

Perhaps the most characteristic use of these pseudo-transitive verbs is to describe the customs and ceremonies of high society, as in the sentence 'Madame de Negra *receives* this evening' (Lytton, *My Novel*, X, chapter 7). Ross reminds us (p. 45) that upper-class language is apt to be curt, and this is a favourite way of producing such curtness.

4.   In W. H. Savage's little book, *The Vulgarisms and Improprieties of the English Language* (1833), the phrase 'I didn't ought to' is corrected to 'I ought not'. For generations 'didn't ought to' and 'didn't use to' have been objected to by purists, though not without difficulty in regard to *use*, where the forms without *did* in the negative and interrogative are unacceptably ugly in sound: 'usedn't he?' etc. Nowadays, forms with *do* are in favour. To quote Barbara Strang (*Modern English Structure*, p. 158), 'With *used to* prescription has taken the form of supporting the *do*-less forms against the forms with *do*. It is my impression . . . that in this case the open-class pattern (with *do*) is . . . most usual, at least in colloquial use and in the speech of the young.' I have very little doubt that many good speakers of English in the last century were abreast of modern youth in this respect, and chose to ignore the dictates of grammarians: 'You *did not use* to like cards' (*Persuasion*, chapter 22); 'But things *did not use* to be so in my young days' (Mrs Oliphant, *The Perpetual Curate*, chapter 2). An interesting passage occurs in *Great Expectations* (chapter 35), where Pip, having made progress in refinement, returns to visit his old home with Joe Gargery and Biddy, and signs of strain appear in their conversation:

'Not to mention your calling me Mr Pip – which appears to me to be in bad taste, Biddy, what do you mean?'
'What do I mean?' asked Biddy, timidly.
'Biddy,' said I, in a virtuously self-asserting manner, 'I must request to know what you mean by this?'
'By this?' said Biddy.
'No, don't echo,' I retarded. 'You *used not* to echo, Biddy.'
'*Used not*!' said Biddy. 'O Mr Pip! *Used*!'

Besides carrying on her inconvenient practice of 'echoing', and also, perhaps, nostalgically recalling happier times, Biddy is here, I believe, criticizing Pip's artificial, over-grammaticized English. She, and Pip in his unregenerate days, would have said 'You did not use to echo'.

5. A further small, but significant point arises from Savage's book quoted in (4) above, in which 'I ought not' replaces 'I didn't ought to'. There was clearly a proscriptive preference for avoiding *to*, which went along with the dislike of *do* in the above context, in so far as *ought*, for example, when not construed with *do*, could be considered on a par with other auxiliaries like *must*: 'You cannot; you must not; you ought not! Kind, generous Digby!' (Disraeli, *Henrietta Temple*, VI, chapter 19). The *to* which we now feel to be necessary in many such contexts is sometimes said to be a latent infinitive, for which the word *to* is the sole indicator. According to the *OED* (*to*, sense B 21), *to* used absolutely at the end of a clause, with ellipsis of an infinitive, is 'rare before the nineteenth century; now a frequent colloquialism'. This *to* is not found, so far as I have observed, in Jane Austen. It is significant also that, down to 1860 at least, it tends not to occur in conversation in Society novels, or where the speakers have any claim to refinement. In view of its greater frequency in present-day English, the absence of *to* is sometimes strongly felt by us, almost as a solecism:

> 'What a splendid music-hall! They should build one at Manchester.'
> 'They *ought*.' (*Conningsby*, IV, chapter 4)

> He does make fun of the Pilgrim's Scrip, and I think he *ought not*. (*The Ordeal of Richard Feverel*, chapter 34)

> I haven't opened a book yet, and don't *mean*. (*Tom Brown at Oxford*, chapter 10)

> I . . . cannot understand why Mamma did not let me read [*Dombey and Son*] when it first came out – I remember she said she *wished me not*. (*The Stanleys of Alderley*, p. 281)

Speakers from the lower ranks of society obviously felt uneasy about this 'resumptive *to*', as it is also sometimes called. They occasionally followed it with the anomalous pronoun *it*: '"She has been my mistress a long time, sir," answered Peggotty. "I *ought to it*"' (*David Copperfield*, chapter 4); '"I wonna stay upo' that man's land a day longer nor I'm forced *to't*"' (Mrs Poyser in *Adam Bede*, chapter 40). In such contexts, the upper-class speaker has the confidence to remain silent, adding no further particles.

In a late (1889) edition of *The Queen's English* (p. 202), Dean Alford has an interesting comment on this:

> 'The proper conventional answer to such a question as "Were you going to do it?" is "I was going to" or "I was not going to" as the case may be; not "I was going", in as much as the mere verb "to go" does not express any mental intention. I know,' he adds, 'in saying this, that I am at variance with the rules taught at very respectable institutions for enabling young ladies to talk unlike their elders; but this I cannot help; and I fear this is an offence of which I have been, and yet may be, very often guilty.'

It is clear from this that omission of this resumptive *to* was seen in some quarters, during the last century, as a mark of refinement.

6.   I have noted in my book, *Jane Austen's English* (p. 142), the novelist's tendency to omit the verb *to be* after auxiliaries. This is in some ways parallel to the omission of *to*, just discussed. In each instance the auxiliary that lacks the infinitive can be referred back to the previous part of the verb *to be*. Again, our sense of omission is obviously stronger than it seems to have been in the early and mid-nineteenth century. It is a usage that is found chiefly among upper-class speakers:

> I ever shall be grateful; I mean, we all *must*. (*Henrietta Temple*, VI, chapter 15)
>
> 'I sincerely hope that she may be happy.'
> 'I think she *will*,' said Mrs Grantly. (*Framley Parsonage*, chapter 30)
>
> 'I mean to be happy, Walter.'
> 'I hope you *may*, dear'. (*The Vicar of Bulhampton*, chapter 33)
>
> Montagu is with me as much as he *can*. (*Disraeli, Letters*, I, p. 56)

7.   It was a refinement in writing and also in speech, judging by the dialogue of the novels, to continue an idiom that had been frequent in the eighteenth century, and which was especially common, for example, in Fanny Burney. This was, the use of a perfect infinitive after a verb in the past tense, particularly when an intended, but perhaps abortive, attempt is being described. It is obsolescent usage once again, but also something of a class-indicator. It is the refined characters in Mrs Gaskell, for example, who have the idiom:

> I quite expected to *have seen* Mr Thornton. (*North and South*, chapter 37)
>
> I did mean *to have returned* to Milton on Thursday. (ibid., chapter 43)
>
> Talked of Clark's boy wishing *to have gone* into the Navy. (*The Girlhood of Queen Victoria*, II, p. 71)
>
> The present Duke... had joined his father in cutting off the entail of the Buckingham estates... and had intended *to have done* the same with regard to the Chandos... This led to delays... and certain insurances to a great amount... which the father had intended *to have converted* into money, were kept up. (Disraeli, *Reminiscences*, p. 134)

8.   We use the construction *is to* frequently today, in a sentence like 'Tom *is to* come home at once.' But the meaning tends to be restricted to contexts of strong compulsion. In eighteenth-century and Regency use the suggestions of arrangement and compulsion are often less strong: 'is likely to' is often a better gloss than 'must'. Again, there were survivals of this usage in Victorian times. Maria Josepha, first Lady Stanley, was thirty when the nineteenth century began, but she lived till 1863. In her youth she had known Gibbon. There are several instances of this older usage in her letters,

and it must have qualified as 'old-fashioned U': 'The safety of England *is to depend* mainly, upon whether the Irish Catholic Church is to be endowed or not' (*The Ladies of Alderley*, p. 199); All one's old historical ideas *are to be turned* topsy turvy in these days' (ibid., p. 107). In a rather different but still old-fashioned way, the negative of the construction can occur meaning 'do not have to': a mere negation of a compulsion rather than a prohibition in the contrary direction:

> 'Mary,' he said, 'I *am not to believe* this message . . . . I do not believe it. I will not believe it.' (*The Vicar of Bulhampton*, chapter 64)
>
> Of course we could change all that. *We're not to settle* every little thing beforehand. (*Mr Scarborough's Family*, chapter 44)
>
> I must speak of him. A man *isn't to hold* his tongue when everything he has in the world is at stake. (*The Last Chronicle of Barset*, chapter 35)

9. The auxiliary combination *must have* now relates to present supposition about the past, as in 'You must have been a beautiful baby'. In old-fashioned nineteenth-century usage, however, it could indicate necessity in the past. We may trust Disraeli, for example, to retain this meaning for the phrase: 'If Gladstone had threatened to resign, as he did about the Paper Duty, he *must have* gained his point' (*Reminiscences*, p. 111). It is also seen in Kingsley: 'If it ever took place I *must have* heard of it' (*Ravenshoe*, chapter 52).

10. Disraeli, who was novelist at the beginning and at the end of his career, liked to recall the usage of his youth. When he writes, in *Reminiscences* (p. 111), of an envious prelate that 'he never *recovered* the appointment of Dr Thomson to York,' he is using *recover* in a quasi-transitive way that is typical of the first quarter of the century. To find another example I had to go back to Bulwer Lytton's *Pelham* (1828): 'I did not *recover* the fright for an hour and a quarter' (chapter 4).

11. In correct writing and even in speech, there was a tendency for the subjunctive to be used more frequently than today. *Had* in the sense of 'would have' and *were* in the sense of 'would be' were both more common, even in main clauses, where they are obsolescent today. The mood was especially likely where the speaker was not only well-connected but also bookish. With Dr Casaubon, for example, in *Middlemarch*, the subjunctives come thick and fast: 'It *had been* easy for me to gain a temporary effect'; 'it *were* well if all such could be admonished' (chapter 20). Or there is the Reverend Josiah Crawley, rebuking Mrs Proudie: 'Madam, you should not interfere in these matters. You simply debase your husband's high office. The distaff *were* more fitting for you' (*The Last Chronicle of Barset*, chapter 18).

It is not irrelevant to notice here, partly because it is a distant memory of the subjunctive ('would have' is often a possible gloss), the use of the pluperfect tense where we now expect a preterite, in clauses following verbs of thinking. This is another small point that is very much a marker of upper-class speech, with a distancing effect comparable to the preterite infinitive in similar contexts just discussed: 'I thought you *had known* him by sight, or I would have prevented your making a mistake by describing him to you' (Surtees, *Ask Mamma*, chapter 24); 'I did not think it *had been* so late' (Mrs Oliphant, *The Perpetual Curate*, chapter 7).

12.   The indefinite pronoun *one* has never been fully naturalized into English, in the way that *on* has into French. Nominally self-effacing, this pronoun paradoxically suggests a certain over-confidence and even arrogance. In a *Punch* article (V, p. 52) of January 1844, which is a burlesque of a series of absurdly snobbish articles by Lady Londonderry ('Journal of a Visit to Foreign Courts'), the author (probably Thackeray) ridicules the excessive use of the pronoun: 'How pretty that way of saying "annoying *one* with *one's* maid at *one's* bedside" – one only finds people of fashion ever use one's language in the proper way – does one . . . I call it the unique way.' It is probably correct to consider such use of this pronoun as typical of upper-class ladies. Here is Lady Canning to Lady Stanley (*The Stanleys of Alderley*, p. 196): 'A few startlingly good characters surprise *one*, and I believe that *one* can hope and wish only that Govt . . . should do their best.'

13.   A curious pregnant use of the demonstrative pronoun *this*, meaning 'this place', especially in the phrase 'leave this', seems to have had aristocratic sanction. The Queen sent Disraeli a telegram from Balmoral, announcing her intention to delay return to London on account of a local funeral:

> 'A valued favourite servant of ours and especially of the Prince's died this morning, and I will not leave without paying the last respect to his memory. I shall therefore leave *this* on Tuesday.' And this morning, a letter containing a long biography of the dear deceased, duly arrives. (Disraeli, *Letters*, II, p. 247)

Likewise in Trollope:

> 'If I can lighten the load—'
> 'You have lightened it – of half its weight; but, Sir Peregrine, I will leave *this*—'
> 'Leave this! go away from the Cleeve!' (*Orley Farm*, chapter 26)

14.   To name diseases with a preceding definite article is one of the instances of older usage (like *town* for London, p. 21), which had been formerly fashionable, but which were later non-U. To quote Lady Grove in *The Social Fetich* (1907), socially unacceptable people 'say they have *the toothache* instead of *a toothache*, and will suggest the necessity of having the offending tooth "drawn" when others would have theirs "pulled out". They will talk about having caught *the measles* instead of *measles*' (p. 37). Ninety

years before, this had been Jane Austen's usage. In *Mansfield Park* Fanny Price has *the headache* and the coachman has *the rheumatism*. As late as 1878, however, Disraeli could write 'I am extremely unwell, having *the bronchitis*' (*Letters*, II, p. 185). But Disraeli was a traditionalist, a connoisseur of archaism, and this would doubtless count, in Ross's terms, as old-fashioned U.

There is an omission of the definite article before the word Government, that seems to have been, and probably still is, establishment usage. The suggestion is that one is on terms of intimacy with the powers that be: 'If his policy or the execution of it does not please *Govt* [*sic*] he begs that he may be relieved immediately' (*The Stanleys of Alderley*, p. 187).

15. Certain uses of adverbs were suggestive of upper-class speakers though it is not always easy to say in what things such distinctions consisted. *Absolutely* in the sense of 'actually, positively, as a simple fact', qualifying the truth of a statement, rather than the fact stated (*OED*, sense 8), is one such use:

> Would he have a cup of coffee, or would he prefer sherbet?
> Sherbet! Was he *absolutely* in an Eastern divan? (*The Warden*, chapter 6)

> 'And you have *absolutely* been with the attorney general?' said the archdeacon. (chapter 18)

> The stupidest fellow that ever lived – the only man who ever stood two contested elections and never opened his mouth; *absolutely*. (Disraeli, *Letters*, II, p. 207)

A further mark of refinement was the positioning of the adverb *quite*, meaning 'completely', to give an effect of crispness and distinction:

> We shall *quite* deserve to be punished by God. (A. H. Clough, *Correspondence*, I, p. 51)

> Yesterday he was very good, and wrote much more copy book than I desired, I believe *quite* to please me. (*The Amberley Papers*, II, p. 510)

> Count Andrassy is a very picturesque gentleman. I have gained him *quite* and he supports me in everything. (Disraeli, *Letters*, II, p. 175)

In upper-class speech, *quite* was much more frequent as an intensive than in the sense of 'moderate': 'The late Duchess of Sutherland... said of Mrs Norton, "She is so nice, what a pity she is not *quite* nice; for if she were quite nice she would be so *very* nice"' (*Mrs Brookfield and her Circle*, II, p. 525).

There was some hesitation, among well-educated Victorian writers, about modifying adjectives which derived from past participles with the adverb of degree *very*. *Very pleased* and *very delighted* were described as 'Americanisms', though in fact these constructions, while going back no further than the middle of the eighteenth century in the language, were British enough. Fitzedward Hall, friend and helper of the *OED* editors, in his *Modern English* (p. 55) quotes *very concerned* from 1760 and *very unqualified* from Gibbon in 1762. Sometimes, to the modern reader, the required addition or substitution of *much* seems unforced, particularly where the verbal element is strong: 'Lady Agnes looking *much* saddened' (*The Stanleys of Alderley*, p. 229); 'He is very sore and *much* hurt and wounded' (*Amberley Papers*, II, p. 322). But where the participle has come to have the force and currency of an adjective, a certain stiltedness is suggested, although the usage is very much the mark of the best people: 'they were *much* vexed at A. leaving so soon' (ibid., p. 292); 'I was *very much* delighted' (A. H. Clough, *Correspondence*, I, p. 55); '"Very nice party," Lord M. said, "and everybody *very much* pleased"' (*The Girlhood of Queen Victoria*, I, p. 329). It is still usual to retain *much* in (*very*) *much obliged*.

THE ACQUISITION, AND THE INFLUENCE, OF UPPER-CLASS SPEECH

Ross (p. 47) asks whether upper-class speech ever can be successfully acquired. He says that in his experience an adult can never be completely successful, though 'there is one method of effective change of voice, provided the speaker is young enough. This is, to send him first to a preparatory school, then to a good public-school.' It all depends, clearly, on the importance to be attached to relatively small, though not insignificant, points of speech. Bulwer Lytton, surprisingly, seems to have acknowledged that there were such people as 'Nature's gentlemen'; but he too has to admit that unpolished language is the last infirmity of noble minds:

> The Countess . . . was struck to find the son of Mark Fairford the carpenter so thoroughly the gentleman. He might not have the exact tone and phrase by which Convention stereotypes those born and schooled in a certain world; but the aristocrat of Nature can dispense with such trite *minutiae*. (*My Novel*, X, chapter 11)

But the father of Harry Richmond, in Meredith's novel, would not have agreed that such things were minutiae:

> 'More than his eating and his drinking, that child's father worrits about his learning to speak the language of a British gentleman,' Mrs Waddy exclaimed. 'Before that child your "h's" must be like the panting of an engine – to please his father. He'd stop me carrying the dinner-tray on meat-dish hot, and I'm to repeat what I said, to make sure the child haven't heard anything ungrammatical . . . . That's because he's a father who knows his duty to the child: – "Child!" says he, "man! ma'am." It's just as you, John, when you sow your seed you think of your harvest. So don't take it ill of me, John; I beg of you be careful of your English. Turn it over as you're about to speak.'
> (*The Adventures of Harry Richmond*, chapter 3)

However, in a manner characteristic of such things in England, the wiser counsels, the pragmatism and moderation of Mrs Waddy's brother-in-law, Farmer Thresher, prevail over these extremes. His is the farm on which young Richmond is brought up:

> 'Change loads on the road, you mean,' said John Thresher. 'Na, na, he's come to settle nigh a weedy field, if you like, but his crop ain't nigh reaping yet. Hark you, Mary Waddy, who're a widde, which's as much as say, an unocc'pied mind, there's cockney, and there's country, and there's school. Mix the three, strain, and throw away the sediment. Now, yon's my view....' 'What John says is worth listening to, Mary. You may be over-careful. A stew's a stew, and not a boiling to shreds, and you want a steady fire, and not a furnace.' (Ibid., chapter 3)

Ross implies (p. 21) that there are few material or even social advantages to be gained from upper class speech in the second half of the twentieth century, though he does suggest the Navy and the Diplomatic Service as enclaves which in 1954 were, to use his own term, not yet 'democratized'. In the last century, on the other hand, an upper-class accent was of enormous advantage. For an illustration we might, once again, consider Henry Kingsley's *Ravenshoe*. Charles Ravenshoe, who has exchanged his identity as a country gentleman for that of a footman in London, penetrates into a London riot on a compassionate errand, to be turned back by an inspector of police. But Charles retaliates by 'forgetting his top-boots, and speaking "de haut en bas", as in old times':

> 'As for you, young man, you march back home double quick. You've no business here. It's seldom we see a gentleman's servant in such company in this part of the town.'
> 'Pooh! pooh! my good sir,' said Charles: 'stuff and nonsense. Don't assume that tone with me, if you will have the goodness. What the young woman says is perfectly correct. If you can assist me to get to that house at the further end of the court, where the poor boy lies dying, I shall be obliged to you. If you can't, don't express an opinion without being in possession of circumstances. You may detain the girl, but I am going on. You don't know who you are talking to.'
> How the old Oxford insolence flashed out even at the last! The inspector drew back and bowed. 'I must do my duty, sir.'

The authority of this is unmistakable, but Charles, be it noted, does not offend unnecessarily. He would like to befriend his opponent once he has his way. There are still various phrases in English like 'If you will have the goodness' and 'I shall be obliged to you', which can be either obsequiously polite or offensively authoritarian depending on context and intonation. Probably it is the upper classes who employ these phrases with most skill and authority. They are part of the language of government by consent. A little later in the novel, the inspector rallies round, but he still mingles deference with his reproaches:

> Sir, if gentlemen disguise themselves they must expect the police to be somewhat at fault till they open their mouths. Allow me to say, sir, that in putting on your servant's clothes you have done the most foolish thing you possibly could. You are on an errand of mercy, it appears, and I will do what I can for you.

Having made his point, Charles is profuse with flattery: '"By Jove ... do you know that you are a deuced good fellow? I am sorry that I was rude to you, but ... I hope you'll forgive me." "Not another word, sir," said the inspector' (*Ravenshoe*, chapter 60). Insolence alternating with good breeding might still carry a young man far in the days when the upbringing of the majority gave them neither the manner, nor the confidence, to retaliate.

2

The Lower Orders

A MULTIPLICITY OF FORMS AND CLASSES

Despite what has been said in the previous chapter about ungrammatical elements in upper-class English, it was language at this level of society that presented the nearest approach to uniformity in nineteenth century England. Ladies and gentlemen going to London for the season, and schoolboys attending public schools, usually within easy reach of the capital, submitted themselves to strong standardizing influences. At the other end of the scale, in the East End, for example, the errors of speech were not only numerous but numerously varied, as that keen observer of the poor, M. E. Loane, pointed out in 1907:

> It is quite incorrect to represent the poor as always making the same errors in speech – to do this would be far more remarkable than to display grammatical accuracy. The same persons will at different times use as the past tense of *see*, *see*, *seed*, and *saw*; while others will ring the changes on *sawed*, *did see*, and *saw*. They will leave h's out one day, and not another; they will say alternatively *he has*, *he have*, and *he haves* ... and so on. A woman entirely alters her phraseology according to whether she is speaking to a child, to her husband, to a neighbour or an employer, and the difference is still more marked among men. In certain districts when men are speaking to one another even upon such general topics as the weather their language is almost unintelligible to a stranger, but they can if they choose make themselves readily understood by him. (*The Next Street But One*, chapter 1)

An important phrase here incidentally, is 'if they choose'. There is no doubt that there was, and still is, a defensive use of substandard English. A small instance occurs in *The Vicar of Bullhampton* (chapter 3), where the vicar collars the ne'er-do-well Sam Brattle:

'That, after all, you should be at this work, Sam!'
'What work is it then?'
'Prowling about my place, after midnight, with a couple of strange blackguards.'
'There ain't so much harm in that, as I knows of.'

'Who were the men, Sam?'
'Who was the men?'
'Yes; – who were they?'
'Just friends of mine, Mr Fenwick.'

Amongst the middle classes, we may be equally aware of a great variety of irregularities and solecisms: a variety that seems strange to us today, influenced as we have been by a constantly broadcast standard English, and by a regular and fairly uniform system of education. The best evidence for this is to be found at the beginning of the period in certain books published for those who wished to aspire socially, and who were prepared to trim their language accordingly: books like *The Vulgarities of Speech Corrected*, published anonymously in 1826 and *The Vulgarisms and Improprieties of the English Language*, published by W. H. Savage in 1833. Such books represented a 'second wave' of improving grammars, following those that had appeared so numerously in the second half of the eighteenth century. They are less systematic, however, and more pragmatic, concerning themselves solely, as their names imply, with correcting offences, chiefly of speech rather than writing. Errors of pronunciation, accidence, syntax, idiom and general taste are dealt with in a haphazard way. They must have been very easy books to write, but, partly because they are not scholarly, they probably faithfully represent the confused and confusing state of the English language for the social climber. They also confirm many of the substandard features of the language to be found in early Victorian novels. When Savage, for example, recommends *I had no occasion* for *I had no call*, *He resembles his father* for *He favours his father*, *on the second floor* for *up two pair of stairs*, *thirsty* for *dry*, *He grieves* for *He does take on so*, *Animals feel as much as men* for *as much as Christians*, *employment* for *employ* and *You've rumpled my dress* for *You've tumbled my dress*, he recalls, in the phrases he rejects, many similar instances from the less refined characters in these novels.

Some expressions, according to Savage, needed to be expunged entirely: *He took me by the scruff of the neck* is a 'sheer vulgarism'. *I was spilt twice* meaning *thrown from a horse* is a 'gross vulgarism'. *I am chuckful* means *I am chokeful*, that is *full up*, but it is a 'low expression'. Colloquialisms frequently needed pruning: *I have never a one* is better rendered *I have none*. *Else* is better omitted from 'Give it to me or *else* I'll tell'; and *tote* from 'That's the whole *tote* of it.' (This word is now no longer an abbreviation of *total* but of *totalizator*!) In the phrase 'a matter of fifty' we can substitute *about* for *a matter of*. *If so be as how you know it* amounts to *If you know it*; rather as *Take and do it* equals *Do it*. With 'Mind *as* you do it' *as* is redundant, as is *for* in 'I'll tell you *for* why,' and the prefix *a-* in 'I can't *abear* it.' In 'leave the door *upon the jar*' the last three words are better reduced to *ajar*. *She's gone dead* is a 'tautological vulgarism'.

Reading the parallel lists of vulgar and correct phrases in *Vulgarities* is like bidding farewell to old friends of good standing. The 'vulgarities' are often phrases that now appear to be hallowed by the very best usage. Abbreviation, more common in earlier English, is out of favour, and to be sacrificed to precise elocution. Yet the really surprising thing is the number of 'Shakespearean' phrases still current at this date:

What's that, i' the name of wonder.	I wonder what that is.
All's in vain.	All is in vain.
The scar on's cheek.	The scar on his cheek.
I'll come t'ye.	I shall come to you.
An't please you.	If it please you.
Thoud'st not refuse me.	You would not refuse me.

As we shall see when considering pronunciation, Savage, in a similar vein, endeavours to put a stop to numerous variant vowels and diphthongs on which Elizabethan punsters had thriven.

This variety in speech was not merely historical in scope, it was geographical also. Provincialisms, far from being in retreat as they are now, flourished in the streets of the capital. Savage lists many words and phrases that must have been in use among Londoners, and that we now feel to be strongly dialectal. *While* for *till*, for example, as in 'She can't come *while* evening', is, according to the *English Dialect Dictionary* (1905), likely to have come from the Midlands or further north, being especially characteristic of Yorkshire. *Slippy* for *slippery*, is also condemned by Savage, but is in general dialectal use, according to the dictionary (and the most recent dialect atlas confines it to the Midlands). Again generally dialectal is *gallows* for *braces*, as in 'Where are my gallowses?' (with characteristic substandard double plural).

There was, in addition, much overlap and confusion of vocabulary. Savage quotes the description of someone '*stinted* in growth and *stunted* in food' and the case of *fear* and *afraid* which had become vulgarly interchangeable: 'She's *afeared*'; 'she won't for '*fraid* of the law'. Pruning was even necessary in matters of morphology, for Savage recommends that *physicianer* and *musicianer* be deprived of their double suffix (one foreign, one native agent suffix). There are hundreds of such 'vulgarisms' in Savage's lists, and presumably they were common in the speech of the middle-class reader sufficiently ambitious socially to invest in a book on such a subject.

In his original article 'Linguistic Class-indicators in Present-day English', Ross wrote of those speakers who were 'non-U' as 'the antonyms' of the upper class. We are reminded of Jorrocks's convenient distinction: 'I'm only a tradesman – a post hoffice directory, not a peerage man' (*Handley Cross*, chapter 23). We shall need to be more precise than this, though linguistic distinctions between the lower classes are not easy to make, largely because they are less well documented. Nevertheless, the classes were in fact becoming more elaborately distinguished as the nineteenth century continued. The author of an unsigned review of *Silas Marner* in 1861 (*George Eliot: The Critical Heritage*, p. 171) admired George Eliot's 'portraiture of the poor, and of what it is now fashionable to call "the lower middle classes"'. Anne Mozley, reviewing *Adam Bede*, also admired the close demarcation of the classes (p. 97).

> Every class that makes up a village community has its representative; and not only is the dialect of the locality given but the distinct inflexion of each order. The field labourers' rude utterance 'as incapable of an under tone as a cow or a stag', receives a touch of cultivation when it is used by a mechanic; and these two, again, are varied in the farmhouse.

It is certainly true that farmers are distinguished in speech from their working-class inferiors in this novel. The latter have the more extreme inflections of dialect, for instance. Contrast a woman from the family of Chad Cranage the blacksmith, with the well-to-do Mrs Poyser:

> 'What's the matter wi' ye?' said Bess the matron . . . . 'Ye'n sweltered yoursen, I reckon, running that fool's race. An' here, they'n gi'en you lots of good grogram and flannel, as should ha' been gi'en by good rights to them as had the sense to keep away.' (chapter 25)

> 'And to think of your knowing no better, Molly, and been here a-going i' nine months, and not for want of talking to, neither – and what are you stannin' there for, like a jack as is run down, instead o' getting your wheel out?' (chapter 6)

As to the villagers' mode of utterance, Anne Mozley is of course quoting the novel she is reviewing:

> Villagers never swarm; a whisper is unknown among them, and they seem almost as incapable of an under tone as a cow or a stag. Your true rustic turns his back on his interlocutor, throwing a question over his shoulder as if he meant to run away from the answer, and walking a step or two farther off when the interest of a dialogue culminates. (chapter 2)[1]

The same careful distinction between the classes appears in *The Mill on the Floss*. The well-to-do Dodson sisters speak, on the whole, in correct grammar, with the exception of *as* for *that* and an occasional adjective form in an adverbial function. Their less than standard pronunciation is indicated

---

[1] In this respect, if in no other, they resemble Cambridge academics: 'When we have succeeded in meeting accidentally, it is etiquette to talk about indifferent matters for ten minutes and then part. After walking five paces in the opposite direction you should call me back, and begin with the words, "Oh, by the way, if you should happen..."' (See F. M. Cornford, *Microcosmographia Academica*, Cambridge, 1908, p. 30).

by the occasional elision of a consonant in words like *allays* and *awk'ard* – letters to her publisher show how much George Eliot was concerned to get such minor points right. For the most part, however, the speech of the Dodson sisters is realized by a faithful and loving recording of idioms and turns of phrase known to the novelist from her youth:

'Did Mr Tulliver let you have the money all at once?' said Mrs Tulliver....
'No; *at twice*,' said Mrs Moss.
They live so back'ard mong the lanes at Basset, they niver hear anything *only when* Mr Moss comes to market.
So far as I know, this is the first time *as here you've been*, since it's been known as the bailiff's in the house. (*The Mill on the Floss*, III, chapter 3)

With Bob Jakin the pedlar, on the other hand, the solecisms are frequent, as his scapegrace character is delineated in his speech: 'They say he'll niver lift up his yead no more – I shouldn't ha come to ax you to gi' me another knife, 'cause you *gen* me one afore' (III, chapter 6). *Gen* for the preterite singular and plural of *give* is still to be heard in the Midlands, but only at working-class level. George Eliot also noticed that every speaker of dialect operates, as it were, on a sort of sliding scale. At times of intimacy and friendliness (perhaps also in times of anger), a man like Adam Bede casts aside standard English:

'Donna thee sit up, mother,' said Adam, in a gentle tone. He had worked off his anger now, and whenever he wished to be especially kind to his mother, he fell into his strongest native accent and dialect, with which at other times his speech was less deeply tinged. 'I'll see to father when he comes home; maybe he wonna come at all tonight. I shall be easier if thee't i' bed.' (*Adam Bede*, chapter 4)

NON-U SPEECH IN COUNTRY AND IN TOWN

I propose now to consider some of these various levels of language below the rank of the gentry, first in the country, and then in the town. In 1844, in *Coningsby* (III, chapter 3), Disraeli talks of the denizens of the country as 'Nobility, clergy, gentry, yeomanry and peasantry'. *Peasantry* was an unacceptable term; as for yeomanry, this was a word used less and less in the nineteenth century, except for archaic and romantic effect. According to the *OED*, a *yeoman* was 'a commoner or countryman of respectable standing, especially one who cultivated his own land'. If Trollope is to be believed, the answer to the question Edward German was to ask in the light opera *Merrie England* (1902), 'Where are the yeomen, the yeomen of England?', was that they had become 'gentlemen farmers':

> There were in the country round sundry yeomanry, as they ought to be
> called, – gentlemen farmers as they now liked to style themselves – men who
> owned some acres of land, and farmed these acres themselves. (*The American
> Senator*, chapter 1)

It is interesting that the two terms are already being bandied about in *Emma*.
Emma does not notice Robert Martin: 'The *yeomanry* are precisely the order
of people with whom I feel I can have nothing to do'; but to Mr Knightley,
defending Martin's right to marry Harriet Smith, he is a 'respectable,
intelligent *gentleman-farmer*!' (*Emma*, chapters 4, 8).

The acid pen of Richard Jefferies is needed to delineate the rise of the
gentleman farmer. Note his word 'Society' with a capital 's' for what the
OED calls (*society*, sense 3c) 'those persons collectively who are recognized
as taking part in fashionable life':

> Today, if you call at such a country house, how strangely different is the
> reception! None of the family come to the meet you. A servant shows you into
> a parlour – drawing-room is the proper word now.... She then takes your
> name – what a world of change is shown in that trifling piece of etiquette! By-
> and-by, after the proper interval, the ladies enter in morning costume, not a
> stray curl allowed to wander from its stern bands, nature rigidly repressed,
> decorum – 'Society' – in every flounce and trimming. (*Hodge and his
> Masters*, chapter 9)

The gentleman farmer may well have lived at a *grange*, defined by the *OED*
as 'a country house with farm buildings attached, usually the residence of a
gentleman farmer'. Trollope noticed this also:

> 'I know the walk well,' said Rawson, 'though I never was inside the park.'
> 'It ain't much of a park. Indeed there isn't a semblance of a park about it.
> Grange is just the name for it, as it's an upper-class sort of homestead for a
> gentleman farmer. We've lived there since long before Adam, but we've never
> made such of a house of it.' (*Rachel Ray*, chapter 26)

Even tenant farmers could be concerned to promote themselves socially,
or at least, as Chaucer knew, their wives would push them into higher
positions. The upward-striving farmer is typified by the Lookalofts in
Barchester Towers. As mentioned before, Miss Monica Thorne in that novel
had tried to arrange her guests in something like traditional social ranking at
the *fête champêtre* she holds, but:

> Where will you put Mrs Lookaloft, whose husband, though a tenant on the
> estate, hunts in a red coat, whose daughters go to a fashionable seminary in
> Barchester, who calls her farmhouse Rosebank, and who has a pianoforte in
> her drawing-room? The Misses Lookaloft, as they call themselves, won't sit
> contented among the bumpkins. (chapter 35)

Mrs Lookaloft forces her way into the drawing-room with the gentry, and feels triumphant, if somewhat uncomfortable: 'It might be fairly expected that from this time forward the tradesmen of Barchester would, with undoubting pens, address her husband as T. Lookaloft, Esquire' (chapter 36). Trollope tells us that Rosebank had formerly been named, more earthily, Barleystubb Farm. 'Rosebank' was probably wishful thinking on Mrs Lookaloft's part. One is tempted to compare this sentimental nomenclature with Ross's note on *home* (p. 44) in which he contrasts 'They've a lovely home' with the more realistic U variant 'They've a very nice house.' The phrase 'The Misses Lookaloft', also, is not the best usage (see p. 159).

At a rather lower level, however, farmers knew that such pretensions to gentility and prosperity would not do:

> 'But they say travelling makes people genteel, Luke. I've been on the Continent with my lady, through all manner of curious places; and you know when I was a child, Squire Horton's daughters taught me to speak a little French, and I found it so nice to be able to talk to the people abroad.' 'Genteel!' cried Luke Marks.... 'who wants you to be genteel, I wonder? Not me for one; when you're my wife you won't have overmuch time for gentility, my girl. French, too! Dang me, Phoebe, I suppose when we've saved money enough between us to buy a bit of a farm, you'll be parlyvooing to the cows!' (Braddon, *Lady Audley's Secret*, 1862, chapter 3)

For the speech of the rural working classes, the influence of Board Schools, set up compulsorily after 1870, was crucial. Frederick Elworthy, writing for the English Dialect Society in 1888, describes the process of correction and modification:

> The children have all learnt to read, and have been taught the 'correct' form of all the verbs they use. The girl would come home, and her mother would say, 'Lize! you didn ought to a-wear'd your best shoes to school.' Eliza would say, 'Well, mother, I wore my tothers all last year, and they be a-wore out.' In this way parents become familiar with the strong forms of literary verbs, but they have no notion of dropping the past inflection to which they have always been accustomed, while at the same time they wish to profit by their children's 'schoolin'. Consequently the next time the occasion arrives, Eliza is told she should have *a-wor'd* her tother hat, & c., and thus *wor'd* and *a-wor'd* soon become household words with the parents; and the same or a like process is repeated by them with respect to other words all through their vocabulary. All children naturally copy their parents' accent, tone and sayings.... Consequently the school-teaching sets the model for written language, and the home influence that for everyday talk. The result is that at the present moment our people are learning two distinct tongues – distinct in pronunciation, in grammar and in syntax. A child, who in class or even at home can read correctly, giving accent, aspirates (painfully), intonation, and all the rest of it, according to rule, will at home, and amongst his fellows, go back to his

vernacular, and never even deviate into the right path he has been taught at school. (*The West Somerset Word-Book*, Introduction, p. xliv)

Did Hardy read Elworthy's book? It is more than likely. At all events, in 1888 he was collecting material, and beginning the writing of *Tess of the Durbervilles*, whose heroine's speech is described thus:

> Mrs Durbeyfield habitually spoke the dialect; her daughter, who had passed the Sixth Standard in the National School under a London-trained mistress, spoke two languages; the dialect at home, more or less; ordinary English abroad and to persons of quality. (chapter 3)

More typical perhaps, particularly in view of the increasing size and number of towns, was the situation described by an HMI, F. H. Spencer, in *An Inspector's Testament* (p. 66), who was at school in Swindon in the 1880s. He claims to have a common, and generalized urban accent that had, nevertheless, a rural base:

> In speech I acquired the accent and the intonation of the common people. That is sometimes a trifling inconvenience; and though the population was of so diverse an origin, so strong is the local speech of the countryside that we all spoke the mid-Wessex speech, the speech of Gloucester, Berks and Wilts, which thickens into Somerset as you go West.... Fifty years of intercourse with people of all kinds and much travel have seemed not entirely to dissipate all traces of that speech.... The grammatical peculiarities of the Wiltshire yokel... were not, however, ours. We did not say 'Her be gwaain whoam' for 'she is going home'. Nor did we use *thic* or *thuc* or the dozen other locutions still in common use in North Wiltshire. But most people who know the vowel sounds of the English provinces, and can recognize the Wessex *r*, would place me today as a native of mid-Wessex.

Spencer admits that he acquired 'all the bad language of the common people', though his father never swore, and his mother would have been shocked at the vocabulary he learnt. But he reflects that other classes too have their bad language: 'Later life has taught me, however, that Eton and Oxford might have infected me with a vocabulary more offensive if less robust, and sanctioned it to a later age.... We of the skilled working classes become respectable earlier than the products of the public-school system.'

Turning from the country to the town and the City of London, we note that in 1877 when Meredith wrote his short story, 'The Case of General Ople and Lady Camper', a member of the landed gentry has the assurance to assert linguistic superiority over someone who clearly cuts some figure in the City. General Ople is a man with many City friends, named, not without satire, by Meredith as 'the Pollingtons, the Wilders, the Wardens, the Baerens, the Goslings'. As a widower, he woos Lady Camper, widow of Sir Scrope Camper, and niece of an Earl. We have already noted her objection to words like *female* and *gentlemanly*. She does eventually bring herself to mention the word *gentlemanly*, only to encounter further vulgarisms:

'You have a gentlemanly residence.'
'It is, my lady, it is. It is a bijou'.
'Ah!' Lady Camper sighed dejectedly.
'It is a perfect bijou!'
'Oblige me, General, by not pronouncing the French word as if you were swearing by something in English like a trooper.'
General Ople started, admitted that the word was French, and apologized for the pronunciation (chapter 4)

As Lady Camper explains to him, 'Vulgar phrases have to be endured, except when our intimates are guilty, and then we are not merely offended, we are compromised by them.' Their conversation continues its chequered career:

'You are still of the mind in which you left me yesterday? You are one day older. But I warn you, so am I.'
'Yes, my lady, we cannot, I say we cannot check time. Decidedly of the same mind. Quite so.'
'Oblige me by never saying "Quite so". My lawyer says it. It reeks of the City of London.' (chapter 5)

It is probably the parade of officiousness and the pseudo-precision of this which gives offence; rather like Mr Elton's habit of saying *exactly so* (*Emma*, chapters 6, 13).

Furthermore, there were worse expressions, it seems, than *female*:

'I have no female relations, but I could send her to the seaside to a lady-friend.'
'General Ople, I forbid you, as you value my esteem, ever – and I repeat, I forbid you ever – to afflict my ears with that phrase, "lady-friend"!' (chapter 5)

Here General Ople thinks, not unreasonably, that Lady Camper is being arbitrary: 'He had never heard Her Majesty speak at levées of a lady-friend, but he was quite sure that she had one; and if so, what could be the objection to her subjects mentioning it as a term to suit their own circumstances?' Had the General been a reader of Shelley, he might at least have been reassured that the compound had been in the language for some decades: ('Bring home with you/That sweet strange lady-friend', *Rosalind and Helen*, l. 91).

One of Lady Camper's final objections is widely shared by the etiquette books of the second half of the century. This is *thanks* for *thank-you*. Lady Camper describes it as a 'vulgar contraction of decent speech', and 'fit for fribbles'. The anonymous author of *Society Small Talk* (1879) rather too complacently believed that the expression had been shown off the premises: 'The courteous "Thank you" has in a measure replaced the uncourteous

"Thanks", and it is no longer considered "very fine" to make this curt curtailment' (p. 119). Before finally accepting General Ople's hand, Lady Camper sums up her instruction by sending him a number of pen-and-ink drawings, with what would now be called sub-titles (chapter 6):

> Wilsonople informs the Moon that she is 'sweetly pretty'. He thanks her with 'thanks' for a handsome piece of lunar green cheese.
> He points to her, apparently telling someone, 'my lady friend'.
> He sneezes 'Bijou! bijou! bijou!'

A generation before the 1870s and Meredith's story, Surtees was writing a series of tales which also turned, but in a broader, less subtle way, on the contrast between the City and the landed gentry. General Ople and his friends, of course, really are 'something' in the City, or at least have connections with City magnates, whereas Surtees' hero, Jorrocks, is but a grocer, though a wealthy one. A great deal must be allowed, also, for the refinement in manners that went on between the 1830s and the 1870s. Jorrocks has a foot in both camps, being a grocer of Great Coram Street and also a huntsman with the Surrey foxhounds. Surtees sets the scene in *Jorrocks's Jaunts and Jollities* with language for City merchants and their activities that was fast dying out: 'the hardy exploits of our fellow *cits*'; '"Let's to business", as they say on *Change*.' Dr Johnson had defined *cit* in 1755 as 'a pert low townsman; a pragmatical trader'. Trade and hunting matters are curiously intermingled: 'Cottons is fell.' 'Hark to Cottager! Hark!' 'Eu in there, eu in, Cheapside, good dog' (chapter 1). At a still lower level, the tradesmen's servants rob the till while the masters are away at the hunt and, appropriately, thieves' slang accompanies the deed: 'He can *prig* as much "pewter" from the till as will take both himself and his lass to Sadler's Wells theatre!' The language of the City allows for a certain coarseness, drawing obviously from a rich store of slang, as seen in the following:

> Tom, however, who is 'large in the boiling piece,' as they say in Whitechapel, is prevented by his weight from being shaken out of the saddle. (chapter 1)
> The fog . . . became denser at every step. 'Hold my 'oss,' said Jorrocks to the Yorkshireman, 'while I run into the "Angel" and borrow an argand burner, or we shall be *endorsed* to a dead certainty.' (chapter 2)

(Surtees's note on *endorsed* reads: 'City – for having a pole run into one's rear.') Catch-phrases are part of the humour. When Jorrocks rides with his fellow-huntsmen through the Strand, he is assailed by Cockney irony: 'Vot a vip the gentleman's got! Vot a precious basternadering he could give us – my eyes, vot a swell! – vot a shocking bad hat!' (chapter 2). (Surtees's note explains that 'Vot a shocking bad hat!' is 'a slang Cockney phrase of 1831'.) On social occasions, the language of the Jorrockses and their associates is inevitably more contaminated by trade than people who moved in the best society might like: Mr Jorrocks used to say that Mrs Jorrocks was '"warranted'" to him as twelve years younger than himself'; someone compliments this same lady on being 'fifty per cent younger' in her appearance than formerly; someone else congratulates the Jorrockses on the amount of soup available at dinner: 'I'm sure you look as if you had your soup "on sale or return", as we say in the magazine line' (chapter 12).

Jorrocks is firmly in the tradition of those Englishmen who regard French as an unfortunate necessity, and he maltreats the language as much as possible. He hopes a guest 'can put up with our homely fare, and do without... *blankets of woe* [blanquettes de veau], and such-like miseries. I hates their '*orse douvers*, their *rots* and their *poisons*' (chapter 12). He prefers good English slang: 'Tell him to *mizzle*, or I'll *mill* him,' that is, 'Tell him to disappear or I'll hit him'; to which we may add rather stale phrases, such as '"Now's the day and now's the hour"; who's for some grouse?' and facetiously ambiguous compliments like: 'Thank you, Mr Crane, for your assistance – your politeness, sir, exceeds your beauty!' Each time one of the company makes an excruciating pun – and this happens quite often – Jorrocks replies 'Werry good – I owes you one.' This repetitive element is not, of course, characteristic of upper-class conversation. In the same way, Jorrocks keeps repeating his favourite proverb, 'Waste not, want not'. But some of Jorrocks's slang percolates upwards. The absolute use of *a few*, meaning by litotes 'a good bit', and possibly, the *OED* suggests, a comic Gallicism based on *un peu*, is used by Jorrocks (chapter 6) when faced with the ridiculous question of whether he hunts:

Stranger: What! you hunt, do you?
Jorrocks: A few.

Charles Kingsley, in *Two Years Ago* (1857), finds this a suitable collocation for gentlemen: 'But, my dear boy, if one man in a town has pluck and money, he may do it. It'll cost him *a few*' (III, chapter 7). There are, in any case, lower forms of conversation than those Jorrocks and his cronies indulge in, and such talk Mrs Jorrocks is determined to avoid: 'Don't let us have any of your low-life stable conversation here' (chapter 12). Reading Jorrocks, as when reading early nineteenth-century colloquial English generally, we may speculate chronologically both ways. Considering, for example, a statement like 'My aunt, who is a werry *feeling* woman, insisted on my staying all night' (chapter 11), we may recall more serious usages like Jane Austen's 'a very feeling letter'; and on the other hand we may gain a foretaste of modern Cockney in '"I must go *and all*" said another gentleman' (chapter 2). When Jorrocks says 'the commercial gentleman (or what were called bagmen in my days' (chapter 13), we may take this along with 'Mr Jorrock's bagman... or "representative", as he calls himself' (*Handley Cross*, chapter 43), and

speculate on the line of ascent, through *bagman, commercial gent(leman)* via
commercial traveller to *rep(resentative)*; each innovation, probably, being a
euphemism.

In *Handley Cross* (1843) Jorrocks is appointed MFH (Master of
Foxhounds), and makes many speeches and gives several lectures, in the
kind of substandard language that frequently recalls Savage's *Vulgarisms*.
Here, for example, are *play-actor* (chapter 10) and *stage-player* (chapter 70),
where Savage recommends either *actor* or *player*. Here too is the redundant
free gratis which Savage had deplored: 'Waxlights are supplied without
charge – or "free gratis", as the waiter says' (chapter 62). Here is frequent
aphesis, as mentioned by Savage: 'When they *"gage* in an undertakin"'
(chapter 32); 'It's a beef-eater – what they stick outside to *'tice* the company
up' (chapter 31). Here also is the free use of *Christians* for 'persons', which
Savage had disliked: 'Foxes like damp beds as little as Christians'
(chapter 26). When Surtees writes (*Plain or Ringlets?*, chapter 1) 'What a
sight of money that man will have!' meaning a spectacular amount, he is
again using a colloquialism condemned by Savage. For *sight* in 'What a *sight*
of nuts!' Savage recommended the U word *quantity*.

More interesting is the tendency to use the catch-phrases of the chase,
stronger no doubt among the masses than among the classes. Jorrocks
suggests some appropriate places for these phrases:

> 'Does your mother know you are out?' is a familiar inquiry that may be safely
> hazarded to a bumptious boy in a jacket. 'More dirt the less hurt!' is a pleasant
> piece of consolation for a friend with a mud mask; and 'One at a time, and it
> will last the longer! is a knowin' exclamation to make to a hundred and fifty
> friends waiting for their turns at an 'unting-wicket.' 'Over you go; the longer
> you look the less you'll like it!' may be 'ollo'd to a friend lookin' long at a fence.
> 'Hurry no man's cattle! you may keep a donkey yourself some day!' is the
> answer to the last. When you see a lawyer floored, sing out, 'There's an 'oss
> alayin' down the law!' If a chap axes if your nag will jump timber say, "He'll
> leap over your 'ead.' These, and such as these, are your ticket for soup, as
> the cook said when she basted the scullion with the hox-tail!

In frosty weather, not fit for hunting, there was a suitable bit of by-play:

> 'Not hung yourself yet, Gillespie?' suitin' the haction to the word by feelin'
> your neck and cockin' your thumb under your hear, is a fine sportin'
> interrogatory to put to a frind in the street durin' a frost. (*Handley Cross*,
> chapter 32)

In his narrative Surtees is fond of a turn of phrase which converts an
adjective to a noun after a definite article: 'Miss, however, did *the fine* by
desiring Frederick to tell her maid to bring a pocket-handkerchief'
(chapter 76); 'as she turned . . . to do *the agreeable* to the caller' (chapter 75);
'He mustered courage to do *the expensive*, and asked me to fetch him a fly'

(chapter 12). Rather different, and based on French, as some of the foregoing may also be, is *to do one's possible (faire son possible)*: 'I shall be most happy to *do my possible*' (chapter 42). The last phrase is found in more reputable contexts: '*Do your possible* to talk my uncle into coming' (*The Small House at Allington*, chapter 8).

There is one curious trick of speech found in Surtees, which happily seems not to have survived. It can never been a U habit. It consists of punning on the name of an eminent man for more general purposes. Anyone being foolish is exhorted to be Cardinal Wiseman; anyone being rude is reminded of Lord John Manners. It is difficult to imagine someone today announcing that he is not so Jimmy Young as he used to be: 'Be Cardinal Wiseman for once, and don't think of it'; 'Bravo, young Chesterfield... what it is to be thick with Lord John Manners!' (*Mr Sponge's Sporting Tour*, chapter 63).

THE LANGUAGE OF TRADE

Town tradesmen like Jorrocks presented a much bigger threat to their social superiors than rural labourers who made no claims:

> Are those the Gormans who made their fortunes at Southampton? Oh! I'm glad we don't visit them. I don't like shoppy people. I think we are far better off, knowing only cottagers and labourers and people without pretence. (*North and South*, chapter 2)

Things were very different with 'shoppy' tradesmen, who of course tended to be townsfolk, lower middle-class and apt to mingle obsequiousness with over-familiarity. It was something that was complained of from the beginning to the end of the Victorian period. Sometimes the assertion of familiarity was grammatical, as with Pelham's tailor in Bulwer Lytton's novel (*Pelham*, chapter 44):

> 'But, sir, *we must* be padded; we are much too thin; all the gentlemen in the Life Guards are padded, sir.'
> 'Mr—,' answered I, 'you will please to speak of *us* with a separate, and not a collective pronoun.'[2]

At the end of the century Gissing, in the posthumously published *Will Warburton* (1905), depicts the same mixture of deference and assertiveness in the grocery trade. The eponymous hero, having lost some of his money,

---

[2] The sartorial use of the first person plural pronoun is happily still current. A friend of mine, hiring morning dress for a wedding in some haste, was sped on his way by a helpful assistant as he put the final touches to the outfit: 'There we are, sir! And when we have done up our flies we shall be ready!'

acquires a grocer's shop under the alias of Jollyman, where his behaviour marks him out as superior to the average shopman:

> Such a gentlemanly man... I never saw a shopkeeper who behaved so nicely.... Mr Jollyman is a shopkeeper, and it's just because he doesn't forget that after all, that his behaviour is so good. Do you remember that horrid Stokes, in King's Road? There was a man who thought himself too good for his business, and in reality was nothing but an underbred, impertinent creature. I can hear his 'Yes, Mrs Cross – no Mrs Cross – thank you Mrs Cross' – and once, when I protested against an overcharge, he cried out, 'Oh, my *dear* Mrs Cross!' The insolence of that man! (chapter 19)

In the end Warburton remains a grocer, and actually marries Bertha Cross – the time is the turn of the century after all – though at one point the idea of being married to a shopman had been unacceptable to her:

> 'Perhaps the truth is yet more awful,' said Bertha solemnly. 'He may have got a place *in a shop.*'
> 'Hush! Hush!' exclaimed the other, with a pained look. 'Don't say such things!'
> A poor clerk is suggestive – it's possible to see him in a romantic light – but a *shopman*! (chapter 29)

Warburton's conclusion is:

> I can't say that I glory in grocerdom, but the plain fact is that I see nothing degrading in it, and I do my day's work as a matter of course. Is it any worse to stand behind a counter than to sit in a counting-house? Why should retail trade be vulgar, and wholesale quite respectable? (chapter 45)

Others asked the same question. The answer was in part that the prejudice against the retail trade, asserted in the more influential etiquette books, filtered down from court drawing-rooms and levées. The frequently re-published *Manners and Tone of Good Society* (1879) makes the following categorical statement (pp. 63–4):

> 'Drawing-rooms' and 'levées' are yearly attended by those ladies and gentlemen who have been presented to her Majesty and at 'drawing-rooms' and 'levées', presentations are made by various of the ladies and gentlemen attending.... The persons entitled to attend drawing-rooms and levées are the families of the aristocracy, the families of the county gentry, persons belonging to either the military and naval professions, the bar, the clerical, medical, and other professions, the families of merchants, bankers, and members of the Stock Exchange, and persons engaged in commerce on a large scale; but at trade, known as retail trade, however extensive its operation, the line is drawn, and very strictly so, as were a person actually engaged in trade to obtain a presentation, his presentation would be cancelled, as soon as the Lord Chamberlain were made aware of the nature of his occupation; but the sons, and daughters, of the wealthy manufacturers, are not themselves

debarred from attending drawing-rooms, and levées, if their wealth, education, and associations warrant them in so doing.

However, as Trollope knew, the line between 'wealthy manufacturers' and the 'retail trade' was not always easy to draw:

> 'Why, he is a tradesman, you know.'
> 'There's no harm that I know of in that,' said Miss Todd. 'My Uncle that left me my money was a tradesman.'
> 'No,' said Miss Baker majestically, 'He was a merchant in Liverpool.'
> 'You'll find it very hard to define the difference, my dear,' said Miss Todd.
> (*Miss Mackenzie*, chapter 10)

There were seeming paradoxes in this matter of occupation and gentility, as this conversation from *Great Expectations* (chapter 22) between Pip and Herbert Pocket shows:

> 'It is indisputable that while you cannot possibly be genteel and bake, you may be as genteel as never was and brew. You see it every day.'
> 'Yet a gentleman may not keep a public-house, may he?' said I.
> 'Not on any account,' returned Herbert.

A more fundamental paradox was that England's wealth and pre-eminence was increasingly to be found in trade and not in the land. In the first chapter of *Dr Thorne* Trollope tackles this contradiction, clearly considering that the image of a trading nation was somewhat demeaning:

> England a commercial country! Yes, as Venice was. She may excel other nations in commerce, but yet it is not that in which she most prides herself, in which she most excels. Merchants as such are not the first men among us; though it perhaps be open, barely open, to a merchant to become one of them. Buying and selling is good and necessary . . . but it cannot be the noblest work of . . . an Englishman.

One cannot imagine Trollope, or his sovereign, speaking of the monarchy, as present-day members of the Royal family sometimes do, as 'a family firm', and even of Buckingham Palace as 'the shop'. This word, at the beginning of Queen Victoria's reign, carried suggestions of vulgarity, so that it was avoided by tradesmen who aspired to higher things:

> At this time there emerged from a milliner's house (*shop* to outward appearance it was not, evincing its gentility and its degree above the *Capelocracy*, to use a certain classical neologism, by a brass plate on an oak door, whereon was graven – 'Miss Semper, Milliner and Dressmaker').
> (Lytton, *Night and Morning*, IV, chapter 44)

Capelocracy is a nonce-word formed by Lytton from the Greek, Κάπηλος, 'a shopkeeper'. The usage is ironic and pseudo-euphemistic. Bearing this in mind, we can savour the irony, also, when Jorrocks, in *Handley Cross* (chapter 26), refers to Lord Bramber's splendid country house as 'a werry good shop here – capital *shop!*' Perhaps the word had declined somewhat. Creevey, in 1824, had written of 'a round of beef at a side table... run at with as much keenness as a *banker's shop* before a stoppage' (*Creevey Papers*, ed. Maxwell, II, p. 81). It is difficult to imagine the word *shop* compounded with anything as exalted as a bank in Victorian times.

As for junior shop-assistants, even the young rural labourer might look down on them, reflecting, perhaps, the superiority felt by the country over the town:

> Now it is well-known that there is nothing more antipathetic to your peasant-boy than a shop-boy. Even on grand political occasions, the rural working-class can rarely be coaxed into sympathy with the trading town-class. (Lytton, *My Novel*, III, chapter 2)

Young Johnny Stanley dismisses a certain Sir H. Havelock, despite the fact that he has won a VC, as 'a most uninteresting shop-boy looking youth with stupid eyes' (*The Stanleys of Alderley*, p. 211). It was thought better for ladies not to speak to shop-girls:

> 'It is not usual, Phillis,' said Mrs Cassilis, directly they were in the carriage, 'for ladies to speak to shop-people.'
> 'Is it not? The poor girl looked pale and tired.'...
> 'You see, my dear, we cannot alter things; and if you once begin pitying people and talking to them, there is an end of all distinctions of class.' (Walter Besant and James Rice, *The Golden Butterfly*, 1876, chapter 11)

Along with *shop*, the word *customer* could partake of the vulgar associations of trade, and an alternative might be preferred. For example, in banking the primary suggestion of the word *client* is one who seeks the services of a professional:

> All were as busy as bees. A double line of customers – *clients*, we believe, is now the term – pressed onwards to the counter, or whatever they call that barrier, some looking extremely unlike the money they were entrusted with. (Surtees, *Plain or Ringlets?*, chapter 32)

When Trollope is being down-to-earth in his criticism of the medical profession, he deliberately chooses the non-professional word: 'As was then the wont with many country practitioners, and as should be the wont with them all if they consulted their own dignity a little less and the comfort of their *customers* somewhat more' (*Dr Thorne*, chapter 3).

The word *trade*, also, carried certain suggestions of tarnish, though its status improved as the century continued. Dickens does not approve, clearly, when the artist Henry Gowan, in *Little Dorrit* (1854), counters Arthur Clennam's statement: 'And your vocation, Gowan, may really demand this suit and service. ... I should have thought that all art did,' with the words: 'Clennam, I don't like to dispel your generous vision.... But what I do in my *trade*, I do to sell' (I, chapter 34). Gissing, however, in *New Grub Street* (1891), seems not to take sides when a rather similar discussion on the vocational versus the mercenary takes place:

> 'What an insane thing it is to make literature one's only means of support....
> To make a *trade* of an art! I am rightly served for attempting such a brutal folly.'
> He turned away in a passion of misery.
> 'How very silly it is to talk like this,' came in Amy's voice....
> 'Art must be practised as a trade... in our time. This is the age of trade.'
> (chapter 4)

Trade as used here, of course, means, not buying and selling goods, but turning into money one's skills as an artisan. This is partly dialectal usage, or as the *OED* puts it, 'local, especially rural English':

> On the other side of the musicians sat the blacksmith, the wheel-wright, and the other tradesmen of the place. Tradesmen means in that part of the country [Hampshire] what we mean by artisans. (*Tom Brown at Oxford*, chapter 18)

An artisan's life, however, was not a calling for a gentleman. The young Lucius Mason, in *Orley Farm* (chapter 2) must undertake some employment, and his mother has her suggestions:

> She had ... another string to her bow. As he objected to be a lawyer he might become a civil engineer.... But Lucius Mason said that civil engineers were only tradesmen of an upper class, tradesmen with intellects; and he, he said, wished to use his intellect, but he did not choose to be a tradesman.

It followed from all this that the word *apprentice* was somewhat objectionable in contexts of the professions. In *Wives and Daughters* (chapter 3) Dr Gibson, an established country doctor, accepted as boarders into his house young doctors-to-be. They were known in the little town of Hollingford as 'Mr Gibson's young gentlemen', and as *pupils:* 'Pupils as they were called in the genteel language of Hollingford – *apprentices* as they were in fact.'

Successful tradesmen who aspired to genteel society (and many did), had to forget some of the habits of the shop. The precision and directness, not to say peremptoriness, of the business letter, for example, was inappropriate to society invitations:

> Polly wrote the letter that evening. 'Mr and Mrs Neefit's compliments to Mr Newton, and hope he will do them the honour to dine with them on Sunday at five o'clock....'
> 'Say five sharp,' said the breeches-maker.
> 'No, father, I won't – say anything about sharp.'

'Why not, Polly?'
'It wouldn't look pretty.' (Trollope, *Ralph the Heir*, chapter 6)

Too much exactitude of this kind savoured of commerce, especially in a letter proposing marriage, as when the 'commercial Jew', Mr Breghert, in Trollope's *The Way We Live Now* (chapter 79), writes to Georgina Longestaffe:

> I shall not interfere with you if you make me happy by becoming my wife, nor, I suppose, will you with me. Should you have a daughter or daughters I am quite willing that they should be brought up subject to your influence.

What gives offence here (apart, presumably, from the different implications about possible sons) is the quasi-legalistic 'daughter or daughters': 'The allusion to the "daughter of daughters" troubled her. She told herself that it was vulgar, – just what a butcher might have said.'

It was difficult, however, to keep the phrases of the counting-house out of the conversation, as, in 1826, the author of *The Vulgarities of Speech Corrected* testifies:

> Some mercantile phrases . . . have become no less common than vulgar, as will at once be obvious by a few examples. For instance, instead of assenting to an opinion by a plain 'yes' or 'I agree with you in that,' the mercantile pedant's favourite expression will be 'I say ditto to that'. Again, instead of observing that a young lady resembles her mother, he will say, 'She is the very ditto of her mother'. This word *ditto* ought to be under an embargo, and ought never to be exported out of the ledger and the invoice, or at least it ought not to be imported into good society. The word *per* and *via* for *by* and *by way of* are other instances of the mercantile pedantic: for example in 'He intends to go *per* the mail, and return *per* the stage'; 'They go *per* the packet *via* Calais, and return *per* the steamer *via* Brighton.' A pedant of this class, instead of 'on the contrary' will say 'per contra'; or instead of 'several' will think *sundries* more elegant. These terms are in his books, but ought never to be heard in his conversations, if he is desirous of speaking elegantly . . . Some mercantile pedants, still more vulgarly, will talk indiscriminately of an Act of Parliament, or a blood-horse, or a celebrated beauty, or an old woman, as 'a pretty piece of goods'. With those persons, also, every thing and every circumstance is vulgarly termed a *concern*, as if it were connected with the transactions of their 'firm'; or involved 'a good or a bad spec', which is the vulgar contraction of the word *speculation*. I am sorry to observe that the word *concern* is by no means confined to the mercantile population, but has now become extremely common as a vulgar by-word among many other classes; as well as the similar word *article* in such phrases as 'Our sheriff is a pretty article, isn't he?' 'The new bridge is a queerish article, and is not, by half, so good as the old concern.'

In the first few decades of the nineteenth century, such expressions found acceptance even among the best people; but later, in Victorian novels for example, they tend to occur with a satirical purpose. The upper classes had to accept strong commercial interests within their midst, but they would not accept their lingo. Thomas Creevey (1768–1838), who had a mercantile background, but advanced to eminence in Whig society, has expressions like 'I start *per* coach at half past ten' (*Creevey Papers*, ed Maxwell, II, p. 100); and 'Such a dumpy rum-shaped ... *article* as Lady Londonderry one can rarely see' (II, p. 80). *Concern*, too, in its use as the 'vulgar by-word' described above, is a favourite of Creevey's: he describes the town of Leamington as 'a half-built skeleton of a *concern*' (II, p. 214). Later Thackeray, and even Matthew Arnold, were to use the kind of expression condemned above, to 'place' characters socially as less than first-rate, or to criticize a mercenary attitude to life:

> 'When you're of a proper age, you'll marry Lady Anne.'
> 'Well, sir, if Anne's agreeable, I *say ditto*. She's not a bad-looking girl.'
> (*Pendennis*, II, chapter 1)

> The Divine Injunction 'Be ye perfect' done into British – the sentence Sir Daniel Gooch's mother repeated to him every morning when he was a boy going to work: 'Ever remember my dear Dan, that you should look forward to being some day manager of that *concern*!' (Matthew Arnold, *Culture and Anarchy*, chapter 2)

Other, more reputable commercial phrases could yet be used disparagingly in conjunction with the worst motives:

> I saw that it was useless to treat him as I should have treated a gentleman. He had evidently put the meanest and foulest construction upon my delicacy and hesitation in speaking to him; so I altered my plan, and came to the point abruptly – '*came to business*' as he would have called it. (Wilkie Collins, *Basil*, chapter 11)

> In the vulgar phrase, he had probably '*taken stock*' of Mr Warricombe's idiosyncracy. (Gissing, *Born in Exile*, III, chapter 1)

> To put it in plain, even coarse language, all social reform must be undertaken *on strictly commercial principles*. (Gissing, *Thyrza*, chapter 11)

No doubt such phrases could be repeated *ad nauseaum*, and often to the irritation of the hearer. There was one phrase that Trollope, who wrote a series of articles in the *Pall Mall Gazette* on 'London Tradesmen', particularly disliked:

> [The publican] uses for his own support and comfort that most pernicious of all commercial phrases – *the custom of the trade*. There is no dishonesty, no robbery to which a man cannot be taught to reconcile himself by that phraseology. (p. 52)

Mrs Gaskell laid down the law at the beginning of *Cranford* concerning the society in that place: 'We none of us spoke of money, because that subject savoured of commerce and trade, and though some might be poor, we were all aristocratic' (chapter 1). But it was difficult for those habituated to trade to keep off the taboo subject when in polite society:

> 'I'm sure there was no trouble spared – nor yet *expense*.' She knew that she ought not to have uttered that last word, and she would have refrained if it had been possible to her; – but it was not possible. The man who tells you how much his wine costs a dozen, knows that he is wrong while the words are in his mouth; but they are in his mouth, and he cannot restrain them.
> (Trollope, *Rachel Ray*, chapter 10)

Neefit the breeches-maker, in *Ralph the Heir* (chapter 6), 'told how he had gone himself to the fishmonger's for that bit of salmon . . . . "And I'll tell you what I did, Mr Newton; I brought down that bottle of champagne in my pocket myself – gave six bob for it at Palmer's, in Bond Street."'

It is rather satisfactory to find, having seen the prejudice against trade, that those engaged in the activity had their own snobberies and their own sense of exclusiveness. In *Orley Farm* (chapter 6) an attorney named Dockwrath is admitted to the commercial room of the Bull Inn, Leeds, only on sufferance. The following conversation takes place between James, a waiter, and a Mr Moulder, a commercial 'gent', i.e. a commercial traveller:

> 'Who's the party, James?' he said to the waiter, speaking in a whisper that was plainly heard by the attorney.
> 'Gen' elman by the 8.22 down,' said James.
> 'Commercial?' asked Mr Moulder, with angry frown.
> 'He says so himself, anyways,' said the waiter.
> 'Gammon!' replied Mr Moulder, who knew all the bearings of a commercial man thoroughly.

When a fellow 'mercial', named Kantwise, tries to display collapsible metal furniture to his fellow-salesmen in the same room, Moulder again appoints himself a guardian of standards: 'As for all that show-off and gimcrack work, I tell you fairly it ain't what I call trade, and it ain't fit for a commercial room. It's gammon, gammon, gammon!' Clearly the commercials were a force to be reckoned with. At an upper room at the Blue Boar in Pip's home town (*Great Expectations*, chapter 13) Mr Wopsle's noisy dramatic entertainment was curtailed when '"The Commercials" underneath sent up their compliments, and it wasn't the Tumblers' Arms.' *Trade*, in the manufacturing sense, can also hold its own, especially in the north, against the socially superior professions. The acerbic Mrs Thornton, mother of the Milton factory-owner and hero of *North and South*, observes of the southerner, Mr Hale: 'He appears a worthy kind of man enough; rather too simple for trade – so it's perhaps as well he should have been a clergyman first, and now a teacher' (chapter 18). There is also this rueful comment from Squire Hamley of Hamley, whose estate is encumbered with debt: 'What family is she of? None of 'em in trade, I reckon, from her being so poor' (*Wives and Daughters*, chapter 35).

Pride in one's class is not something peculiar to the higher echelons of society. Mrs Tozer, for example, wife of the butterman in Mrs Oliphant's *Salem Chapel* (chapter 15), glories in the implication of trade that her social superiors would have found demeaning; thus making a virtue of necessity: 'It's a thing well known as the Salem folks are all in trade, and don't drive their carriages, nor give themselves up to this world and vanity.' As the young minister of Salem, Beecher, put it, with typical smugness (chapter 21): 'These sort of people are the strength of our connection – not great people, you know, but the flower of the middle classes.' The word used by 'the flower of the middle classes' with deadly effect against those claiming to be above them in rank, is *fine*. 'Dinner or supper,' boasts Mrs Tozer (note the significant meal-times), 'we never can be took wrong, not being *fine* folks but comfortable' (chapter 34). Inevitably, one recalls the fabled Elsie Marley:

> Elsie Marley's grown so *fine*,
> She won't get up to feed the swine,
> But lies in bed till half past nine:
> Lazy Elsie Marley.

At a lower level in society, the suggestion of fineness was less unacceptable. Arthur Hugh Clough writes to his sister Anne:

> On the whole, I should incline to study arithmetic and grammar perhaps, but you must remember that a great advantage is given by any sort of cultivation (music, drawing, dancing, German, French etc.) for intercourse with the poor. They ... carry their liking for a lady almost to the vice of liking a *fine* lady. (*Correspondence*, I, p. 184)

Both *fine lady* and *fine gentleman* have separate entries in the *OED*, though the nineteenth-century quotations grow increasingly critical and sarcastic, for the concept offended against the work ethic. The two sons of Squire Hamley in *Wives and Daughters* (chapter 22) may well illustrate the difference between a *gentleman* and a *fine gentleman*:

> Roger was practical; interested in all out-of-door things .... Osborne, on the contrary, was what is commonly called 'fine'; delicate almost to effeminacy in dress and in manner; careful in small observances.

THE LANGUAGE OF THE POOR

Hitherto we have considered linguistic class-indicators as used by the upper and middle classes; but we should also examine the efforts towards acquiring new language habits made by those who wished to rise from the ranks. For the earliest part of our period, there is little direct information on the language of the poorest classes. James Kay-Shuttleworth in his *First Report of the Training College at Battersea* (1841) paints a rather grim picture of the situation in the early 1840s:

> Those who have had close intercourse with the labouring classes well know with what difficulty they comprehended words not of a Saxon origin, and how frequently addresses to them are unintelligible from the continual use of terms of a Latin or Greek derivation; yet the daily language of the middle and upper classes abounds with such words . . . hardly a sermon is preached which does not on every page contain numerous examples of their use. Phrases of this sort are so naturalized in the language of the educated classes, that entirely to omit them has the appearance of pedantry and baldness, and even disgusts people of taste and refinement. . . . It seems impossible to avoid using them, and the only mode of meeting the inconvenience alluded to is to instruct the humbler classes in their meaning. (p. 339)

Accordingly, at Battersea training college, great stress was laid, we are told, on Latin and Greek roots. This affords an interesting contrast with writers of books on etiquette, many of whom advocate plain English to the middle class. The two-fold aspect of English etymology was clearly in the air in the early and mid-Victorian period (Trench, *On the Study of Words*, appeared in 1851). Henry Kingsley, who has a way of becoming bored with novel-writing and proceeding to make some stylistic or other comment, observes in a footnote to *Ravenshoe* (1861):

> As a matter of curiosity, I tried to write this paragraph . . . without using a single word derived from the Latin. After having taken all possible pains to do so, I found there were eight out of forty-eight. I think it is hardly possible to reduce the proportion lower, and I think it is undesirable to reduce it so low. (chapter 47)

Deprived of words of classical derivation, the language of the poorest classes was apt to be monosyllabic, as was that of Jo the crossing sweeper in *Bleak House* (1852-3):

> And I ain't had much of the sov'ring neither . . . fur I had to pay five bob down in Tom-all-Alone's, afore they'd square it fur to give me change, and then a young man he thieved another five while I was asleep, and another boy he thieved ninepence, and the landlord he stood drains round with a lot more on it. (chapter 19)

Mayhew, too, is full of monosyllabic speech; for example this 'passionate' soldier's woman:

> You wants to know if them rowses is common. Well, they is, and it's no good one saying they ain't and the sodgers is such – cowards they think nothing of sticking a woman when they're riled and drunk, or they'll wop us with their belts. I was hurt awful onst by a blow from a belt; it hit me on the back part of the head, and I was laid up weeks in St. George's Hospital with a bad fever.

The sodger who done it was quodded, but only for a drag [three months] and he swore to God as how he'd do for me the next time as he comed across me.... You see this public; well, I've smashed up this place before now. (*London Labour and the London Poor*, IV, p. 236)

Mayhew may well have been surprised, after this, to encounter one of those 'degraded creatures', the Park Women (prostitutes in Hyde Park), who talked as follows:

I was very pretty. I may say so without vanity or ostentation, for I had many admirers, among whom I numbered the only son of the people in whose house I lived. I was engaged to teach the two sisters, and altogether I gave great satisfaction to the family. The girls were amiable and tractable, and I soon acquired an influence over their generous dispositions that afforded great facilities for getting them on in their studies. (Ibid., IV, p. 243)

The lady alleges that she was the daughter of a curate in Gloucestershire. It is difficult to believe that she can have been quite as fluent as this, but there is no doubt that, whatever the chosen career, a knowledge of Greek and Latin roots is an advantage! Yet, as G. L. Brook points out (*The Language of Dickens*, p. 104), a monosyllable can be emphatically precise: 'When Jo in *Bleak House* (chapter 25) is asked if he is hungry, there is real emotion in his reply, "Jist!"' There is some subtlety, too, in even the baldest language; as when the soldier's woman quoted above, accused of being 'passionate', replies 'Passionate! *I believe yer*. I knocked my father down and well-nigh killed him with a flat-iron' (IV, p. 236). The phrase *I believe you*, with its suggestion of a hidden and secondary conversation, is not a straight answer; but too many straight answers, in such society, would give a dangerous impression of naivety.

Fifty years after Mayhew, and writing from the point of view of a very shrewd and well-educated district nurse among the poorest classes, M. E. Loane, in her book *From Their Point of View* (1908), paints a very different picture of the vocabulary of the poor. For one thing, universal education had been in force for thirty years; for another 'like children and foreigners, the poor understand and appreciate a much wider range than they use.' Given literacy, the middle-aged and elderly continued to read, especially newspapers, in increased leisure, and thus their vocabulary was enlarged (chapter 3). She quotes instances such as 'Bad boots was the instigation of my illness'; 'I see your new fence is under course of construction'; and 'Our monarch would appear to be upon amicable terms with the majority of the foreign royalties.' Many of the poor in 1908, she says, 'talked like a book'. In the country, too, there was the same liking for the polysyllabic. Hardy loved to show his rustics chancing their arm with big words: 'Haymoss' Fry, in *Two on a Tower* (chapter 13), looks forward to the possibility of seeing a comet from Swithin St. Cleeve's observatory tower with the words:

'I'd as soon miss the great peep-show that comes every year to Greenhill Fair as a sight of such a immortal spectacle as this!'
'"Immortal spectacle" – where did ye get that choice mossel, Haymoss?' inquired Sammy Blore. 'Well, well, the Lord save good scholars.'

One factor here, undoubtedly, was increased confidence. The difference is well illustrated in that dual personality, Charles Ravenshoe, in Henry Kingsley's novel (chapter 61). The gentleman who, with 'the old Oxford insolence' flashing out, could daunt an Inspector of Police, sinks, in a delirious illness, into his *alter ego*, the footman and former trooper at Balaclava. In doing so, he falls back upon proletarian monosyllables and an elementary sentence structure:

> 'Charles, Charles, don't you know me?'
> 'That is my name, sir. That is what they used to call me. I am no common beggar, sir. I was a gentleman once, sir, and rode a horseback after a blue grey hound.... I was in the light cavalry charge at Balaclava. An angry business. They shouldn't get good fellows to fight together like that. I killed one of them sir. Hornby killed many, and he is a man who wouldn't hurt a fly.'

Something should be allowed here for Kingsley's reading of Shakespeare, whose delirious characters also tend to eschew the polysyllabic; even so, there is no doubt that the *persona* of footman has made a deep impression on the hero, and that habits of servitude have induced a monosyllabic humility.

Charles Ravenshoe was a fictional character whose life was split between the upper and the working classes; but this happened in real life at least once. A. J. Munby, whose life was chronicled by Derek Hudson in *Munby, Man of Two Worlds*, was a man accustomed to living in the forefront of educated London society, who fell in love with Hannah Cullwick, a servant girl from Shropshire. Hannah had made up her mind, as she wrote in her diary, 'that it was best and safest to be a slave to a *gentleman*, nor [*sic*] wife and equal to any vulgar man – still with the wish & determination to be independent by working in service and without the slightest hope o' been rais'd in rank either in place or by being married' (p. 345). Nevertheless, after nearly twenty years of his attentions, she agreed to marriage. Munby loved her for the hardworking woman that she was. He loved to see her working 'in her dirt'; he also loved her way of speaking, which he did not regard as erroneous:

> When she says 'It lugs so' [looks so?] or 'I'd as lief do it' or 'never did nothing' or the familiar 'she says, says she', the phrase sounds precious as an epigram.... 'Them taters', also: she sat on the hearth in the fireglow, and peeled them deftly into her blue checked apron... (p. 149)

Often when the two extremes of society met, at least in the early Victorian period, the result would be mutual incomprehension, as with Lady Dedlock and Jo the crossing-sweeper: "'I'm fly," says Jo. "But ten larks, you know! Stow hooking it!" "What does the horrible creature mean?"' (*Bleak House*, chapter 16). Matters improved during the next fifty years; but yet M. E. Loane, a great optimist, wonders whether,

> any real conversation between members of two classes is possible. All my conversations with my patients and their friends have been of an exceedingly one-sided character; that is to say, in some cases I talked, and in some cases they did, but we never took anything like equal parts. A question, a shade of surprise, the faintest dissent from their views, the lack of instant approbation, would generally be enough to silence them, and in many instances cause them to veer round suddenly, and bring forward opinions in direct opposition to those they had already expressed. (*From Their Point of View*, chapter 10)

Nevertheless, Loane's books throw some interesting sidelights on what we have considered earlier. She devotes a whole chapter of *The Queen's Poor* to the language of the lowest working classes. For them, ladies are defined as 'people who lies on the sofa all day and reads novels'. A girl is pleased that the mistress she works for is not a lady: 'Ladies is people that must have things just so. Rhoda's missis isn't one, so she just suits her.' I can find no comparable bouquet for gentlemen in Loane, but I have culled one from a rural source:[3]

> They were asked by the friends after as to how they got on with entertaining me. They said they misjudged me – they thought I was a gentleman but I was no gentleman at all as I was as humble as anyone.

The upper-class tendency to enquire after health without expecting an answer had percolated downwards, according to Loane: 'Old Mr Waters he do have such old-fashioned ways: he always ask how you are as if he wanted to know!' Conversation is repetitious: 'the most ignorant will repeat themselves commonly five or six times during the same interview, and even those of superior culture will do it in all times of excitement.' Sharp, definite statements are generally avoided. In reply to the question 'Did you go and speak to him about it?' a man said, 'Well, I kinder went over there, and I sorter remarked as you might stay . . .' It is a nice thought that a tendency to ironic understatement, found in the earliest Anglo-Saxon poetry, manifests itself again, according to Loane, in the speech of working-class men. She overheard comments on a good-looking girl who passed when workmen were employed on upper windows in a street: '"Hm," said one, "that's a nice sort of girl, Bill?" Bill surveyed her critically. "Hm, yes. Do to go out walkin' with – weekdays."' To a lady who remonstrated with a man for working his horse too hard, the driver was ready with an answer: '"That's a

[3] C. T. Trevail, *The Life and Reminiscences of C. T. T.*, Luxulyan, *Cornwall* (Bristol, 1926), p. 55.

very heavy load for your horses!" "It is, ma'am ... in fac', if 'tworn't for the ladies pityin' of 'em and given' 'em sponge-cakes, I dunno how they ever would get up the 'ills.'"

As for bad language, it was so abundant among some sections of the working classes at the end of Victoria's reign that 'I have known mothers who, contrary to the usual custom of poor people, put all her children to bed at six so that they might be asleep "before the language begins".' Loane considers it a blessing that, with more schooling, more neutral adjectives were made available:

> I saw five or six little ragamuffins playing together in a London park: 'Let's cross that rustic bridge' said one, and they clattered over. I could not help wondering what adjective would have been used by children in their position a few years previously.

A mother who had slapped her child for using bad language in ignorance, felt sorry afterwards: 'Poor little soul. I don't believe she knew what she was saying ... but at nine years old she did ought to have some feeling for words, so I give her something to remember.'

Even among the very poor, however, there were euphemisms: 'The workhouse in all refined circles, is called the Infirmary, and it seems to be a point of honour with most of the elderly inmates to speak of it as a well-managed place to which they have voluntarily retired.' It is interesting, too, that, according to Arthur Morrison, the forbidden word *expense* (p. 100) becomes, at this lower level of society, a mark of refinement:

> In the East End, when a woman has not enough money to buy a thing much desired, she does not say so in plain words; she says the thing is an 'expense' or a 'great expense'. It means the same thing, but it sounds better. (*Tales of Mean Streets*, 'On the Stairs')

One is reminded of the nice euphemistic distinction made by the villagers of Lark Rise in Flora Thompson's *Lark Rise to Candleford* (chapter 1): 'Poverty's no disgrace, but 'tis a great inconvenience.' Educational distinctions were sources of pride, as Loane reminds her readers: 'A child's "standard" has become of exactly the same concern to the poorest mother as the public schoolboy's "form".' The word *standard* was the name for a form or class in the old elementary schools. It disappeared after the 1944 Education Act.

A typical, if partial, rise from the working classes is chronicled by Gissing in *Demos* (1886). Richard Mutimer, the hero, learns as a youth to be careful of his pronunciation, especially when he begins to speak at socialist meetings. He has, in Gissing's words, his 'struggles with the h-fiend' (chapters 4, 6). Yet, presumably because of family feeling, he cannot 'bestow the aspirate' upon his younger brother Henry, known to all their working-class friends as *'Arry*; to everyone, in fact, until Richard's middle-class wife calls him, quite naturally, *Harry*. Richard himself, as a young man, appeared to a member of the landed gentry, Hubert Eldon, as 'not quite the man I had expected; more civilized. I should suppose he is the better class of artisan. He talks with a good deal of the working-class accent, of course, but not like a wholly uneducated man' (chapter 7).

Richard is far from reticent about his lowly origins. His future mother-in-law, Mrs Waltham, does not approve of this:

> There are certain things to which in good society one, does not refer, first and foremost humiliating antecedents. The present circumstances were exceptional to be sure, but it was to be hoped that Mr Mutimer would outgrow this habit of advertising his origin. Let him talk of the working-classes if he liked, but always in the third person.

Sometimes such conversation with the middle classes elicits an amusing clash of contexts (chapter 8):

> 'We put our money by for the *club* every week, what's more.'
> 'The club?' queried Miss Waltham, to whom the word suggested Pall Mall and vague glories which dwelt in her imagination.
> 'That's to make provision for times when we're ill or can't get work,' Mutimer explained.

Owing to a chance inheritance, the Mutimer family become rich, and while their mother remains assertively her old self, Richard continues his progress up the social ladder, along with his sister Alice, known for her presence and spirit as 'The Princess'. Richard gives her instructions as to how to behave before servants (chapter 15):

> 'Put on just a bit of the princess,' he said. 'Not too much, you know, but just enough to show that it isn't the first time in your life that you've been waited on. Don't always give a "thank you"; one every now and then'll do.'

When Richard and his wife Adela, recovering from a miscarriage, go for dinner to Alice's house, Richard is agreeably surprised at his sister's progress (chapter 22):

> 'I do hope it won't be too much for you,' she said. 'Pray leave as soon as you feel you ought to. I should never forgive myself if you took a cold or anything of the kind.'
> Really, Alice had supplied herself with most becoming phrases. The novels had done much; and then she had been living in society. At dinner she laughed rather too loud, it might be, and was too much given to addressing her husband as "Willis'; but her undeniable prettiness in low-necked evening dress condoned what was amiss in manner.

Alice has recently married a man named Willis Rodman, and we see here that Richard Mutimer has acquired sufficient knowledge of upper middle-class *mores* to know that, while the meaningless hyperbole 'never forgive myself' is acceptable, being too conventional to have any emotional content, genuine expression of emotion for a married partner by the repetition of his Christian name is bad form. The suggestion that one can improve one's conversation by reading is still current in the 1880s.

A change occurs in the fortunes of Richard Mutimer by the discovery of a second will reversing the first. Poverty develops the domineering and jealous side of his nature; it also has an interesting effect on his accent:

> The thin crust of refinement was shattered; the very man came to light, coarse, violent, whipped into fury by his passions.... Even his accent deteriorated as he flung out his passionate words; he spoke like any London mechanic, with defect and excess of aspirates, with neglect of g's at the end of words, and so on. Adela could not bear it. (chapter 28)

Gissing faces the fact that an alien accent can antagonise. When Hubert Eldon, the landowner, has to interview unemployed artisans from the disused industrial plant standing on land which he has re-acquired, he exclaims to his friend Wyvern, a vicar: 'They are our enemies, yours as well as mine; they are the enemies of every man who speaks the pure English tongue and does not earn a living with his hands' (chapter 29). Young 'Arry Mutimer, who becomes a ne'er-do-well, does not help his case with his still ambitious brother Richard when, on being asked what kind of job he requires, answers (chapter 31): '"A clerk's, of course." He pronounced the word *clerk* as it is spelt; it made him seem yet more ignoble.' This, while an acceptable pronunciation in America, is of course still a class shibboleth in Britain.

Richard Mutimer was a Londoner, and it is an interesting fact that the speech of the working-class Londoner was looked down upon by his social equals in the provinces. Mrs Gaskell, in *Mary Barton: A Tale of Manchester Life* (1848) has one of her characters dismiss London speech as 'mincing': '"You're frightening them horses," says he, in his mincing way (for Londoners are mostly all tongue-tied, and can't say their a's and i's properly).' In the journey which two of her Manchester characters make on foot from the capital, it is not until they get beyond Birmingham that they begin to feel reassured in this matter of accents: 'So we left Brummagem ... and th'day were fine, and folk began to have some knowledge o' th' proper way of speaking' (chapter 9). This antipathy to the vernacular of London is nowhere more felt than in the novels of the fastidious Gissing, born in the West Riding of Yorkshire in 1857:

> The father spoke with a strong Midland accent, using words of dialect by no means disagreeable to the son's ear – for dialect is a very different thing from the bestial jargon which on the lips of the London vulgar passes for English. (*Born in Exile*, 1892, VII, chapter 3)

There was, Gissing felt, something irremovable about Cockney:

> Mrs Yule's speech was seldom ungrammatical, and her intonation was not
> flagrantly vulgar, but the accent of the London poor, which brands as with
> hereditary baseness, still clung to her words, rendering futile such propriety
> of phrase as she owed to years of association with educated people. (*New Grub
> Street*, 1891, chapter 7)

It is easy to smile at Gissing's obsession, but this is a matter from which
anxiety has been removed relatively lately, so that one can now observe
University colleagues retaining traces of residual Cockney as a matter of
pride in their idiosyncrasy. How different from one of the characters,
daughter of a laundress, in Gissing's *New Grub Street* (chapter 8), who was
'unpresentable'! 'Mrs Hinks still spoke the laundress tongue, unmitigated
and inimitable.'

Writing of training college life in the 1890s, F. H. Spencer, *An Inspector's
Testament* (p. 145), describes how 'the provincials' (in the teaching
profession) eagerly looked for evidence of metropolitan inferiority. One Ike
Bowen, from Warrington, 'doing' teaching practice at Isleworth, reported:
'When oi sez "Paat yer aands aap", y'paats em dahn; when oi sez "Fowld y'r
ahms", ye tawks; owld yer jawr.' 'That,' said the man from Warrington, 'is
how they talk in the sunny south.'

The accent of the working class in London was, indeed, unmistakable.
Young Harry Goslett in Besant's *All Sorts and Conditions of Men* (1882)
lowers himself socially by working in London as a cabinet-maker, but he
deceives no-one: 'He is – he says – only a cabinet-maker. And Dick Coppin
says that though he can use a lathe, he knows nothing at all about the trade,
not even how they talk, nor anything about them' (chapter 40). Whether
man or woman worked in a London factory, they had to accustom
themselves to uncouth language: 'You will find yourself in a workshop full of
disagreeable people, who pick out unpleasant adjectives and tack them on to
everything' (chapter 17). Nevertheless, Goslett seems to have adopted some
of the more innocuous expressions: 'He had been working, and was now,
following the example of Miss Kennedy's work-girls, '*knocking off*' for half
an hour' (chapter 10). Among work-girls, working together for long hours in
a close atmosphere, there is often a tendency to exasperation, which
manifests itself in quarrels and in indignant gossip about quarrels: 'Their
talk is a narrative of indignation full of "sezee", "sezi", and
"sezshe" – mostly the last, because what "she" said is generally the cause of
all this wrath' (chapter 11). It is interesting that Gissing, too, writes of 'the
eternal "says I", "says he", "says she" of vulgar converse' (*Thyrza*,
chapter 4). Already in 1833, this use was listed among Savage's *Vulgarisms*;
Savage corrects, however, such sentences with the past tense but without
reversing the inversions: 'said he, said I'. As to more recent use, these

inverted forms seem largely to be confined to Ireland now, where they can still be heard occasionally in television interviews from that troubled country; but the uninverted formula: 'She says to me, she says' can still be heard in England.

The hero of *All Sorts and Conditions of Men* is free from all doubts, such as may have perplexed his social superiors, about dinner-time: '"Dinner in the middle of the day, of course," Harry went on, with a cheerful smile. "At the East End everybody stokes at one. We have tea at five and supper when we can get it. A simpler life..."' (chapter 17). M. E. Loane, in *The Next Street but One* (chapter 1) explains other East End terminology on this point for her upper and middle class readers:

> She was a little slow in answering the door, and when she came, said she was just getting her husband's *tea*. Knowing that tea really meant dinner, and that the comfortless meal a workman calls his dinner is really his lunch, I declined to go in.

Even a phrase like 'in the army' can, for one from a superior background, produce, like the word *club*, an interesting clash of contexts, and can have different implications for the 'humbler creation':

> 'You always told me,' said Harry, 'that my father was in the army?'
> 'What do you call a Sergeant in a line regiment, then?'
> 'Oh! of course, but among gentlemen – I mean – among the set with whom I was brought up, to be in the army means to have a commission.' (*All Sorts and Conditions of Men*, Prologue)

It will have been noticed that in dealing with the language of the working classes, I have drawn my examples from the 1880s and 1890s, from the end of the period. This is because writers like Gissing and Besant are among the first to see the workers as a class, and not, as so often in early Victorian novels, as picturesque individuals. Similarly, whereas George Eliot was complimented (p. 84) for depicting something as precise as a lower middle class, it is left to Gissing to select, with the ear and observation of a sociolinguist, a few language traits typical of that class. He characterizes them with the phrase *really nice*:

> Never had it been their lot to serve 'really nice' people – this phrase of theirs was anything but meaningless. They had lived with more or less well-to-do families in the lower middle class – people who could not have inherited refinement, and had not acquired any, neither proletarian nor gentlefolk, consumed with a dread of vulgar pretentiousness, inflated with the miasma of democracy. (*The Odd Women*, 1893, chapter 2)

Among their speech habits, Gissing detects a meaningless use of the phrase 'of course':

Then she remarked inconsequently that she was awaiting the arrival of her brother by train.
'He's a traveller for a West-end shop; makes five hundred a year. I keep house for him, because *of course* he's a widower.'
The 'of course' puzzled Marcia for a moment, but she remembered that it was an unmeaning expletive much used by people of Miss Eade's education. (chapter 28)

At a lower level of society, at least in the first half of the century, *of course* had alternated with *in course*: '"Of course you told that to Miss Hale." "*In coorse* I did"' (*North and South*, chapter 29). Here the factory-owner Thornton is speaking to the obstreperous northern workman Higgins. The reconciliation they attempt is rather cleverly signalized by Mrs Gaskell with linguistic means:

'So, measter, I'll come; and what's more, I thank yo'; and that's a deal fro' me,' said he, more frankly, suddenly turning round and facing Mr Thornton fully for the first time.
'And this is a deal from me,' said Mr Thornton, giving Higgins's hand a good grip.

Does *deal* have its more provincial meaning of 'a good deal, a considerable amount' (as the phrase had been used by Higgins), or the more standard, if colloquial 'agreement, business transaction'? Suffice it to say, that in this way Mrs Gaskell attempts to build a small bridge acrosss the increasing gulf between master and man. For she is clearly behind Thornton's aim of attaching 'class to class as they should be attached', through 'that sort of common interest which invariably makes people find means and ways of seeing each other, and becoming acquainted with each other's characters and persons, and even tricks of temper and modes of speech' (chapter 52).

Gissing would not have been so sanguine, at least as far as speech was concerned. Instead of a coming together of different accents in mutual understanding, he believed that the speech of the lower orders would prevail. Here, for example, is the complaint of a character in *Born in Exile* (1892) named Godwin Peak, of whom Gissing wrote 'Peak is myself – one phase of myself':

My own experience ... has been among the lower classes of London. I don't mean the very poorest, of whom one hears so much nowadays .... But the people who earn enough for their needs, and whose spiritual guide is the Sunday newspaper .... They set the tone in politics; they are debasing art and literature; even the homes of wealthy people begin to show the effects of their influence. One hears men and women of gentle birth using phrases which originate with shopboys; one even sees them reading print which is addressed to the coarsest million .... When commercial interest is supreme, how can the tastes of the majority fail to lead and control? (III, chapter 5)

Perhaps Gissing's view was an unduly pessimistic one (it would be hard to find a more cheerless writer); or perhaps things had changed from thirty years before, when Mrs Oliphant found in periodicals the opposite fault – a snobbish assumption of an exclusively aristocratic readership:

> Somehow the tone of public writing has changed of late days. Scarcely a newspaper writer condescends now to address men who are not free of 'society', and learned in all its ways. The 'Times' and the magazines take it for granted that all their readers dine out at splendid tables, and are used to a solemn attendant behind their chair. (*Salem Chapel*, chapter 1)

The poorest classes were not without the linguistic means of defending their position, if not of asserting their claims. Disraeli describes how, in Lancashire in the 1830s, workmen were calling themselves *operatives*; and the operatives were objecting to referring to their superiors as *masters*: '"My employer," said the operative. "They call themselves masters, but we do not"' (*Endymion*, chapter 62). Probably one of the words used by the employer instead of *operatives* was *hands*. This is a term that Mr Thornton, in *North and South* (chapter 15), as an employer in process of enlightenment, is learning not to use:

> My theory is, that my interests are identical with those of my workpeople, and *vice-versa*. Miss Hale, I know, does not like to hear men called 'hands'; so I won't use that word, though it comes most readily to my lips as the technical term, whose origin, whatever it was, dates from before my time.

As to rural workmen, there was at least one word that they would not endure:

> What do you think, Coningsby, the other day we had a meeting in this neighbourhood to vote an agricultural petition that was to comprise all classes. I went with my father, and I was made chairman of the committee to draw up the petition. Of course I described it as the petition of the nobility, clergy, gentry, yeomanry, and peasantry of the county of—: and, would you believe it, they struck out *peasantry* as a word no longer used, and inserted *labourers*. (*Coningsby*, III, chapter 3)

There is indeed something profoundly un-English about this word. The *OED* has a note: 'in early use, properly only of foreign countries'. Charles Kingsley in *Yeast* (chapter 13) has a reference to this passage in *Coningsby*, and to one other passage, and suggests a better word than either *peasantry* or *labourers*:

> That amusingly inconsistent, however well-meant, scene in *Coningsby*, in which Mr Lyle is represented as trying to restore 'the independent order of peasantry', by making them the receivers of public alms at his own gate, as if they had been serfs or vagabonds, and not *citizens* of modern England.

'IN SERVICE'

There was a widespread feeling among those of the poor with any claim to standing, that to go 'to service' or to be 'in service' was demeaning. Even in the East End, Arthur Morrison tells us, 'domestic service is a social descent'. Mr Poyser, as a prosperous farmer, is opposed to the idea of his niece, Hetty Sorrel, becoming a lady's maid: 'I niver meant you to go to service, my wench; my family's ate their own bread and cheese as far back as anybody knows, hanna they father? You wouldna like your grandchild to take wage?' (*Adam Bede*, chapter 31). In America, indeed, Mrs Trollope found (*Domestic Manners of the Americans*, chapter 6), that the very word *servant* was taboo: 'The greatest difficulty in organizing a family establishment in Ohio, is getting servants, or, as it is there called, "getting help", for it is more than petty treason to the Republic, to call a free citizen a "servant".'

There were, and still are, words which treat euphemistically what, considered at its lowest terms, may well be servitude. Throughout the nineteenth century the word for 'a post of employment; a position in which one works for wages' was *situation*. The first *OED* quotation is from 1813: 'He obtained *the situation* of army-agent.' The word in this sense is still, of course, current; but from time to time the grimmer realities of employment might cause people to see through its euphemistic tendencies: 'Having "accepted Mr Puffington's *situation*," as the elegant phraseology of servitude goes' (*Mr Sponge's Sporting Tour*, chapter 33). Surtees was writing in 1853. Later in the century a new word began to appear in such contexts. Richard Jefferies, in *Hodge and his Masters* (1880), complains that farmers' daughters often turn their backs on farming:

> As for the loud-voiced young farmers, with their slouching walk, their ill-fitting clothes, and stupid talk about cows and wheat, they were intolerable. A banker's clerk at least – nothing could be thought of under a clerk in the local banks; of course, his salary was not high, but then his '*position*'. (chapter 10)

This last must be the *OED* sense 9b 'place in the social scale', first illustrated from Trollope. In Mrs Gaskell's *Wives and Daughters* of 1865 (chapter 31), the word occurs in this sense twice, in inverted commas, clearly as something new. From here it is but a short step to sense 9c 'an office, situation, place of employment', with the first *OED* quotation from 1890: 'a *position* in a bank'. Clearly, while *situation* covers all social contexts, *position* is a middle-class word. It is amusing, incidentally, running up and down the gamut of society, to find that a *clerk* should be found so acceptable in the Jefferies' quotation above. In 1832, and admittedly higher up the social scale, the word was attended by problems:

Durham told me Tennyson is moving heaven and earth to get the name of his
office changed from 'clerk' [to the Board of Ordnance] to that of 'secretary' or
anything else, alleging gravely as a reason that a very advantageous marriage
of his eldest daughter had gone off, solely from the lover not being able to
stand the father's being a clerk. (*Creevey Papers*, ed. Maxwell, II, p. 241)

Servants and dependants upon the upper classes found it politic to guard
their language. A useful formula when attempting what might be construed
as familiarity was 'making so bold' or 'may I make so bold': '"Why, if that
bain't Mr Eames!" said the gardener. "Mr John, *may I make so bold?*"' (*The
Small House at Allington*, chapter 54). There was boldness and boldness,
however, as the encounter of the parvenu Titmouse with the aristocracy
demonstrates: '"Excuse me, my lady, but what an uncommon fine piano
that is!" said he – "*If I may make so bold*, will your ladyship give us a tune?"'
(Warren, *Ten Thousand a Year*, IV, chapter 1). Even an outspoken character
claims to be more guarded in her speech when talking to relatives of the
nobility: 'Now, if you were Sally, I should say "Answer me that, you goose!"
But as you're a relation of my lady's, I must be civil and only say, "I can't
think how you can talk so like a fool!"' (Mrs Gaskell, *My Lady Ludlow*,
chapter 10). Surprisingly, servants seem to have had more latitude in the
previous century. Not without *hauteur*, Lord Melbourne speaks of the
household of Lady Holland: 'Lord M. said she had excellent servants, who
were like those in former times and put in a word in the conversation
occasionally' (*The Girlhood of Queen Victoria*, II, p. 79).

Not all employers were as strict in forbidding *followers*, that is, young
men who came courting housemaids, as Miss Matilda Jenkyns in *Cranford*
(chapter 3). When Jowett comes to dinner with the Stanleys, the family are
much exercised to ensure a limited and congenial party to meet him, for 'He
wrote such a jocose note to Mama to accept,' writes Kate Stanley, 'saying he
was like the housemaids "no followers allowed".' (*The Amberley Papers*, I,
p. 131).[4] Many servants made it their rather smug boast that they 'always
gave satisfaction' (Mrs Oliphant, *The Perpetual Curate*, chapter 11); if they
did not, they might be given *warning*, that is, notice of dismissal. Hannah
Cullwick, A. J. Munby's working-class 'flame', did heavy work with a will,
but was not neat enough to wait at table: 'But i couldn't be clean, & besides
i'd liefer be dirty ... at last i got *warning*' (*Munby, Man of Two Worlds*,
p. 184).

Not infrequently, certain expressions used by servants were found
appropriate by their employers, and were quoted by them, not necessarily
condescendingly: 'I ... sweep the parlour ... then *clean myself*, as the
servants say' (Mrs Carlyle, *Letters* p. 53). This is rather a specific meaning:

[4] Part of the joke is that the visit occurred soon after the publication of the immensely
controversial *Essays and Reviews* (1860), to which Jowett had contributed.

the *OED* (*clean*, sense 1b), defines it as 'said, by servants or operatives employed in dirty or dusty work, of making themselves clean and tidy in the afternoon or evening'. Other instances of employers quoting servants can be seen in the following:

> It's better for Royalty to 'keep itself *to* itself' as servants say of one another when they mean the highest praise. (*The Amberley Papers*, II, p. 378)

> But having *talked*, as Wee [a nurse] would call it, *nicely*, about missions I have been badgered by them for subscriptions. (*The Stanleys of Alderley*, p. 213)

Very occasionally, the same phrase might have a different meaning with a different class of speaker. An example is *a good cry*: 'I should like to have *a good cry*, as the servants say' (*Endymion*, chapter 68). With which compare the very different political use of the same phrase; what we might call a good slogan: 'It's a very *good cry*, though . . . I'm all for a religious *cry*' (*Coningsby*, II, chapter 2).

A similar desire for the freedom of an occasional colloquial or slang phrase led writers like Trollope, whose subject was so often high society, to embroider their narrative with the language of the streets. In Trollope, there is often an ironically apologetic note as to its provenance:

> He seemed to be at some loss for words: he shut up, as the slang phrase goes. (*Dr Thorne*, chapter 5)

> Undy Scott, among his other good qualities, possessed an enormous quantity of that which schoolboys in these days call 'cheek'. (*The Three Clerks*, chapter 44)

An Americanism (though it no longer seems so to us) that Trollope was fond of using was the phrase 'a good time':

> An American when he has spent a pleasant day will tell you that he has had a 'good time'. I think that Mrs Dobbs Broughton, if she had ever spoken the truth of that day's employment, would have acknowledged that she had had 'a good time'. (*The Last Chronicle of Barset*, chapter 51)

An almost identical mixture of the occasional slang phrase and the odd Americanism is found in Henry Kingsley:

> Turn Lady Ascot once fairly to bay, you would (if you can forgive slang) get very little change out of her. (*Ravenshoe*, chapter 46)

> It was evident that, since John Marston's arrival, he had been playing, with regard to Mary, second fiddle (if you can possibly be induced to pardon the extreme coarseness of the expression). (Ibid., chapter 58)

> On this occasion, Mary struck the old lady dumb – 'knocked her cold', our American cousins would say. (*Geoffrey Hamlyn*, chapter 9)

COURTSHIP, MEDICINE, DISSENT

In affairs of love, the language of the different classes became especially evident. For the upper classes there was a legacy of terminology from Regency times and before to describe the various stages of courtship, and these were only gradually discontinued as the century proceeded: *distinguishing notice*, being *particular*, *attachment*, *engagement* (see the index of *Jane Austen's English* for each of these words). The process was less complicated in the lower ranks, but phraseology such as *to keep company*, and (rather later) to *walk* (*out*) *together* represent the freer, less chaperoned life of the lower middle classes and the working class. Joe Gargery, in *Great Expectations* (chapter 7), demonstrates the usage: 'I offered to your sister to *keep company* and to be asked in church.' For a doctor's daughter in prim, provincial Hollingford to behave like this, however, was quite another matter. An unchaperoned affair was a scandal in upper middle-class society: '"What did you hear from Mrs Dawes?" "Why, that Molly and Mr Preston were *keeping company*, just as if she was a maidservant and he was a gardener"' (*Wives and Daughters*, chapter 47). One Peter Prosper, Squire of Buston Hall, in Trollope's *Mr Scarborough's Family* (chapter 44), is incensed when this middle-class phrase is used of his affairs: 'That it should be said of him, Mr Prosper, of Buston, that he was "keeping company" with any woman!' As for such a phrase as *to walk together*, it is one of those which Elizabeth-Jane Henchard must lose if she is to obey her father's instructions to be less provincial and more refined: 'She . . . no longer said of young men and women that they "walked together" but that they were "engaged"' (*The Mayor of Casterbridge*, chapter 20).

Surviving into the 1930s, Mary, Countess of Lovelace, wrote a reminiscent essay in a compilation entitled *Fifty Years* (1882–1932) *Memories and Contrasts* (London, 1932). Her essay was on 'Society and the Season'. She characterized the new freedom of Society girls in the 1930s in a manner that was not without its *hauteur*:

> For dinners and entertainments other than balls, apparently the girls do not need any female protection whatever. They go about anywhere and everywhere with any male friend whom they choose. In fact, they 'walk out' and 'keep company' just as our friends in the servants' hall do.

One profession increased its hold on the public esteem during the century, and that was the medical profession. 'Sam is only a surgeon,' says a character in Jane Austen's unfinished novel *The Watsons*. We may be sure that Mr Woodhouse, in *Emma*, would have obtained the best medical advice available; yet his physician does not have the title of 'Dr', being known simply as *Mr Perry* or *Perry*. 'Doctor' is reserved for doctors of divinity in Jane Austen's novels. A few decades later, there are more titles and more gradations and types of medical skill, as we can see from *Vanity Fair* (I am assuming here that Thackeray is reflecting, as in his ilustrations to the novel, the manners of 1848 rather than of the 1820s and 1830s, when *Vanity Fair* purports to be set). We find the wealthy Miss Crawley in chapter 19, attended by Dr Squills, the physician, but also more constantly by Mr Clump, the apothecary, who administers the medicine.

A certain air and bearing were expected from a physician. Unlike Dr Thorne in the novel of that title (chapter 3), a physician should not pocket his fee too ostentatiously: 'it showed that this Thorne was always thinking of his money, like an apothecary'. Nevertheless, Dr Thorne in fact was a 'graduated physician', entitled 'beyond all dispute to call himself a doctor'. But he charged seven and sixpence instead of 'the guinea fee', and this was thought 'democratic'; he ignored the principle of giving advice and selling no medicine, which blurred the 'distinct barrier between the physician and the apothecary'. Lower forms of medical life in this novel are 'Mr Rerechild' (chapter 24), and Dr Thorne's predecessor, 'a general practitioner' – the phrase seems to have been just coming in in 1858, when *Dr Thorne* was published (see the OED, *practitioner*). This man had never put himself on a par with his betters in the profession, though he had been allowed to *physic* the servants – the latter word, unlike *physician*, has deteriorated.

The improvement was even reflected in the status of medical students and the names given to them, according to G.A. Sala in *The Baddington Peerage*, a novel written in 1860, but purporting to narrate events of thirty years before that date:

> The 'Blue Pump' parlour was deserted by its usual frequenters – medical students attached to the neighbouring Hospitals; St. Fawkes's, St. Griddle's, and St. Catherine Wheeler's; and sometimes even nascent practitioners from the great West-End Hospital of St. Lazarus. Medical students are more choice nowadays in their houses of entertainment, and would indignantly resent being called 'Sawbones'. (chapter 6)

Among the really great, however, the medical man did not count for much socially. '"As to *mésalliance*, there's no blood on any side," said Lady Pentreath. "Old Admiral Arrowpoint was one of Nelson's men, you know – a doctor's son. And we all know how the mother's money came."' (*Daniel Deronda*, chapter 35). Nevertheless, the really outstanding physician might arrive at a baronetcy; though, to quote a character in Disraeli's *Sybil* (1845), 'A baronetcy has become the distinction of the middle class; a physician, our physician for example, is a baronet; and I dare say some of our tradesmen; brewers, or people of that class' (chapter 11).

Jorrocks describes his medical man as 'a wonderful M.D.' (*Jorrocks's Jaunts and Jollities*, chapter 6). This use of initials, in Victorian times, counted as slang (p. 43), and presumably the modern abbreviation GP would not have been acceptable either.

One linguistic concomitant of the successful bedside manner has been noted by Thackeray: it is the use of compliments in the third person:

> Persuade her to rise, dear Madam; drag her from her couch and her low spirits; insist upon her taking little drives. They will restore the roses too to your cheeks, if I may so speak to Mrs Bute Crawley. (*Vanity Fair*, chapter 19)

The language of Methodism and other Nonconformists was, by very definition, non-U: 'It's on'y tradesfolks as turn Methodist, you niver knew a farmer bitten wi' them maggots', says Mr Poyser (*Adam Bede, chapter 18*). Dissenters with social pretensions were sometimes aware of what they had lost in terms of gentility by their secession: 'Some chapel-going ladies were fond of remembering that "their family had been Church"' (*Felix Holt*, chapter 18). As Disraeli points out (*Sybil*, chapter 11) 'Going to church was held more genteel than going to meeting. The principal tradesmen of the neighbouring great houses deemed it more "aristocratic", using a favourite and hackneyed epithet, which only expressed their own servility.' Both George Eliot and Mrs Oliphant took an obvious delight in deploying the language of Nonconformity for their own purposes: sometimes humorously, as when Mrs Oliphant enjoys the unctuousness of Tozer, senior deacon of *Salem Chapel*; sometimes with more serious purpose, as in the masterly study of Dinah Morris's vocation in *Adam Bede*. It is Nonconformist usage to speak of God *owning* the work of a preacher, that is, acknowledging it by enabling him or her to make converts (*OED*, *own*, sense v. 4). Dinah says 'God . . . has called me to speak his word, and he has greatly *owned* my work' (chapter 3). When Dinah describes her co-religionist, Seth Bede (chapter 8), as 'a *gracious* young man and without offence', she means 'endowed with divine grace', usage already obsolescent in the nineteenth century (*OED*, *gracious*, sense 6). Writing to Seth, Dinah says (chapter 30) 'I have all things and *abound*,' a verb for 'to prosper' which she would have read in several places in St. Paul's epistles. In much the same way Mr Lyon, dissenting minister in *Felix Holt*, has the Biblical *apparel* for 'clothes' ('There is that in *apparel* which pleases the eye' chapter 18); and *to glorify* for 'to boast' ('Not – to use his own phrase – not that he "*glorified* himself herein",' chapter 24).

Even among the chosen vessels of Dissent, however, there are gradations of usage that have their basis, doubtless, in the society of this world. When Lyon had the temerity to mention Felix Holt and his troubles by name in both prayer and sermon, this was thought unduly familiar by his congregation of old-fashioned Independents. Felix was mentioned by 'the naked use of a non-Scriptural Treby name' – not as, for example, 'a young Ishmaelite, whom we would fain see brought back from the lawless life of the desert... etc.' In the opinion of Mr Lyon's congregation, such things might pass 'in a low unlettered local preacher of the Wesleyan persuasion: but a certain style in prayer was demanded from Independents, the most educated body in the ranks of orthodox Dissent' (chapter 37). Felix, they did not scruple to point out, had done no good to 'the cause', a word still meaningful in some Free Church circles. As the *OED* points out (*cause*, sense 11c), this has often a very localized meaning, referring to a particular organization or church.

This last is less a word of the Biblical traditions of Nonconformity such as George Eliot relished, than a term appropriate to what would now be called the sociology of religion. Such a word, too, is Mrs Oliphant's *charge*: "Ah! – going to be married, I suppose?" said the man from 'Omerton; "that's the natural consequence after a man gets a *charge*" (*Salem Chapel*, chapter 18). A *charge* is the responsibility, under God, of a congregation. The man from 'Omerton, here mentioned (actually named Beecher), takes over the charge at Salem when the hero of the novel, Arthur Vincent, relinquishes the ministry. Beecher proves to be a more complaisant, less intractable pastor; but his less than heroic status (which his congregation, after Arthur, doubtless find comforting, or to use Mrs Tozer's word *comfortable*) appears in his unctuous but incorrect English, here and elsewhere. After a year's experience at Salem, the man from 'Omerton is acknowledged, by himself and others, to have made an 'it' (chapter 43). Arthur Vincent is a man with higher social aspirations, and reluctantly, as a dissenting minister, he envisages for himself a humdrum future, unerringly choosing appropriate lower middle-class phraseology to describe it (chapter 2): 'To circulate among their tea-parties, and grow accustomed to their finery, and perhaps "*pay attention*" to Phoebe Tozer; or, at least, suffer that young lady's attentions to him.' Frequently, in *Salem Chapel*, the word *connection* occurs, in the originally Wesleyan sense of a body of persons connected together, a religious society. The word *people* alone can also mean a minister's congregation. Mrs Oliphant has 'chapel people' in inverted commas as a usual phrase, which in some places it still is (chapter 18). Mrs Vincent warns her son: 'Arthur, with a troublesome flock like yours you must not commit yourself! You must not let your sister's name be talked of among the *people*' (chapter 29). This expression, though much used by Dissenters, had its origin in the Prayer Book.

Like Dinah Morris, Tozer, deacon and butterman, echoes the Bible in his language, but by describing Vincent as 'precious' and 'a shining light' he somehow manages to confer dignity neither on his protegé nor himself, though there is ample Biblical precedent for both epithets (for example, Psalm 49:8; John 5:35).

Sober and discriminating as the Methodists were in their speech, it is amusing to find the eccentric but orthodox Miss Galindo, in *My Lady Ludlow* (chapter 11) avoiding, as a rule, their expressions: 'But, however, it was a mercy, and I don't mind saying so, ay, and meaning it too, though it may be like Methodism.'

VULGARIZED WORDS

There were various words and usages that, though they had been acceptable in Regency times, acquired vulgar, ironic or other overtones as the nineteenth century proceeded. The word *genteel* (p. 15) is a sort of paradigm of this process; but there were others. Sometimes a legal term could be downgraded from the professions, and intrude into conversation. The commonest word of this kind was *party* for a person. The more technically legal contexts sounded less offensive, as in 'it would be better for the *parties* to divide the loss, Mr A taking one-third, and Mr B two-thirds,' or 'Miss A was a *party* to that business.' But sentences like 'I told the *party* what you said, and he was satisfied' and 'I never knew she was the *party* concerned' are to be, by 1826, condemned, though Jane Austen could use such expressions as 'They all joined in a very spirited critique upon the *party*' (*Sense and Sensibility*, chapter 37). One of the reasons for the decline of this usage may be that it renders the word ambiguous. We have to check the context of *Sense and Sensibility* to see that it is actually to one person, and not more, that the reference is made. It is the kind of ambiguity that Dickens loved to exploit:

> 'In one moment, my dear, I'll introduce the party.'
> Running downstairs as fast as she had run up, Miss Tox got the party out of the hackney-coach, and soon returned with it under convoy. It then appeared that she had used the word, not in its legal or business acceptation, when it merely expresses an individual, but as a noun of multitude, or signifying many. (*Dombey and Son*, chapter 2)

Dickens of course knew the usage that had extended from the legal use, and employed it in the substandard way for comic effect. An undertaker in *David Copperfield* (chapter 30) complains: 'When a *party* is ill, we can't ask how the party is.' It is usage that is described by the *OED* (*party*, sense 14) as 'formerly common and in serious use; now shoppy, vulgar or jocular, the proper word being *person*'.

It follows from such changing usage that linguistic authority often passed to younger and more aware members of a family. Blanche Amory, in *Pendennis*, checks her mother Lady Clavering, and Rosamond and Fred Vincy, in *Middlemarch*, correct Mrs Vincy. Rosamond is critical of her mother's remark that she has refused 'the pick of' the young men in Middlemarch. 'If I had had time to think', says Mrs Vincy, 'I should have said "the most superior young men".' But here her son Fred interrupts: 'There are so many superior teas and sugars now. Superior is getting to be shopkeepers' slang' (chapter 11). So a word which Jane Austen could use with a straight face becomes contaminated with the dreadful suggestion of trade.

The use of the word *line* meaning 'a department of activity' has long been frowned on by the pundits. Under this sense (28) the *OED* quotes Boswell: 'Johnson was ... prompt to repress colloquial barbarisms ... such as *line* for *department*, or *branch*, as the civil *line*, the banking *line*.' This barbarism throve in the following century, nevertheless, and was more or less acceptable: 'We are getting very much into the Reform *line*, I assure you,' writes Creevey in 1821 (*Creevey Papers*, ed. Maxwell, II, p. 6). Much later in the century, Martin Tupper boasts: 'If an author can be accounted a fair judge of his own writings, this is my best effort in the imaginative *line*' (John Drinkwater 'Martin Tupper' in *The Eighteen Eighties*, p. 214). So with the pleasant but ineffectual Mary Snow in *Orley Farm* (chapter 48), who says: 'He is quite a genteel young man and very respectable in the medical *line*.' Among his *Vulgarisms* (1833) Savage includes 'in the tobacco *line*' which he emends to *trade*.

A particularly interesting example of this process of vulgarization is the word *tasty*. Now confined to describing eatables with the meaning of 'appetizing', *tasty* could also mean, at the beginning of the nineteenth century, 'tasteful, displaying good taste', and this meaning it vulgarly retained to the mid-Victorian period. In *Orley Farm* (chapter 6), a commercial traveller describes a hideous iron table he is attempting to sell as 'the tastiest present for a gentleman to make to his lady'. 'It was certainly a "tasty" article,' writes Trollope, tongue in cheek. The *OED* has an interesting quotation from Coleridge, showing what had happened to this word: 'I wish I could find a more familiar word than *aesthetic*....To be sure there is *tasty*; but that has been long ago emasculated for all unworthy uses by milliners, tailors and ... dandies.' Bulwer Lytton uses the word with typical condescension in *Godolphin* (chapter 49) to describe suburban villas in Brompton: 'and the windows were plate-glass, with mahogany sashes – only, here and there, a Gothic casement was stuck in by way of looking "*tasty*".'

A word that had become vulgar through acquiring suggestions of unctuousness was *treasure*, meaning a valuable person. It could be used without irony by Jane Austen: of Frank Churchill, Emma Woodhouse says: 'Well if he has nothing else to recommend him (except good looks) he will be a *treasure* at Highbury' (*Emma*, chapter 18). In Parliament, according to Creevey (*Creevey Papers*, ed. Gore, p. 139), Wilberforce made a speech in

1815 on the death of Whitbread, politician and member of the distinguished brewing family, describing him as 'one of the public *treasures*'. However, when the vulgar Mr Sherwin, in Wilkie Collins's *Basil* (1852) uses the word, we recognize that it contributes to a general impression of vulgarity: 'That's what I call having a *treasure*! And yet, though he's been with us for years, Mrs S. there won't take to him!' (chapter 15). The word *object* applied to persons, sometimes in deeply felt contexts, meaning the person for whom, or to whom, one's aims and ambitions are directed, also occurs in Jane Austen. Edmund Bertram in *Mansfield Park* (chapter 27) describes Mary Crawford and Fanny Price as 'the two dearest *objects* I have on earth'. By the time of *Orley Farm* (1862), however, the word so used has become threadbare, and the meaning depersonalized, as when the rather pathetic Mr Kenneby confesses: 'I've had my *object*, and though she's been another's, still I've kept her image on my heart' (chapter 43).

Mr Kenneby is imitating an upper-class expression. Reversing this process, Tom Brown (*Tom Brown at Oxford*, chapter 40), brings himself with much hesitation to fill something of a gap in upper-class speech with a word from the lower orders. Talking to a village lad he has befriended, he says 'Why, I haven't seen – I've scarcely heard of – my *sweetheart* – there, you'll understand that – for this year and more.' This is indeed a word of the lower classes. When there is talk of Maggie Tulliver getting a place as a teacher, her Uncle Glegg protests, 'You must ha' picked up half-a-dozen *sweethearts* – isn't there one of 'em the right sort of article?', and Aunt Glegg interposes 'not *sweethearts*, if I'm to use such a word, though it was never heard in my family' (*The Mill on the Floss*, VI, chapter 12).

To step for *to come* or *to go* is listed by Fowler as one of his 'Genteelisms'. Already in Victorian times it was the rather pompous use of tradesmen and servants:'"Mistress is in her boudoir," said the consequential butler.... "Please *step* into the parlour"' (*Handley Cross*, chapter 8). When Foker describes Pen in *Pendennis* (I, chapter 10) as 'as good a fellow as ever *stepped*', there is a further irony, for this was something of a horse-dealer's cliché: 'He's as good a horse as ever stepped' (*Mr Sponge's Sporting Tour*, chapter 41).

Even the most fashionable words, with usage, could become provincial and passé. In the following passage an upper middle-class provincial lady is talking to her maid, who speaks first, and we are able to see how far the word *beau*, the fashionable Regency term for a dandy, has sunk: '"But I won't say but what I've had a *beau*, young as I look." "But you don't suppose that I want beaux, as you call them?" "I don't know, ma'am, as you wants 'em exactly"' (*Can You Forgive Her?*, chapter 47). We may assume that it is not fashionable usage when Peggotty offers the opinion that Dora might think herself well off to have 'such a beau' as David (*David Copperfield*, chapter 33). There was in any case a disposition no longer to use the noun *beauty*, in the sense of *beau*, of males, as both Jane Austen and Thackeray had done. Thomas Hardy, in *Two on a Tower* (1882), chronicles this change with regard to the adjective *beautiful*:

> He was a youth who might properly have been characterized by a word the judicious chronicler would not readily use in such a connexion, preferring to reserve it for raising images of the opposite sex .... To say in these days that a youth is beautiful is not to award him that amount of credit which the expression would have carried with it if he had lived in the times of the Classical Dictionary. (chapter 1)

(This is Lemprière's *Classical Dictionary* of 1788).

The use of *lady* meaning 'wife' is to be found in Disraeli's first novel *Vivian Grey* (1826–7), and also in Jane Austen: 'Mr Grey was for Eton, but his *lady* was one of those women whom nothing in the world can persuade that a public school is anything else but a place where boys are roasted alive' (*Vivian Grey*, chapter 2). This is the usage, the *OED* informs us, of the first half of the nineteenth century. We can observe the word's demotion in Laurence Oliphant's *Piccadilly* (1870):

> The stairs were so crowded that Bodwinkle, who looked like one of his own footmen, and stood on the top of them, facing his wife, was red and apoplectic from pressure. His 'lady', as I heard one of his City friends call her, had achieved the greatest object of her ambition in life. (p. 207)

However, in 1879 Disraeli continued with the old-fashioned usage, unless he was being ironic, which is possible in the context: 'Sir Beach ... could not stay ... as his *lady* in London is in a delicate situation; hourly delicacy' (*Letters*, II, P. 235).

The twenty years before Victoria's reign do seem to have been a time for observing the ironic overtones of words that had hitherto been used naturally. Once again, *genteel* is the type for such words. With the influx of mercantile elements into the hitherto stable landed classes, old values were threatened, and certain words that had been complimentary were modified and used ironically, to convey criticism of new elements in society. Even the most acceptable adjectives are found to be susceptible to ironic and mercenary interpretation. In Peacock's *Crotchet Castle* (1831) the following dialogue takes place:

> *Captain Fitzchrome*: Is it come to this, that you make a jest of my poverty? Yet is my poverty only comparative. Many decent families are maintained on smaller means.
>
> *Lady Clarinda*: Decent families: aye, *decent* is the distinction from *respectable*. Respectable means rich, and decent means poor. I should die if I heard my family called decent. And then your decent family always lives in a snug little place; I hate a little place. (chapter 3)

Respectable meaning 'rich' seems to have been City usage: 'He was "highly respectable" as they say on 'Change – that is to say he was very rich' (Surtees, *Handley Cross*, chapter 7). Thirty years later, Trollope has Lady Midlothian congratulate the flighty Alice Vavasor on the fact that she is 'going to be married so *respectably*', and Alice is angry at the application of 'that odious word *respectable* to her own prospects'. The trouble was that her engagement 'was very respectable' but 'lacked other attractions which it should have possessed' (*Can You Forgive Her?*, chapter 2). Here too *respectable* obviously means financially respectable.

If meanings of words fluctuate, so too do idioms and turns of phrase alter in acceptability. In Jane Austen's novels, and in fashionable, sophisticated contexts, the curious inversion *and reason good*, meaning 'and with good reason', occurs more than once. Consider this conversation between Emma and Mr Knightley, for instance: '"To be sure – our discordancies must always arise from my being in the wrong." "Yes," said he, smiling – "And *reason good*. I was sixteen years old when you were born"' (*Emma*, chapter 12). By the time of *Felix Holt* (1866), the phrase is a part of the Midlands dialect, being used by Mrs Holt, the garrulous mother of the hero: 'There was no more smell nor strength in the mustard than so much flour. And *reason good* – for the mustard had lain in paper nobody knows how long' (*Felix Holt*, chapter 22).

There were several turns of phrase which acquired associations with trade as the nineteenth century progressed: phrases, for example, on the pattern of 'self and family', with no possessive adjective attached to either element. Such collocations had been respectable enough in the eighteenth century, and the idiom had been especially frequent in the diary of the well-to-do eighteenth-century clergyman James Woodforde: 'My Nephews *and self* took a ride to Mattishall'; 'Neither any from my House at Church but *self and two Servants*' (*Diary of a Country Parson*). But by the time of *Middlemarch* (1872) – and perhaps more characteristic of that date than of the time, forty years earlier, when the events are alleged to have taken place – [5] this particular collocation had come to epitomize the smugness and limited horizons of a provincial community such as Middlemarch. Mr Maumsey, a grocer, says of the Reform Bill: 'Few men have less need to cry for change than I have, personally speaking – that is, *for self and family*' (*Middlemarch*, chapter 51). With his usual sharpness in matters of speech and social level, Trollope has Lucy Robarts adapt the phrase for her own sarcastic purposes, when she is due to be reprimanded by Lady Lufton for setting herself up as a possible match for Lady Lufton's son: 'Have I not

[5] In Bulwer Lytton's *Pelham* (1828), that most proscriptive of novels, a version of the idiom, but with a possessive adjective, is still acceptable: 'A bench which, for a certain number of *sous*, one might appropriate to the entire and unparticipated use of *one's self and party*' (*Pelham* ch. 21).

desired King Cophetua to take *himself and sceptre* elsewhere?' (*Framley Parsonage*, chapter 35). This is very neat. The ironic blend of the heroic legend of King Cophetua and the beggar-maid, with the commercialese of 'self and sceptre', manages to convey the suggestion that even the venerable Lady Lufton herself is not entirely free from worldly self-seeking.

An interesting instance of a respectable Regency idiom that develops into a vulgar Victorian catch-phrase is the collocation *to wish one may*. Jane Austen writes in one of her letters: 'Since I wrote last, my 2nd Edit. has stared me in the face – Mary tells me that Eliza means to buy it. *I wish she may*' (*Letters*, p. 372). One can compare with this a line from *The Blue Bells of Scotland*, the well-known song written at the time of the Napoleonic wars: 'But it's Oh! in my heart, I wish he may not die,' now usually modernized to 'I hope he will not die.' With the addition of *get*, however, this phrase emerges as vulgar, Victorian town slang. It is the language of political hecklers in Disraeli's *Coningsby*, for example: 'He brought in his crack theme, the guillotine, and dilated so elaborately upon its qualities, that one of the gentlemen below could not refrain from exclaiming, "I wish you may get it"' (*Coningsby*, V, chapter 4). The phrase occurs to Trollope when Lady Desmolines and her daughter Madeline attempt to compromise John Eames. John, into whose arms Madeline has 'swooned', must perforce help Lady Desmolines to lay her out on a sofa: 'The old woman looked at him with eyes which asked whether he didn't "wish he might get it" as plainly as though the words had been pronounced' (*The Last Chronicle of Barset*, chapter 80). Probably the nearest equivalent today, in import and register, for many Victorian contexts in which this phrase occurs, is 'Chance would be a fine thing!'

To say 'not half', as in 'I don't half like chocolates,' is now to make an extreme, if rather vulgar statement. 'Don't half' is a deliberate under-statement implying a great deal more than fifty per cent. Earlier, Victorian statements with this adverbial use of *half* often had the literal meaning of 'not up to half, therefore only to a limited extent': 'They congratulated me again, and went on to express so much wonder at the notion of my being a gentleman, that *I didn't half like it*' (*Great Expectations*, chapter 18). Here Pip is by no means pleased that the idea of his being a gentleman is seen somewhat incredulously. So also in this passage from Thomas Hughes's *The Scouring of the White Horse* (1859): 'So we sat down with them, but *I didn't half like* the way in which Miss Lucy was running on with two young farmers, one on each side of her' (chapter 6). Even this literal use of 'not half' may have been slightly vulgar. If it was necessary to speak with more precision and care, 'not above half' could be used; for instance by a high court judge, father of the heroine in *Orley Farm* (chapter 58): '"Papa, is that review you were speaking of here at Noningsby?" "You will find it on my study table; but remember, Madeline, *I don't above half* go along with him."' The modern meaning, implying understatement, is found as early as *Handley Cross* (1843) but it is not the best usage: 'Doleful at length took his departure, feeling that Sir Archy was *not half* a bad fellow, and vowing that he would return without fail on the morrow' (chapter 75).

A frequent occurrence in novelists and playwrights who render eighteenth-century and Regency conversation is what we might call the enclitic *however*, meaning 'at any rate', now obsolete, according to the *OED*. There is a suspicion, even in Jane Austen, that this is not the best usage; as when Mrs Bennet says: 'If I wished to think slightingly of anybody's children, it should not be of my own *however*' (*Pride and Prejudice*, chapter 7). By the time of *Mary Barton* (1848), this is a provincialism: '"Did you know he were in Halifax, Mary?" "No," she answered, faintly and sadly ... "Well, he's there, *however*"' (chapter 12). *Somewhat* now tends to be restricted to adverbial usages in standard English, as in 'He declined *somewhat*; That is *somewhat* different.' Yet it could formerly be used by Jane Austen, for example, as a pronoun, where we now prefer *something*: 'As if he had *somewhat* in particular to tell her' (*Sense and Sensibility*, chapter 27). It was also used, to quote the last *OED* example of this usage (*somewhat*, sense 1b), by Charles Kingsley in *Westward Ho!* (1855): 'Some folks say he's not right in the head, or turned miser, or *somewhat*.' It is easy to see what has happened to this usage if we read these quotes aloud. The temptation to pronounce *somewhat* as it is often pronounced dialectally, as [sumət], is very great. With this word the process of provincialization went on apace in the nineteenth century. With her superior Manchester characters, however, Mrs Gaskell continues to spell the word according to standard English pronunciation: 'Grandfather would have known there was *somewhat* the matter' (*Mary Barton*, chapter 5). A glance at Orton's *A Word Geography of England* (map 24) will show how widespread, dialectally, is the use of *somewhat* for *something*. Instances to represent a dialectal pronunciation are plentiful: 'I'd give ye *summut* to run for' (*Handley Cross*, chapter 44).

Since so many words were ceasing to be genteel, it behoved those mindful of their station in life to avoid 'low' expressions, and to rebuke members of their families who indulged in them: '"There you go, Polly; you are always having a shy at Lady Ann and her relations," says Mr Newcome, good-naturedly. "A *shy*! How can you use such vulgar words, Mr Newcome?"' (Thackeray, *The Newcomes*, I, chapter 16). Even a reputable English word like *brisk*, in moments of ill-will, can become a weapon in this war of words: '"What should be the matter with me?" "You don't seem very *brisk*, Ma," returned Lavvy the bold. "Brisk?" repeated her parent. "Brisk? Whence the low expression, Lavinia?"' (*Our Mutual Friend*, III, chapter 4). This is Mrs Wilfer, who elsewhere shows her gentility by euphemism: '"By-the-by, ma'am," said Mr Boffin, turning back as he was going, "you have a *lodger*?" "A gentleman," Mrs Wilfer answered, qualifying the low expression, "undoubtedly occupies our first floor"' (ibid.' I, chapter 9). Like Mrs Lookaloft, she thinks of life 'beneath our humble roof' in grandiloquent terms:

> 'Very pleasant premises,' said Mr Boffin, cheerfully.
> 'Pardon me, sir,' returned Mrs Wilfer, correcting him, 'it is the abode of conscious though independent Poverty.'
> Finding it rather difficult to pursue the conversation down this road, Mr and Mrs Boffin sat staring at mid-air. (ibid., I, chapter 9)

Mrs Wilfer's daughter, Lavinia, is capable, not only of taking, but of giving a reprimand in the cause of genteel English (IV, chapter 16):

> 'Really, George,' remonstrated Miss Lavinia ... 'I think you might be more delicate and less personal.'
> 'Go it!' crid Mr Sampson ... 'Oh yes! Go it, Miss Lavinia Wilfer!'
> 'What you may mean, George Sampson, by your omnibus driving expressions, I cannot pretend to imagine.'

G. M. Young, in *Portrait of an Age* (p. 2), has put the situation very well: 'The world is very evil. An unguarded look, a word, a gesture ... might plant a seed of corruption in the most innocent heart, and the same word or gesture might betray a lingering affinity with the class below.'

3

Pronunciation

In matters of pronunciation and accentuation, it is curious to see how far back the tradition of certain features labelled by Ross in 1954 as upper-class do in fact go. *Medicine* and venison, for example, are correctly pronounced, according to Savage in *Vulgarisms* (1833), with no medial vowel. In 1954 [mɛdisən] and [vɛnizən] are categorized by Ross as non-U, just as 'meddysun' and 'vennysun' were so spelt to indicate a vulgar pronunciation by Savage in 1833. With these acceptable elisions of a medial vowel, Savage also includes *nominative* as in 'the nominative case'. 'Nommynative', he says, is a vulgarity. *Syrup* in the pronunciation [sʌrəp] is said by Ross to be non-U; and Savage condemns 'surrup', along with 'surringe' for *syringe*. In the rather curious phrase 'I took the altitude', *altitude* is spelt by Savage with two 'll's' by way of indicating a vulgar pronunciation. This may correspond with a pronunciation with [ɔ] instead of [ɔ:] in words like *fault, salt, Balkans* etc., described as non-U in 1954 by Ross. Already in 1833 Savage warns against an unacceptable pronunciation of *length* as [lɛnθ], which Ross too considers to be non-U. For the numeral zero the U word in 1833 was *nought* and the non-U word was *ought*: 'Put down five and *ought*.' The same was still true, according to Ross, in 1954.

However, as one might expect in view of the century and more that intervenes between these two authorities, the strictures of Savage and Ross do not always tally. Thus it is interesting that what Ross describes in 1954 as 'a U-pronunciation until comparatively recent times' should, in 1833, have been condemned by Savage as vulgar. This is the vowel in *staunch* and *launch*, now almost universally with [ɔ:], but formerly often with [a:]. Since Savage often uses the consonant 'r' to indicate a preceding long vowel, the latter would seem to be the pronunciation of 'starnch' and of 'He went to the *larnch*'; a pronunciation variously described by the two authorities as vulgar (Savage), and as old-fashioned U (Ross). In the contentious matter of *er* spellings, also, in words like *sergeant, clerk* and *Derby*, Savage's advice differs from Ross's, and from modern usage, at some points. It is true that a sentence rendered 'He keeps six clurks,' which is condemned, indicates Savage's disapproval of the pronunciation of this word with [ə:] (a disapproval found in Victorian novels, p. 108). It is also true that Savage follows J. A. Walker's *A Critical Pronouncing Dictionary... of the English Language* (1791) in considering the pronunciation implied by the spellings 'consarn', 'clargy', 'sarvice' and 'varsal world' (universal world) as vulgar. But Savage also disapproves of this vowel in the place-names *Derby* and *Berkshire*, favouring instead the spelling pronunciation in [ə:] now considered by Ross and speakers of British English generally as substandard. Here Savage's desire for 'correctness' obviously took him too far. The word *vase* is given one acceptable and one unacceptable pronunciation by Savage: [vɔ:z] and [veiz]. Both these pronunciations are rejected a hundred and twenty years later by Ross, who favours [vɑ:z].

With words like *real* and *ordeal* there were more contenders for non-U equivalents. The U-pronunciation, however, seems to have remained the same: at least this is suggested by Savage's spellings 'rēăl' and 'ordēăl', so accented, no doubt, to suggest the modern diphthong: [riəl] [ɔ:diəl]. Different vulgar pronunciations of these words are rendered 'rale' and 'ordeel' respectively. The latter represents the very frequent non-U pronunciation [ɔ:di:l], while the former is probably the diphthong [reil], unlikely to be heard with this word now, except perhaps in Ireland. A further possibility is suggested in Creevey: '*Ra-ally*, as Mrs Taylor would say, Peel makes a great figure' (1828 *Creevey Papers*, ed. Gore, p. 253). Writing at the end of the century, Lady Grove, in *The Social Fetich* (p. 5), speaks of a 'gateless barrier' set up against those who pronounce *real* as 'reel' and *really* as 'reelly'.

With the vexed question of accentuation, there is interesting continuity in the word *formidable*, which both Savage and Ross agree is pronounced by the best people with accent on the first syllable. One can perceive, in Savage's lists, many prescriptive attempts, not always ultimately successful, to push the accent backwards to the first syllable from a later one to which it naturally seems to gravitate. Therefore in Savage lámentable is to be preferred to laméntable, éxquisite to exquísite, révenue to the Shakespearean revénue, mércantile to mercántile, índustry to indústry, cóntroversy to contróversy, chástisement to chastísement, fánatic to fanátic, déspicable to despícable, and cómpulsory to compúlsory. Contrary to this, however, Savage disapproves of *commenting* with the now normal initial accent, preferring to accent the second syllable.

The best usage, in Savage's view, generally exacted precise elocution of syllables, preferring 'lukewarm' to 'loowarm' and 'empty' for the more provincial 'empt' (as a verb). Consequently the upper-class tendency to elide syllables, in words like *extraordinary* and *interested*, noted not only by Ross but by overseas visitors in the nineteenth century, does not appear in Savage's lists; though *toward(s)* is to be pronounced as one syllable, and a warrant for this is found in the scansion of a line from *Paradise Lost* (I, 669):

'Hurling defiance *toward* the vault of heaven'. It was right, too, to say 'maintain', but wrong to talk of 'maintainance', right to say 'pronounce' but wrong to talk of 'pronounciation'. *Southern* must not be pronounced, like *south*, with a diphthong, nor *knowledge*, with the diphthong of *know*. *Breeches* must have a short vowel[i], but *teats* must have a long [i:] – 'Look at the cow's teats (not tits).' *Theatre* must be accented on the first syllable, not the second, and *plebeian* on the second syllable, not the first. The habit of cheerfully ignoring the niceties of French pronunciation, as in 'reservoy' for *reservoir*, and 'a claw' for *eclat* ('He came out with *a claw*'), was not approved of. It was wrong to consider the French loan-word *chaise*, meaning a light carriage, as a plural noun, and form a new singular, *shay*. Moreover Savage, stricter than the *OED*, insists that *trait* should always have its French pronunciation, and that it was vulgar to speak of a 'trate of character'. Surprisingly, he condemns the pronunciation of *lieutenant* as 'leftenant', doubtless following Walker, who had expressed the hope that 'the regular sound, "lewtenant" will in time become current'. Walker's hope seems likely to be realized.

In general, there were more untidy ends and anomalies of pronunciation in 1833 than today, and Savage set himself to remedy matters by trimming overlaps, where these occurred. Thus, in the matter of the centuries-old confusion of the two sounds that eventually became [ɔi] and [ai], he condemns both 'Does the water *bile*' and 'I'm subject to the *boil*,' and also the pronunciation of *ointment* as 'hyntment', thus aiding the process of differentiation. Already in 1828 confusion on this matter was something of a joke: 'I mention the *pint* to show the terms on which we parted' (*Creevey Papers*, ed. Gore, p. 251). Savage warns both against substituting palatal consonants where they should not exist, as in 'non-plushed', and omitting them where they are necessary, as in 'srimps'. There was confusion between voiceless alveolars and affricates, as contrary variants like 'larfture' for *laughter* and 'picter' for *picture* show. He requires the now universal voiced affricate in *soldiers* ('solejers' not 'soadyers', as he puts it), but insists that *educated* be always pronounced with a semi-vowel, not a palatal ('edyucated, not edjucated'), though this is practically impossible at speed. Interestingly, he has one or two examples of palatal consonants in place of [s] or [z], as in 'The very refuge of society' and 'Don't squeege so' – both, of course, deplored. On this minor point of lower-class speech, Dickens was to build a substantial part of Mrs Gamp's idiolect.

Some of the pronunciations Savage recalls, like some of the vocabulary, must have been dialectal. The cockney interchange of [w] and [v], still common in 1833, and soon to be brilliantly exploited by Dickens in *The Pickwick Papers* (1837), is noted: the change of [w] to [v] is illustrated with what was clearly a catch-phrase: '"Vot are they made of ?" "Vy with vax, vicks and all."' The still more common change from [v] to [w] is shown in 'wittles', 'wishus' for *vicious*, 'conwulsed' etc. This phenomenon of the interchange of [w] and [v] seems to have died out about the middle of the nineteenth century (see Jespersen, *A Modern English Grammar*, I, 13.8). Also characteristic of cockney speech is the substitution of [f] for [θ] in Savage's example, 'He was very lofe at first'; and [d] for [ð], as in 'three *fardens*' and 'The horse was all of a *larder*' (lather). Also very prevalent in London, as well as much more widespread, was the use of epenthetic, or additional consonants. This is a feature of earlier substandard English that has quite dramatically diminished, doubtless owing to increased literacy. Savage has 'scholard', 'margent' for *margin* (formerly this had had literary currency), 'fust' for *fuss*, 'wunst' for *once*, 'wyned' for *wine*, 'townd' for *town* etc. Occasionally, as with dialect words (p. 83), some pronunciations seem to have come from further afield: 'My *wive's* bonnet', with the voicing of the final labio-dental, suggests Devon; 'He came from the *heelands*', corrected to *highlands*, suggests that Savage will have no dealings with Scottish vowels.

We have noted in *The Vulgarities of Speech conected* of 1826, forestalls any more puns on the lines of Falstaff's 'If *rweasons* were as plenty as blackberries'. He warns that a *Seville* orange should be distinguished in Thackeray's: 'a Calcuttar attorney' (*Pendennis*, II, chapter 22). Allied to this 'r' is the kind of metanalysis Savage exemplifies: 'She's a nold dooman,' and the curious 'He's quite an *ottomy*', meaning 'a skeleton', from *anatomy*, with misunderstanding of the first syllable as an indefinite article. Also a product of considerable illiteracy is frequent aphesis, in words like 'She was *ticed* away' and 'to *strain* for debt'. But it is owing to literacy without benefit of the broadcast word that we find, in Savage's lists, 'catastroaf' for *catastrophe* and 'antipoads' for *antipodes*.

We have noted in *The Vulgarities of Speech Corrected* of 1826, several phrases which recall, over two centuries after his death, the idiom of Shakespeare. In *Vulgarisms*, we find Savage, in turn, trying to put a stop to numerous pronunciations that had been a fruitful source of Shakespearean puns. It is wrong, he says, to pronounce *raisin* with a vowel ('currants and *reasons*' is his example), and not (as now) with a diphthong. Thus, he forestalls any more puns on the lines of Falstaff's 'If *reasons* were as plenty as blackberries'. He warns that a *Seville* orange should be distinguished in pronunciation from the adjective *civil*, though he does direct us to Beatrice's pun in *Much Ado about Nothing*: 'Civil, count, – civil as an orange'. The alternative pronunciations of *ache* as [eitʃ] and of *Rome* as [ru:m] – two fruitful sources of Tudor puns – are forbidden; as is the Shakespearean 'apricock for *apricot*, justified etymologically as being from *praecox*, 'early ripe'. As for the rejected pronunciation suggested by the spelling 'orrizon' instead of *horizon*, this would have been instantly recognized by Chaucer! Again, one is surprised by the number of earlier pronunciations surviving to the comparatively late date of 1833.

Savage seems to have written under the shadow of the famous orthoepist
J.A. Walker, whose influential *Critical Pronouncing Dictionary* underwent
numerous revisions, to be finally overhauled and re-published in 1836 by
B.H. Smart as *Walker Remodelled: A New Critical Pronouncing Dictionary of
the English Language*. Such an influence, elocutory rather than observant in
tendency, was totally against detailing the numerous elisions and abbrevi-
ations to be found in even the most 'correct' speakers. We have to wait until
the 1870s for that bright American, R.H. Dana, to anticipate some of the
remarks about elision made later in 1954 by Ross. Dana comments more
than once on differences between British and American pronunciation in
this respect:

> They pronounce *interesting* in three syllables. We naturally slur the second,
> but they omit it altogether. We pronounce *extraordinary* 'eks-tror-dinary',
> while here many of them drop the third syllable, making it *exstrornery*.

However, Dana goes on to note: 'It was noticeable that Mr and Mrs
Gladstone pronounced these words as we do in America' (*Hospitable
England in the Seventies*, p. 25). There have, nevertheless, always been fairly
strict limits in this matter of elision of syllables in good speech. *Medicine* and
venison were, and still are, acceptable di-syllables; but even today he would
be a foolish man who imagined that the omission of the middle syllable in,
for example, *cigarette* was anything but a non-U class indicator. The
anonymous author of *Vulgarities* warns against reducing syllables in words
like *traveller* and *suddenly*; though it must be a rare occurrence that the
mispronunciation of a fiancée's Christian name in this way could have such
unfortunate consequences as it has in Gissing's *Demos* (chapter 14):

> It was unfortunate that Richard did not pronounce the name of his bride-
> elect [Adela] quite as it sounds on cultured lips. This may have been partly
> the result of diffidence; but there was a slurring of the second syllable
> disagreeably suggestive of vulgarity. It struck on the girl's nerves, and made it
> more difficult for her to grow accustomed to this form of address from
> Mutimer.

So the use the female Christian name, so significant, as well shall see, in
Victorian courtship, becomes a stumbling-block.

M. R. James, writing of Eton in the 1880s (*Eton and King's*, p. 127), notes
some remarkable elisions from one of the masters (though we must
presumably allow for schoolboy exaggeration):

> His oratory was a little difficult to follow. Such words as *laboratory* he was
> supposed to be able to pronounce in one syllable; *fish sauce* stood for 'official
> sources', *hair pin* for 'high opinion', *temmince* for 'ten minutes', and so on.

The pronunciation and intonation of the Reverend Austen Leigh, nephew
and biographer of Jane Austen, was studied by the boys of Eton: 'We loved

to hear him speak of a *queshtion*, *a pidgin*, *a lagune*; but do not let it be imagined that his division was one in which liberties could be taken' (p. 34). There was also a master named Joynes, whose 'simple piety and sincerity could not be misconstrued', but who 'did not escape being burlesqued' (p. 85): 'Before he doyed he wrote me a lettur ... Look at the Chinaman. He's industrious, not oidle.' This pronunciation with [ɔi], by the way, is perhaps an upper-class retention of what in previous centuries had been a very common rendering of the [ai] diphthong. Ross (p. 51) quotes Walker's *Critical Pronouncing Dictionary* of 1791 to the effect that, in the House of Commons in the late eighteenth century, the phrase 'the *ayes* have it' was 'frequently, but not correctly' given this 'coarse, rustic pronunciation'. Vestigially, it may still survive. I once visited, as one of a coach-party, a library in the company of, among others, a distinguished librarian from the Bodleian, an undoubted U-speaker. When, on the return journey, the coach-load of people joined in a rendering of 'I will sing you One-O,' and inspiration and memory flagged after number eight, he shouted back from the front seat, 'Noine broight shoiners!'

To return to the subject of elision, Lady Agnes Grove in *The Social Fetich* (p. 9) recognized that it was possible to follow spelling too closely:

Nothing ... is more irritating than the sedulous pronunciation of mid-verbal 'h's' [I presume she means with words like *adhere* and *exhibit*] or the sounding of the 't' in *often* .... That it is as fatal to over-value syllables as to under-value them is seen in the words *topaz*, *marmalade*, *Judas* and the name *Seymour*, which becomes vulgarized when the final syllable is pronounced *more* and *mer*.

The accepted, that is in practice the correctly elided, pronunciation of many aristocratic surnames was a matter of such importance that many etiquette books published lists of families with tricky surnames, adding home-made 'phonetics' to indicate the received pronunciation of these names. Thus *Gifford* has a 'soft' 'g', and *Gillot* and 'hard' one: *Beauclerk* was 'Boclair', *Villiers* was 'Villers' and *Waldegrave*, 'Walgrave'. These long lists are sufficient to dispel any idea that the pronunciation of the upper classes followed the spelling slavishly. Indeed, as Ross points out, it was the non-U who clung to spelling pronunciations in words like *waistcoat* and *forehead*. That it was important to get the right elision with surnames is amply demonstrated by an anecdote from the *Recollections* of Louisa, Countess of Antrim (p. 57):

Lady Morton was for many years lady-in-waiting to Queen Alexandra, then Princess of Wales. When she was dying, her nurse, hoping to rouse her, read aloud a kind letter of inquiry written of behalf of the Princess by Miss Charlotte Knollys, her Secretary. The nurse pronounced the signature phonetically – Knollies – on which a sepulchral voice from the bed put in drily – 'Commonly pronounced "Noles".' These are said to have been the last words of the patient.

The surname of one of Queen Victoria's best-known equerries, Sir Frederick *Ponsonby*, demonstrates a notable characteristic of upper-class pronunciation, the tendency to pronounce [ɔ] before a nasal as [ʌ], in a dwindling number of words such as *accomplish*, *Brompton* and *constable*. Formerly, according to Smart (*Walker Remodelled*, p. xxii), this sound was heard also in *combat* and (though there is no nasal) in *sovereign*, 'but since [the latter word] has been the name of a current coin, the regular sound of "o" has been getting into use, and bids fair to be completely established.' Comparable with *Ponsonby* in having the pronunciation with [ʌ] are *Cholmondeley* which the etiquette books write as 'Chumley' and *Conyngham*, which they write as 'Cunningham'.

In some contexts, Lady Grove likes (p. 8) 'a true, clean, clear pronunciation' for unaccented syllables: 'a clear "e" sound in *jewel*, *towel*, *moment*; an unmistakable "i" in such words as *possible*, *evil*, *devil*, *animal* and *beautiful*.' When she says that these sounds must not be pronounced 'as if the "i" or the "e" were a "u"', she is asserting a characteristic of U speech that is still observable. To quote J.C. Wells (*Accents of English*, II, p. 281): in received U pronunciation (U-RP) '[i] is distinctly preferred over [ə] in the cases which are variable within RP, as *wait[i]d*, *hors[i]s*, *poss*[i]*bly* . . . *carel*[i]*ssn*[i]*ss*.' Medially, the upper-class Englishman has *tel[ʃi]phone*, where the American, by contrast, often has *tel[ʃə]phone*.

Ross notes (p. 40) that some U-speakers have a long vowel in what he calls 'many "o" words', particularly those followed by [s] [f] and [θ]; in words like *lost*, *off* and *broth*, pronounced [lɔ:st] etc. That this is now a rapidly diminishing phenomenon we can observe by listening to broadcasts by U-speakers recorded from the 1930s. More and more words from this group have gradually lost the sound of [ɔ:], which has been replaced by the spelling pronunciation [ɔ]. If we are to believe Lady Grove (p. 26) a word like *coffee* formerly had this pronunciation with [ɔ:] (it must have sounded rather American):

> In the democratic ardour of my youth, I did what is now a source of regret to me. I carefully modernized my pronunciation, and endeavoured to 'get away' from what I considered the unenlightened peculiarities of the generation above me. Alas! I can no longer say 'corfy' naturally, so I resign myself to the less distinguished and more general sound, except on the occasions when, to my joy, I unconsciously revert to the pronunciation of early youth.

The fact that, by coincidence, this sound is in many words identical with that of what she is pleased to call 'the Cockney Ruffian' did not worry Lady Grove at all:

A highly refined writer of fiction will, in depicting his low-life scenes, make his barbarians say 'I'm orf!' And when one sees the word spelt like that as a sign of the coarseness and ignorance of the character, the writer has betrayed his own hideous, mincing mispronunciation of the word which the ruffian has enunciated quite as it should be.

There were Victorians who pronounced the word *God* with the same vowel [ɔ:], the pronunciation with a long vowel having in this particular word a good pedigree, from an opened syllable in Middle English. Lady Grove grows somewhat quizzical, accordingly, over a spelling she occasionally finds in Kipling:

> Mr Rudyard Kipling is rather an offender in this respect. I know a highly cultivated, ultra-refined person who always speaks of a *gawd-mother*, not using the word in any ironical sense, however... but simply because she happens to pronounce such words in the same way as Mr Kipling's soldiers.

Curiously enough, the pronunciation of *God* indicated by Kipling's spelling survives, albeit humorously; whereas the same sound in the other words illustrated above is now considered, to quote J. C. Wells (*Accents of English*, I, p. 234) 'a laughable archaism of "affected" or aristocratic U-RP'.

Another of Lady Grove's 'gateless barriers separating without hope of appeal the sheep from the goats' is the pronunciation of the word *girl*.

> Anyone saying 'gurl' is beyond the pale. 'What on earth else can you call it?' I can hear someone exclaim. Believe me, my friends, there are those of us with whom that exclamation does for you. Banish all hope of ever being considered of the elect.

Thus, Lady Grove, in *The Social Fetich* (p. 4). The Countess of Munster, however, in *My Memories and Miscellanies* (p. 176) is more helpful: 'The higher classes pronounce "girl" as though it were spelt *gairl* whereas [the lower classes] pronounce it as if the were spelt *gurl* or as it is written, *girl*.' It seems clear from this that the pronunciation [gɛl] or [gɛəl] is desired. The objection to the present-day pronunciation as non-U is implied earlier in the century, in Thackeray's *Pendennis* (I, chapter 34):

> 'The Capting is an Irishman,' Mrs Bungay replied; and those Irish I have always said I couldn't abide. But his wife is a lady, as any one can see; and a good woman, and a clergyman's daughter, and a West of England woman, B., which I am myself... and O Marmaduke! didn't you remark her little *gurl?*'

The variant 'gal is also found in Thackeray, but this is seen as dandified and raffish: 'A young officer of the Life Guards... said "A dem fine gal, egad!"' (*Vanity Fair*, chapter 2).

Men hoping for a successful political career already felt the need, in the first half of the nineteenth century, to shed any provinciality in their pronunciation. It was felt necessary, to quote Smart (*Walker Remodelled*, p.

xl) to acquire 'the standard dialect – that in which all marks of a particular place of birth and residence are lost, and nothing appears to indicate any other habits of intercourse than with the well-bred and well-informed, wherever they may be found'. When the Yorkshireman, he continues, is 'no longer guilty of saying *dool* [dul] for *dull*, he must not carry the change so far as to say *bull* [bʌl] for *bull*." Sir Robert Peel (d. 1850), born near Bury in Lancashire, had, according to Disraeli, some difficulties here. 'Peel always *put* a question' – by using italics Disraeli obviously means [pʌt] – 'and to the last said *woonderful* and *woonderfully*. He guarded his aspirates with immense care. The correctness was not spontaneous. He had managed his elocution like his temper; neither was originally good' (*Reminiscences*, p. 93).

Savage in 1833 had warned against 'plat' for *plot*, and had tried, unsuccessfully in the long run, to substitute *razor-strap* for 'razor-strop.' According to Disraeli, this confusion of [a] and [o] was to be heard in the House of Lords:

> Lord Derby was very punctilious in his pronunciation of English, though his son talked a Lancashire patois. Lord Derby would insolently correct Lord Granville across the House of Lords. Lord Granville always said 'wropped up' – 'wrapped' Lord Derby would say in a tone clear to the reporters.

In England, though often not in America, a distinction is made between [u:] and [ju], as in '*Do* not walk in the *dew*'. The pronunciation [u:] in words like *lute*, *lucid* and *lunatic* (sic) is described in 1836 by Smart (*Walker Remodelled*, p. x) as vulgar. The author of *The Vulgarities of Speech Corrected* advises against the pronunciation indicated by the spelling 'dooty' and by 'doo' for *due*. Henry Alford in *The Queen's English* (1870) described it as 'an offensive vulgarism, most common in the midland counties, but found more or less everywhere'. But there was also a tradition of such pronunciation amongst dandies of a previous generation. Major Pendennis, a Regency dandy grown old, has 'the course for us to *pursoo*' and '*a doosid* deal' (*Pendennis* II, chapters 16, 19). Edmund Sparkler in *Little Dorrit*, another man-about-town, has 'a *doosed* fine gal' (I, chapter 21).

In present-day English the centring diphthong [uə] is increasingly merged with the lower centring diphthong [ɔə]: *mourning* and *morning*, for example, are becoming homophones. The first of these sounds was more common in the nineteenth century, and seems to have been particularly frequent in upper-class speech. *Poor* will sometimes be spelt 'pore' to indicate what was then a non-U pronunciation and is now the norm. M. R. James (p. 86) quotes the guide showing visitors around the chapel at Eton: '"What a *pore* face that is, if we may say so," was the constant remark of old Burgess, the Chapel clerk, when he showed visitors round, and pointed to the principal scene in the window.' The exact converse of this occurs in *The*

Queen's Poor (1905), where a working-class woman mimics the vicar complaining: 'There are so many *poo-er* in my pah-rish' (chapter 12).

The pronunciation of *oblige* with a vowel and not the modern diphthong became more and more archaic and provincial as the nineteenth century proceeded. One of those who had retained the vowel pronunciation was George IV. In his admirable *Sound and Symbol* (p. 128), Gerson gives three versions of an anecdote dealing with the process of the monarch's being forcibly thrust into the nineteenth century in this matter. The most colourful account is in Mrs Matthews' *Memoirs of Charles Matthews, Comedian* (1839). The monarch is reported as saying that he had offered the famous actor Kemble some snuff, with these words:

> 'If you will take a pinch ... you will much obleege me.' Kemble paused for a moment, and, dipping his fingers and thumb into the box, replied, 'I accept your Royal Highness's offer with gratitude; but, if you can extend your royal jaws so wide, pray, another time, say oblige.' And I did so, ever after, I assure you.

The old eighteenth century pronunciation is still heard from Mr Peggotty in the Yarmouth of *David Copperfield* (chapter 3); and also in Trollope's Wiltshire, where Miller Brattle in *The Vicar of Bullhampton* (chapter 51) has 'I'm *obleeged* to you ... Master Fenwick – very much *obleeged*.'

Confident departure from apparent regularity was sometimes a mark of U-speech, for example in the use of the definite article *an*, normally only found before vowels or an *h* that was not aspirated and that was therefore considered silent. There is not much scope for variable usage in this matter today, though Ross in 1954 (p. 41) cites *hotel* with no aspirate as U-usage. In this matter Lady Grove is at her most dogmatic (*The Social Fetich*, p. 5): 'A book ... becomes barely readable if the article *a* instead of *an* is placed before the word *hotel*.' Savage, in 1833, is much concerned to preserve a silent 'h' in as many words as possible and gives a four-page list of them: words like *herbal, habitual, heroical, historical, hospitable, humble* and *homage*. This list is clearly a counterblast to a tendency he greatly deplores, whereby people, in an access of false refinement, add the aspirate redundantly:

> The rustics attach their rough breathing indiscriminately to every letter capable of receiving it. We thus hear of *H-India, h-orthography, h'ell-wide, h'ebony, h'instinct, h'oxen*, lacerating at the same time their own larynx and afflicting the more delicate tympana of their metropolitan auditors by a cacophonous phraseology as nauseous as it is falsely imagined to be proper.

Predictably, for usage with the relatively rare semi-vowel, Savage considers our 'He's a Uropean' [*sic*] to be vulgar, and prefers 'an European'.

We are now arrived at the vexatious eighth letter of the alphabet, and the subject is very germane to our purpose for, to quote the *OED*, 'the correct treatment of initial "h" in speech has come to be regarded as a kind of shibboleth of social position.' Unfortunately, not every 'h' is sounded, and thus the problem is compounded by tendencies to hypercorrection. 'Even in educated pronunciation', the dictionary goes on to say, 'there are cases in which 'h' is usually mute.' Thackeray spells 'hhonest' with two 'h's' to indicate the kind of solecism that can arise here. It must also be clear from Savage's list above that it was not necessarily the same words that were aspirated throughout the course of the nineteenth century. Samuel Lysons (b. 1806) in *Our Vulgar Tongue* (1868) remarks:

> I have lived to see great changes in this respect. I have known the mute 'h' to become audible, and the audible 'h' to become mute. I was taught to pronounce the words *humble, hospital, herbs, honest* without an 'h', and can't get out of my old fashion without a struggle. Nevertheless people now talk of *humble, hospital, herb*, and I have heard people talk of *a honest* man. (p. 36)

The anonymous author of *An Essay on the Science of Pronunciation* (§. 287) writes in 1850: 'We have but eight words (and their compounds) in our language wherein the "h" must be suppressed: – *heir, honest, honour, hospital, hostler, hour, humble, humour.*'

The problem of the aspirate can be seen dramatically, as with Richard Mutimer's 'struggles with the h-fiend' (p. 106); and even dynastically, as when George Eliot discusses the rise and fall of families in *Middlemarch* (chapter 11): 'Some slipped a little downward, some got higher footing; people denied aspirates, gained wealth, and fastidious gentlemen stood for boroughs.' Lady Grove's observation that one man may steal a horse while another is not even allowed to look over the hedge at it applies to the question of aspirates also. An Eton master of the 1880s, secure in his eccentricity, is exempt from censure:

> As we turned homeward from Sheep's Bridge, we were met by Rouse, smoking a nocturnal cigar, and he – who by accident or design played fast and loose with his h's – said to us, 'Har the great gates not shut?' We didn't know. 'Then 'ow in the world did you come 'ere?' (M.R. James, *Eton and King's*, p. 60)

Failure to pronounce 'h' was especially characteristic of newly-rich people 'who, if there was talk of a statue to the Queen or the Duke, would come down to the Town 'All and subscribe their one, two three 'undred apiece' (*The Newcomes*, II, chapter 17). The inclusion of superfluous 'h's' was more likely when someone of the lower orders was giving information to his social superior: 'Artises come and take hoff the Church from that there tree – It was a Habby once sir' (*Pendennis*, I, chapter 15). The consonant was particularly liable to be maltreated in the south. Samuel Lysons in *Our Vulgar Tongue* (p. 36) observes: 'Its misuse is very much confined to the southern provinces, and not a little to the metropolis.' Thus it does not appear to be one of the endearing 'kitchen errors' of A.J. Munby's Hannah Cullwick, who comes from Shropshire. As to the attitude to be adopted, Thomas Hughes advises the upper-class speaker not to allow the misuse of the aspirate to grate on his ears, as it was clearly liable to do: 'There is much to be learnt in a third-class carriage if we will only not look while in it for cushions . . . and will not be shocked at our fellow-passengers for being weak on their "h's" and smelling of fustian' (*Tom Brown at Oxford*, chapter 17).

Another issue of some moment was the final consonant in present participles and verbal nouns. H. C. Wyld, in his *Studies in English Rhymes* (p. 112), observes that 'down to the thirties of the last century -*in* and not -*ing* was the almost universal pronunciation among all classes of speakers – in fact, many thousands of excellent speakers never use any other form today.' Wyld was writing in 1923. By the time of Ross's article, the 'many thousands' have dwindled, and this pronunciation is in retreat. Ross writes (p. 39), '[in] for [iŋ] in verbal forms (*huntin' shootin'* and *fishin'*) was undoubtedly once a U-indicator and it still survives among a few elderly U-speakers; among younger ones, it seems, today, to be altogether dead.' It is likely that many more thousands, including most of the 'Upper Ten Thousand', had this pronunciation in Queen Victoria's day. It was one of the things that struck the American R. H. Dana, and he comments on it twice in his book *Hospitable England in the Seventies* (pp. 25, 112):

> I notice that the majority of people I have met so far drop their 'g's' in the present participle. It is *huntin'*, *ridin'* etc.
> Many of my friends here [in Scotland] as in London, drop their 'g's' in the words ending in '-ing'; saying *talkin'* for *talking*.

The abandoning of the form in [n] was a parallel case, in many ways, to the discontinuance of forms like 'he ain't' and 'he don't'. Almost certainly all these forms will have been lost more rapidly after 1870, with the advent of universal education. But the tendency to insist on [ŋ] began earlier than this and was a strong one. It accounts for the many hypercorrect forms, which, as Gerson points out (*Sound and Symbol*, p. 214), are occasional in Dickens and quite common in Thackeray: forms like 'capting' for *captain*, 'foring' for *foreign*, 'sovering' for *soverign* and so on.

The anonymous author of *Vulgarities* has more to say about the final consonant of the present participle. He notes 'the contraction, or rather, mispronunciation of the syllable -*ing* at the end of words', and exemplifies with 'lovin' and 'somethin'. But he also goes on to disapprove of 'the opposite of what I have just reprehended; that is, where the "g" is sounded more strongly, as in *nothingg, somethingg, lovingg*; or, still worse, *somethink, lovink, nothink, writink*. All of which vulgarities,' he concludes, 'are very different from the correct sounds, in which the "g" should not be heard, except it mingle with the ringing tones of the "n"' (p. 39). These are not, of course, upper-class pronunciations: the first is probably regional. The emphasized 'g' is a characteristic of what was formerly called the North-West Midlands, and Munby lovingly records it from his enamorata, Hannah Cullwick. He took her to the Albert Hall to hear *The Creation*, and her comment was '"What a deal of money it must take to pay all them *singers!*" Shropshire fashion' (*Munby, Man of Two Worlds*, p. 324). The development 'somethink' is, according to Gerson (p. 226), 'a widespread vulgarism in Modern English'. He gives many illustrations from Dickens, both from cockney speakers and from the Yarmouth episodes in *David Copperfield*.

There were, of course, a great many old-fashioned pronuciations continuing through the century. Since the fashionable expressions of former times are apt to become the vulgarisms of the present, many such pronunciations and idioms would have branded the speaker; unless his position in society gave authority to the archaic. Such an exceptional person was recalled in G. W. E. Russell's *Collections and Recollections* (p. 2):

> 'There was an old Lady Robert Seymour, who lived in Portland Place, and died there in 1855, in her ninety-first year . . . . She carried down to the time of the Crimean War the habits and phraseology of Queen Charlotte's early court. *Goold* of course she said for *gold* and *yaller* for *yellow*, and *laylock* for *lilac*. She laid stress on the second syllable of *balcony*. She called her maid her *ooman*; instead of sleeping in a place she *lay* there, and when she consulted the doctor she spoke of having 'used the "pottecary".'

Much the same old-fashioned pronunciations are remembered by Augustus Hare in *The Story of My Life* (I, p. 138), from his childhood in the 1840s, fifty years before:

> Grannie used to talk of *chaney* (china), *laylocks* (lilac) and *goold* (gold); of the *Prooshians* and the *Rooshians*; of things being 'plaguey dear' and 'plaguey bad'. In my childhood, however, half my elders used such expressions, which now seem to be almost extinct. '*Obleege* me by passing the *cowcumber*' Uncle Julius always used to say.

By 1907, Lady Grove was beginning to find such archaism affected and trying:

> I confess, however, that people who ostentatiously and with effort affect to be 'old-fashioned' are somewhat trying. I know, for instance, an old 'beau' . . . who inststs upon *yalla*, *balcony* and *cowcumber*, who invariably says 'Thankee' to those he considers beneath him, and 'Thanks' (which is worse) . . . to his 'equals'. (*The Social Fetich*, p. 16)

Samuel Rogers (1763–1855) obviously went much further back in his reminiscences of earlier pronunciation:

It is curious how fashion changes pronunciation. In my youth everybody
said 'Lonnon' not 'London'. For said 'Lonnon' to the last.... The now
fashionable pronunciation of several words is to me at least very offensive:
cóntemplate – is bad enough; but *bálcony* makes me sick. (*Recollections
of the Table-talk of Samuel Rogers*, p. 252)

Many of these pronunciations were being criticized quite early in the
century as not the best usage, for example in Savage's *Vulgarisms*. Savage
warns against 'laylock' for *lilac*: – the earlier pronunciation [leilɔk] being
described by the *OED* as 'now chiefly dialectal or US'; and he also does not
allow *cucumber* with a diphthong in the first syllable. The *OED* quotes
Smart's *Walker Remodelled* (1836) to the effect that the pronunication
[kaukʌmbə] was no longer fashionable: 'no well-taught person, except of
the old school, now says *cowcumber* ... although any other pronunciation ...
would have been pedantic thirty years ago.' Savage disapproves of 'goold'
for *gold*, 'yaller' for *yellow* and the formerly fashionable pronunciation of
china as 'chaney'. So too with 'sparrowgrass', which according to the *OED*
remained a polite name for *asparagus* during the eighteenth century.
Walker's *Critical Pronouncing Dictionary* of 1791 states '*Sparrowgrass* is so
general that *asparagus* has an air of stiffness and pedantry.' 'Sallery' for
celery is also condemned by Savage. With Lady Grove's 'thanky', above, we
can compare 'looky', in Savage's list for condemnation. Both 'thanky' and
'looky' (for *thank you* and *look you*) retain the old subject form *ye*, in the
incorrect and correct grammatical function respectively.

There seems to have been an acid test for correct pronunciation: this was
the word *phaeton*, for a four-wheeled carriage of light construction, usually
drawn by a pair of horses, and named for the charioteer of the sun. But
how to pronounce it? The *OED* suggests [feitən]. What was clearly wrong
was to be misled by the spelling into a rising diphthong; as was the case with
Mrs Jorrocks: '"You think Captain Doleful will do for Belinda?"
"Undoubtedly, if he has what you say, and will keep her a gig." "A *fe-a-ton*"
replied Mrs Jorrocks, with a look of exultation' (*Handley Cross*, chapter 72).
Likewise a man with very affected pronunciation in Lytton's *Night and
Morning* (II, chapter 5): 'I am waiting for my *phe-a-ton*, which my faellow
[*sic*] is to bring down.' Names for carriages seem to have presented
problems. 'Mrs Humphry', in *Manners for Men* (p. 30), published in the last
decade of the century, observes that 'the proper pronunciation of the word
brougham is as though it were spelt *broom*, quite short and monosyllabic.
This is a trifle, of course, but like many another equally small matter, it is
indicative of those accustomed to good society.'

Finally, we may note that French place-names could sometimes be
pronounced in an uncompromisingly English way; though already in the
1830s the practice was being discontinued:

Lord M. thinks it better to pronounce the French and other names as they ought to be pronounced; but he says some people wouldn't do so; that Mr Fox, who could speak French very well, used always to say *Touloon* instead of *Toulon*; *Bourdeaux*, pronouncing the 'x' at the end; *Fontblanky* instead of *Fontblanque*. (*The Girlhood of Queen Victoria*, II, p. 141)

Even at the end of the century, Lady Grove still seems to be standing out for an English pronunciation for *Calais*: 'It is as bad,' she writes in *The Social Fetich* (p. 6) 'to talk about a *valley* for a *valet* or *Callay* for *Calais* as it is to sound the 'h' in *hotel*.'

4

Modes of Address

IN SOCIETY

The aspect of social life in which class language makes itself particularly clear is that of modes of address; a matter of much more importance in the more formal and demarcated society of Victorian England than today. Of course, even today it is true that a mode of address can be a matter of pride, and that, as Trollope points out (*The Warden*, chapter 19): 'A vicar or fellow is as pleased at becoming Mr Archdeacon or Mr Provost, as a lieutenant at getting his captaincy.'

Greeting, on introduction to a stranger, today still takes, in upper-class circles at least, the accepted form 'How do you do?' Ross (p. 45) is very explicit on this point: '*Pleased to meet you* ... is a very frequent non-U response to the greeting *How do you do?* U-speakers normally just repeat the greeting; to reply to the greeting (e.g. with *Quite well thank you*) is non-U.' This may be felt to be cold by some; and was obviously felt to be so by Henry Kingsley:

> Densil said, 'Father Mackworth, Mr Marston;' and Marston said, after a moment's glance at him, 'How do you do, sir?' Possibly a more courteous form of speaking to new acquaintance might have been used. But Marston had his opinions about Father Mackworth, and had no objection that the holy father should know them. (*Ravenshoe*, chapter 16)

Even the somewhat warmer greeting 'How are you?' hardly requires a reply:

> 'Ah, Bold! how are you? You haven't breakfasted?'
> 'Oh, yes, hours ago. And how are you?'
> Did any reader of this tale ever meet any friend or acquaintance without asking some such question, and did anyone ever listen to the reply? (*The Warden*, chapter 15)

As to ways of addressing one another, the usual neutral way for upper-class males, for men in the professions, for instance, to address their colleagues, was by surname alone. We are apt, nowadays, to find such usage cold, and to use Christian names more readily. Today, for instance, the absence of a courtesy title, Mr, is what distinguishes the accused in newspaper reports of police court-cases, from the witness, who is exempt from suspicion. It seems odd now that Mr Meagles, in *Little Dorrit* (I, chapter 16), should ask Arthur Clennam for permission to address him with surname alone by way of increasing their friendship: 'We are delighted to see you, Clennam (if you'll allow me, I shall drop the Mister).' We may also miss the overtones of competence and manliness which the simple surname could formerly imply.[1] Thus when John Eames has administered a thrashing to the faithless Adolphus Crosbie at 'The Paddington Station', and is back promptly at his office, unscathed, soon afterwards, the simple surname serves to underline this briskness: 'It was then a quarter past eleven, but nevertheless Eames appeared at his office precisely at twelve' (*The Small House at Allington*, chapter 34).

At a lower level in society, where a position in the scheme of things needs to be asserted and cannot be assumed, address by surname alone may become less common.[2]

> They entered a house which Rodman did not know ... when a man who stood there taking refreshment called out 'Hallo, Rodman!' To announce a man's name in this way is a decided breach of etiquette in the world to which Rodman belonged. He looked annoyed.... But at the same moment the barmaid addressed him.
> 'What is yours, Mr Rodman?' (Gissing, *Demos*, chapter 32)

The following contrast on this same point of nomenclature represents the social superiority of those working in a profession to those working in trade:

> The two men were very civil to each other in their salutations, the attorney assuming an air of patronizing condescension, always calling the other Grimes; whereas Mr Scruby was treated with considerable deference by the publican and was always called Mr Scruby. 'Business is business' said the publican as soon as these salutations were over: 'isn't it now, Mr Scruby?' (*Can You Forgive Her?*, chapter 13)

---

[1] One very honourable annual context for the surname alone still survives: the Wimbledon tennis tournament. The simple male surname, coupled with the more formal addition of a title, *Mrs* or *Miss* for the ladies, is pleasantly archaic. Curiously, however, in the unfortunate event of a dispute between player and umpire, *Mr* occurs: 'Mr McEnroe', for example.
[2] An article by E. R. Chamberlin entitled 'Sanitation Kills Villages' in *The Guardian* (5 March 1980) represents Norfolk villagers as still preferring what they would doubtless call 'a handle to their name'. Complaints against 'the newcomers' (usually people retiring to the neighbourhood) mentioned their tendency to be either stand-offish or over-familiar: 'Newcomers are on Christian name terms on arrival and introduce themselves as "Joe and Jenny". Most village people are somewhat embarrassed at appearing so intimate and are "Mr and Mrs" to all but close friends'. This sociological phenomenon is also noticeable in the south-west of England.

Harry Goslett,[3] hero of Besant's *All Sorts and Conditions of Men* (1882), has elected to forgo his inheritance and live in the East End; but he finds that this involves a humiliating absence of any prefix to his name, on a note bringing an offer of employment:

> A mere note sent by a clerk, inviting 'H. Goslett' to call at the Accountant's office at ten in the morning. The name, standing bare and naked by itself, without any preliminary tile of respect, Mister, Master, or Sieur, presented, Harry thought, a very miserable appearance. Perhaps it would be difficult to find a readier method of insulting a man than to hurl his own name at his head. One may understand how Louis Capet must have felt when thus reduced to a plain simplicity. (chapter 15)

Yet, if one were on sufficiently friendly terms, even a lord's title might be dispensed with. Disraeli writes to Lady Bradford: '*Bradford* paid me a visit this morning on his way to the races' (*Letters*, II, p. 164). This habit, however, like marriage, was not to be undertaken by anybody lightly:

> Puffington made the acquaintances of several very dashing young sparks — Lord Firebrand, Lord Mudlark, Lord Deuceace, Sir Harry Blueun, and others, whom he always spoke of as 'Deuceace', 'Blueun' etc., in the easy style that marks the perfect gentleman. (*Mr Sponge's Sporting Tour*, chapter 31)

Surtees modifies this with a footnote to *gentleman*, 'Query "snob"?' In a very exalted family, with a titled son or sons, there might be, in effect, a use of surnames within the family: 'St. George! Have you read his letter?' asks the Marquis of Trowbridge of his son, Lord St. George (*The Vicar of Bullhampton*, chapter 57). And so on up to royalty itself: 'Prince Albert commanded, "*Wales*, come and shake hands with Mr Tupper"' (John Drinkwater, 'Martin Tupper' in *The Eighteen-Eighties*, p. 212). At this level of society there are thus more varied forms of nomenclature. When young Blanche Stanley is engaged to David, seventh Earl of Airlie, how are they to proceed?

> He wants us all to call him Airlie which makes Blanche and me shy, but he particularly dislikes B. calling him Lord Airlie and she was afraid the first quarrel would be about David, which she says she never could have stood. (*The Stanleys of Alderley*, p. 12)

Ladies did not address gentlemen by surname alone, and were not supposed to refer to them without the courtesy title of *Mr*.[4] In Jane Austen's

---

[3] His guardian, Lord Jocelyn, suggests that Harry pronounce his name with the accent on the second syllable!

[4] In his tract for the Society for Pure English (SPE) no. 47, 'Names, Designations and Appellations', written in 1936, R. W. Chapman expressed a hope that this state of affairs would continue, and that a lady might refer to, and address, her husband's friends as 'Mr Smith' or 'John', but never as 'Smith'. His anxiety in this matter, however, has hardly been justified: the problem has been avoided by a greatly increased use of Christian names.

novels the great offender in this matter is Mrs Elton in *Emma* ('Knightley!'
Emma protests, '– never seen him in her life before and call him Knightley!'
chapter 32). In the following passage from *The Last Chronicle of Barset*, Lily
Dale is discussing with Sir Raffle Buffle, John Eames' superior, the journey
made by Eames to discover the Arabins and exonerate Josiah Crawley from
an accusation of theft. Lily speaks first, more formally, and Sir Raffle Buffle
second: '"That is just what *Mr Eames* has gone abroad to learn." "It is very
well for *Eames* to go abroad . . . The thing couldn't have happened at a more
unfortunate time"' (chapter 52). Similarly, because David Copperfield has
been the friend of his youth, Mr Micawber addresses him as 'Copperfield'
(as opposed to *Mr Traddles*, of whom, unlike David, Micawber occasionally
takes advantage); but to Mrs Micawber, David, when an adult, is 'Mr
Copperfield' (*David Copperfield*, chapters 27–8). It is a mark of ill-breeding,
despite her attempts at gentility, that Mrs Kirkpatrick (later Mrs Gibson)
refers to her late husband by surname alone: 'I did, when poor *Kirkpatrick*
was alive. Heigh ho! it's a sad thing to be a widow' (*Wives and Daughters*,
chapter 9). For a wife not merely to refer to her husband, but to address him
by surname alone, as Mrs Poyser, secure in her provinciality, does Poyser
(*Adam Bede*, chapter 14) indicates that she is happily free from any
pretensions to gentility. So also is Peggotty, who calls out on her husband's
death-bed '*Barkis* my dear!' (*David Copperfield*, chapter 30).

Provincial middle-class society was reluctant to use Christian names. To
Mr Deane, his brother-in-law Mr Tulliver is 'Tulliver' and even (shades of
Bunyan!) 'neighbour Tulliver'. Christian names are rare even between man
and wife, at least in company. Mrs Glegg addresses her husband as 'Mr
Glegg', and he replies with the vulgar 'Mrs G.'; only in entreaty does he
protest, 'Softly, softly, *Jane*, be reasonable' (*Mill on the Floss*, I, chapter 7).
Aunt Pullet refers to her husband as 'Pullet' (I, chapter 9). Mr Tulliver
addresses his impecunious sister as 'Mrs Moss', but cannot maintain his
obdurate stance, and proceeds with 'Gritty' (I, chapter 8).

It was not allowable for a young woman to call a young man, outside her
family, by his Christian name. For a married woman to do so, as here Mrs
Dobbs Broughton does to Conway Dalrymple, could well carry a
suggestion, in the higher ranks of society, of adultery:

> 'But she's awful in another way, too,' said Dalrymple.
> 'Indeed she is, Conway,' Mrs Dobbs Broughton had got into a way of calling
> her young friend by his Christian name. 'All the world calls him Conway,' she
> had said to her husband once when her husband caught her doing so. (*The
> Last Chronicle of Barset*, chapter 24)

A similar danger occurred when men addressed married women by their
Christian names. Johnny Eames warns his friend Cradell that he is asking
for trouble from her husband in calling the not very respectable Mrs Lupex

by her Christian name: 'If you go on calling her Maria you'll find that he'll have a pull on you. Men don't call other men's wives names for nothing' (*The Small House at Allington*, chapter 41). People universally known by their Christian names were exceptional, and in 1876 Besant and Rice ventured this generalization about them:

> When a woman is always called by her Christian name, it is generally a sign that she is loved and lovable. If a man, on the other hand, gets to be known, without any reason for the distinction, by his Christian name, it is generally a sure sign that he is sympathetic, but blind to his own interests. (*The Golden Butterfly*, chapter 14)

Just occasionally, and in emotional circumstances, a mature woman could address a man unwontedly by his Christian name, and then she spoke with power. In the following incident one Harry Gilmore has been crossed in love, and Janet Fenwick, the wife of the Vicar of Bullhampton, tries to comfort him:

> Of course it is nonsense to talk about dying, but I feel as though if I didn't die I should go crazy. I can't settle my mind to a single thing.
> It is fresh with you yet, *Harry*, she said. She had never called him Harry before, though her husband did so always, and now she used the name in sheer tenderness. (*The Vicar of Bullhampton*, chapter 23)

It is practically unthinkable today that a wife should not use the Christian name of her husband's friend when her husband uses it, but this withholding of a given name was commoner than today among ladies also:

> Before much further could be said between them, the Countess de Saldar drove up.
> 'My dearest Rose!' and 'My dearest Countess!' and Not Louisa then?' and I am very glad to see you!' without attempting the endearing 'Louisa' – passed. (Meredith, *Evan Harrington*, chapter 13)

While men could use Christian names to each other, if they were close friends, the unprefixed surname was then the norm in good society. Too liberal a use of Christian names was thought free-and-easy: 'Bohemia,' writes Thackeray (*Philip*, I, chapter 5), 'a land where men call each other by their Christian names'. The Irish poet, Aubrey de Vere, enjoyed meeting Tennyson in the early 1840s in friends' rooms in the Temple and elsewhere, where there was 'an air of informality, so that only Christian names were used, even by the newest of acquaintances' (R. B. Martin, *Tennyson: The Unquiet Heart*, p. 257). This was clearly exceptional. More typical, probably, of 'correct' circles, was the young Arthur Hugh Clough, writing in 1836 to a Rugby friend: 'I saw Brodie a good deal at Oxford, and have made another friend in him, of whom I hope my dear Simpkinson will not be jealous' (*Correspondence*, I, p. 55). It is curious that, whereas Steerforth calls David Copperfield 'David', and also by his nickname, 'Daisy', David replies with 'Steerforth', never with 'James': 'You have no best to me *Steerforth*... and no worst. You are always equally loved' (*David Copperfield*, chapter 29). At one point in *Framley Parsonage* a conversation occurs between two friends that is potentially if not actually acrimonious. Lord Lufton has given offence and tries to placate Mark Robarts by using his Christian name; upon which Mark, in his annoyance, reacts by becoming more formal, changing his manner of address from 'Lufton' to 'Lord Lufton': '"As to you personally Mark," he said, coming back to the spot on which Roberts was standing, "I do not wish to say anything that shall annoy you." "You have said quite enough, Lord Lufton"' (chapter 19). Men, as well as women, could object to being addressed by their Christian names. Mark Roberts repudiates any friendship between himself and Sowerby, a man who, he considers, has cheated him: '"But Mark—" "Call me by my name, sir, and drop that affectation of regard. What an ass I have been to be so cozened by a sharper!"' (chapter 33). There were other men who disliked such familiarity. In his *Reminiscences* (p. 59), Disraeli has this anecdote of Sydney Smith (d. 1845) and Monckton Milnes:

> Sydney Smith used to call him [Milnes] 'the cool of the evening' when he went about to his parties. Being terribly familiar he called the great witty critic 'Sydney', who looked astounded, but said nothing at the time. Shortly afterwards Milnes very fussily regretting that he could not meet S. S. at Lady Ashburton's because he was engaged to dine with the Archbishop of Canterbury, Sydney Smith said 'Ah! well by the bye, let me give you a friendly hint, don't call the Archbishop 'Harley', because, perhaps, he might not be used to it.'

However, noble birth brings with it the authority to overrride normal conventions. When a young man, like Johnny Eames, is so fortunate as to be taken up by the nobility, Lord de Guest and Lady Julia de Guest, he would have been foolish to complain at what, at that level of society, might be thought a very rapid promotion to Christian-name terms: 'He was first welcomed by Lady Julia: "My dear Mr Eames," she said, "I cannot tell you how glad we are to see you." After that she always called him John' (*The Small House at Allington*, chapter 52). As for the Earl, he had got into the habit of calling his young friend, still more familiarly, Johnny, 'having found that Mrs Eames generally spoke of her son by that name'. Pre-eminently, indeed, Christian names are for usage within the family; but in a family as august as the Proudies, they may become infrequent even here.[5] In

---

[5] If a man was very exalted, by the way, he might rarely hear his own Christian name. Up to the time of his marriage, only his uncle the Duke of Omnium called Plantagenet Palliser by his Christian name 'though there were some scores of men who talked of Planty Pal behind his back' *The Small House at Allington*, Ch. 43].

The Last Chronicle of Barset (chapter 54) Mrs Proudie attempts to overcome an estrangement between herself and the Bishop by calling him unwontedly by his Christian name (she normally calls him 'bishop', just as Mrs Grantly calls her husband 'archdeacon'):

> 'What has happened that you should speak like that?' she said to him once. 'What has broken your heart?'
> 'You,' he replied. 'You; you have done it.'
> 'Oh, Tom,' she said, going back into the memory of very far distant days in her nomenclature, 'how can you speak to me so cruelly!'

This neat stroke of Trollope's greatly adds to the tragi-comedy at the Palace. Somehow we had not suspected the Bishop of having a Christian name – any more than of having the power of whistle (in chapter 3 of *The Warden* Trollope tells us that bishops lose the power of whistling on being consecrated)! An interesting real-life parallel to the last quotation is provided by young Clough, writing in 1836 about his revered Headmaster: 'I cannot indeed conceive anyone calling "the Dr" Tom even at Fox-how' (*Correspondence*, I, p. 50).

Pushing, ambitious young men like Mr Slope of Barchester Towers, men moreover who are not familiar with the best usage, will be premature in using Christian names. Here Mr Slope is quietly put in his place by the Signora Vesey Neroni: '"Oh, Madeline!" he sighed. "Well, my name is Madeline," said she, "but none except my own family usually call me so. Now look me in the face, Mr Slope. Am I to understand that you say you love me?"' (*Barchester Towers*, chapter 27). On the other hand, here is a much rarer instance of a young lady encouraging the rather stiff and very wealthy Mr Palliser, whose travelling companion she has been for some months, to address her more informally:

> 'I'll go to her at once,' said Alice, rising.
> 'I'm so much obliged to you; – but, Miss Vavasor –'
> 'You called me Alice just now, Mr Palliser, and I took it as a great compliment.'
> He blushed again. 'Did I? Very well. Then I'll do it again – if you'll let me.'
> (*Can You Forgive Her?*, chapter 73)

Considering that Alice Vavasor was his wife's cousin, Plantagenet Palliser seems to have been unduly starchy. Cousins, as Trollope points out in a chapter headed 'Cousinhood' in *The Vicar of Bullhampton* (chapter 14) have certain advantages. In contrast with the freer usage he has observed in America, the novelist finds that:

> Here with us, there is restriction, and it is seldom that a girl can allow herself the full flow of friendship with a man who is not old enough to be her father, unless he is her lover as well as her friend. But cousinhood does allow some

escape from the hardship of this rule. Cousins are Tom, and Jack, and George, and Dick . . . . Cousins are almost the same as brothers, and yet they may be lovers.

A vicar of a parish who has watched over the upbringing of a young lady might also be accorded special privileges in this matter of names. 'Pardon me, Mary,' says Mr Farebrother in *Middlemarch* (chapter 52) to Mary Garth, 'you know I used to catechize you under that name'; but all the same he frequently addresses her more formally: 'Mr Farebrother used to say "Mary" instead of "Miss Garth", but it was part of his delicacy to treat her with the more deference because, according to Mrs Vincy's phrase, she worked for her bread' (chapter 40).

To press for a freer use of a young man's Christian name was a method by which others could urge on his suit; and Mary Bold does so with Eleanor Harding on behalf of her brother John (*The Warden*, chapter 11). When there has been family opposition, the daughter may have to urge her fiancé's Christian name on her family:

'Oh! mamma, I think it must be delayed.'
'But why, my love? Mr Graham has not said so?'
'You must call him Felix, mamma. I'm sure it's a nice name.'
'Very well, my dear, I will.' (*Orley Farm*, chapter 80)

There is pathos in the use of the Christian name in the following passage. Here, Mrs Dale calls the faithless Crosbie for the first time by his Christian name, thus signalling admission to her family of the man she mistakenly believes is to be her son-in-law:

'God bless you, Adolphus,' Mrs Dale said to him, as she parted with him at her own door. It was the first time that she had called him by his Christian name. 'I hope you understand how much we are trusting you.' (*The Small House at Allington*, chapter 15)

The most significant use of Christian names in novels, is undoubtedly to mark a stage in courtship. Not only much subtlety, but a good deal of emotional power has been lost by the discontinuance of these nicely graded modes of address:

'Mrs Bold – ' at last he said, and then stopped himself. If he could not speak, how was she to do so? He had called her by her name, the same name that any merest stranger would have used! She withdrew her hand from him, and moved as though to return to her seat. 'Eleanor!' he then said, in his softest tone, as though the courage of a lover were as yet but half assumed . . . . 'Eleanor!' he again exclaimed; and in a moment he had her clasped to his bosom. (*Barchester Towers*, chapter 48)

The young man guarded his right to his fiancée's Christian name jealously. Frank Churchill, in *Emma* (chapter 50), is incensed at Mrs Elton's free use of Jane Fairfax's Christian name: '"Jane" indeed! . . . You will observe that I have not yet indulged myself in calling her by that name.' Lord de Guest speculates, in *The Small House at Allington* (chapter 52), whether John Eames, assuming he even has the authority, will allow the Earl to call Lily Dale, 'Lily'. 'I wish I might have the power of letting you,' says Johnny, ruefully. A more rarefied situation occurs in *Tom Brown at Oxford* (chapter 49), when a young man apologizes to a young lady for calling her fiancé by his Christian name: 'You mustn't mind me calling him Jack. The only thing that it gives me any pleasure to think about, is your engagement.'

These gradations of address had their uses: to insist on something more formal than a Christian name was a way of setting the barriers up against too close a friendship: '"Stop, Lucy!" he said, putting himself between her and the door. "It must not be Lucy any longer, Lord Lufton; I was madly foolish when I first allowed it"' (*Framley Parsonage*, chapter 16). Nevertheless, Lord Lufton has got into the habit of using Lucy's Christian name. Later, in a conversation with Griselda Grantly, whom his mother wants him to marry, he reveals a close acquaintance with Lucy by the use of her first name that is crucial for the outcome of the novel:

> 'And Miss Robarts; I thought you admired her very much?'
> 'What, Lucy Robarts?' said Lord Lufton.... 'I do like Lucy Robarts certainly...' To this Griselda made no answer, but drew herself up, and looked as cold as Diana. (*Framley Parsonage*, chapter 20)

This last instance, of Christian name with surname, occasionally occurs; it usually represents a cutting through of ceremony to a 'moment of truth'. Thus in Trollope's *Mr Scarborough's Family* (chapter 50) the affronted Miss Thoroughbung calls for frankness from her vacillating suitor, using a form of address with which, as a country squire, he is totally unfamiliar: '"Peter Prosper, why don't you answer like a man, and tell me the honest truth?" He had never before been called Peter Prosper in his whole life.' More seriously, Little Dorrit forestalls a proposals of marriage from John Chivery by using his full name (having first, to show a certain respect for him, returned his 'Miss Dorrit' and 'Miss Amy' with the equally formal 'Mr John') '"If you please, John Chivery," she returned ... "since you are so considerate as to ask me whether you shall say any more – if you please, no"' (*Little Dorrit*, I, chapter 18).

The following quotation presents the much rarer situation, in fiction if not perhaps in fact, of a man's severance of his relationship with a woman, signalized by the deliberate avoidance of Christian names:

> 'You have sent for me, Mr Eames,' she said...
> 'Yes, Miss Roper, I did want to see you very particularly.'
> 'Oh dear!' she exclaimed, and he understood fully that the exclamation referred to his having omitted the customary use of her Christian name. (*The Small House at Allington*, chapter 51)

This is Amelia Roper, with whom John Eames flirts. Amelia refers to herself in the third person, with her own Christian name. Such usage is artificial and 'stagey', and indicates her second-rate status: 'I have got your promise, but I'd scorn to take advantage. If *Amelia* hasn't got your heart, she'd despise to take your hand', (chapter 5).

Besides 'Miss Robarts' and 'Lucy' or 'Miss Roper' and 'Amelia' there was a third possibility: the use of the title *Miss* with the Christian name. Perhaps because it was general usage with well-born little girls, its use with adults carries a suggestion of condescension and superciliousness in many contexts. Thus Lady Lufton says to Fanny Robarts: 'That *Miss Lucy* of yours seems to be a very determined young lady' (*Framley Parsonage*, chapter 41). Similarly, when Mrs Proudie is being a Job's comforter to Mrs Grantly about difficulties encountered in the Grantly-Dumbello alliance: 'I trust that this sorrow may eventuate in a blessing to you and *Miss Griselda*' (chapter 45). In other contexts, with young men or young women, this could be a convenient half-way house between formality and informality – for family retainers, for instance. Thus a family servant warns the hero of *Orley Farm* (chapter 74), 'But now, Mr Graham, if you don't treat our *Miss Madeline* well! – '. Much play is made with this form of address in Clough's poem, *The Bothie of Tober-na-Vuorlich*, where Philip Hewson falls in love with a Scots girl of inferior station to himself, while on vacation with the reading-party:

> Do as I bid you, my child; do not go on calling me Mr.
> Might I not just as well be calling you Miss Elspie?

Formalities in nomenclature can in such circumstances be seen as foothills leading to the ascent on virtue:

> No, Mr Phillip, no – you have kissed me enough for two nights;
> No – come Philip, come, or I'll go myself without you.
> You never call me Philip, he answered, until I kiss you.

A final case of *Mr* with the Christian name is its use to distinguish father from son: "Mr Millbank is there, sir, but very much engaged" ... "Perhaps his son, *Mr Oswald Millbank*, is here?" ... "*Mr Oswald* is in Belgium," said the clerk' (*Coningsby*, IV, chapter 3). The case of Mr Dick in *David Copperfield*, incidentally, was different. His full name was Richard Babley; but he objected to it from his having been ill-used by others of the family bearing his surname (chapter 14).

A still further stage of informality could be the abbreviation of the Christian name. People with a proper sense of the fitness of things reserved this kind of familiarity for rare occasions:

> 'So we're sold after all, Sue!' said he to his wife, accosting her with a kiss as he
> entered his house. He did not call his wife Sue more than twice or thrice in a

year, and these occasions were great high days. (*Barchester Towers*, chapter 50)

This is Archdeacon Grantly, delighted that his sister-in-law is to marry Mr Arabin and not Mr Slope. Similarly Mr Gresham, squire of Greshamsbury, 'never called his wife Bell, except when he wanted her to be on particularly good terms with him' (*Dr Thorne*, chapter 31). At a lower level of society, however, hypocoristic, or endearing forms were more common, and the use of the full name might be the significant, even the sinister thing:

> 'I won't have any more of it. Mary Anne, you'll have that table cleared out after breakfast tomorrow.'
> When a man, to whom his wife is usually Polly, addressed her as Mary Anne, then it may be surmised that that man is in earnest. (Trollope, 'The Spotted Dog')

That this reluctance to use hypocoristic forms in the higher classes is not merely a convention observed in novels is shown in *The Queen's English* (p. 242), where Dean Alford tells of his meeting with a man whose conversation at first impressed him, until, at the end of the evening on which they met, his wife called out to him 'Sammy, love!'

> All is out. He has a wife who does not know better, and he has never taught her better. This is the secret. The skeleton in their cupboard is a child's rattle. A man may as well suck his thumb all his life, as talk, or allow to be talked to him, such drivelling nonsense.

One minor formality that remained throughout the century was that of referring to, and addressing, the elder sister (less frequently the elder brother) as 'Miss' (or 'Mr') followed by the surname alone, and using the Christian name, with or without surname, for younger members of the family. Becky Sharp explains the usage in a letter to Amelia Sedley: 'Then there are Mr Pitt's apartments – Mr Crawley he is called – the eldest son, and Mr Rawdon Crawley's rooms – he is an officer . . . and away with his regiment' (*Vanity Fair*, chapter 8). For an illustration of this usage concerning ladies, we can consider the following extract from Princess Victoria's journal, which shows incidentally that these varying titles entailed responsibilities:

> Miss Harcourt is a very nice person. She ought by rights to be called Miss Georgiana Harcourt, the Archbishop's eldest daughter being unmarried, but as she never goes out and does not make the honneurs in the house, Miss Georgiana is always called Miss Harcourt. (*The Girlhood of Queen Victoria*, I, p. 134)

This carefully differentiated nomenclature the middle and upper classes seem to have taken in their stride: 'Look, look!' says a certain Miss Piper in

Wives and Daughters (chapter 26) 'that's our Mr Cholmley, the magistrate . . . and that's Mrs Cholmley in red satin, and Mr George and Mr Harry from Oxford, I do declare; and Miss Cholmley; and pretty Miss Sophy.'

There was one circumstance in which women might be referred to and addressed by surname alone: when spoken to, or of, by their superiors in an upper-class family. For a female servant to be so named was not thought demeaning, on the whole, though young Tom Gradgrind objected to addressing Sissy Jupe, employed in attendance upon his mother when not being educated, as 'Jupe' (*Hard Times*, I, chapter 8). Lady Hainault, in *Ravenshoe* (chapter 21) addresses her paid companion with the words '*Miss Hicks*, ring the bell!' when a stranger, Charles Ravenshoe, is present. When he has left, 'Miss Hicks' becomes 'Hicks': 'You know perfectly well, *Hicks*. You know I only had her to spite old Ascot.' Sometimes a married woman might retain her maiden name, as did Mrs Hickes, wife of the butler at Transome Court, who had entered Mrs Transome's service forty years before, and was still called Denner by her mistress. Such relationships of long standing, while retaining their formality partly through nomenclature, could be close, though the closeness might appear only in a crisis:

> 'Denner,' she said, in a low voice, 'if I could choose at this moment, I should choose that Harold should never have been born.'
> 'Nay, my dear' (Denner had only once before in her life said 'My dear' to her mistress), 'It was a blessing to you then.' (*Felix Holt*, chapter 39)

Children of well-to-do parents might expect to be addressed as 'Master' or 'Miss'. When she went to America, Mrs Trollope (*Domestic Manners of the Americans*, 1832) found a democratic absence of such appellatives. She speaks of the 'violent intimacy' of an American neighbour: 'My children, including by sons, she always addressed by their Christian means, excepting when she substituted the word "honey"; this familiarity of address, however, I afterwards found as universal throughout all ranks of the United States' (chapter 10). *Master* was the title for boys and youths of superior birth, not fully grown. When Dr Gibson's articled pupil in medicine, living in the same house, addresses a 'flaming love-letter' to the Doctor's daughter Molly, he replies with a scathing rebuke addressed inside the letter to 'Master Coxe': 'That "Master" will touch him to the quick' said Dr Gibson to himself as he wrote the word.' More mercifully, he addresses the outside to 'Edward Coxe, Esq.' (*Wives and Daughters*, chapter 5). As to the children of the very great, they were not addressed with Christian names even by their nurses and tutors at the beginning of Queen Victoria's reign:

> Talked of the Nurse and Tutor calling children by their Christian names, which my brother said was done abroad, and which Lord M. said no one would ever think of doing here, that they always called them Lord, and Mr. (*The Girlhood of Queen Victoria*, II, p. 196)

(A note by the editor, Viscount Esher, says that nurses and tutors began to use Christian names to their charges about 1880.)

'Above all', says a mid-Victorian etiquette-book, *Mixing in Society* (p. 245), 'never name anybody by the first letter of his name. Married people are sometimes guilty of this flagrant offence against taste.' Strong-minded women, not in good society, might attempt to reverse this edict, but it was not good usage:

> 'Laws, T., don't be so foolish,' she said to her husband. She always called her husband T., unless when the solemnity of some special occasion justified her in addressing him as Mr Tappit. To have called him Tom or Thomas would, in her opinion, have been very vulgar. (*Rachel Ray*, chapter 2)

With the growing refinement of the young, it might sometimes be they who rebuked, from an almost equally uncertain standpoint, their elders in this matter:

> 'Should you like that Mendelssohn for the Sunday after next? Julia sings it splendid!'
> 'No, I don't, Ma.'
> 'You do, dear! She's a good, good dear, Mr H., that's what she is.'
> 'You must not call – a – him, in that way. Don't say Mr H., Ma,' says Julia. (*The Newcomes*, II, chapter 6)

The author of *Manners and Rules of Good Society*, (1888) is adamant that wives of military men should not be addressed as 'Mrs General A', 'Mrs Colonel B', etc., but as 'Mrs A' etc., without reference to their husbands' rank. So 'Mrs Captain Osborne' and 'Mrs Major O'Dowd' (*Vanity Fair*, chapter 27) represent either old-fashioned or incorrect usage. Surtees, in *Handley Cross* (chapter 62) records an amusing episode of a man writing ADC after his name, the letters standing for Assistant Drains Commissioner. It was the kind of thing, however, that occurred in reality to Mrs Trollope in America. There, such was the love of military titles, the name 'General M' was borne by Mr M, the Surveyor-General of the District (*Domestic Manners of the Americans*, chapter 17).

The nobility were often addressed in the third person, or at least with a reference in the third-person to their title. This was a mode of speech that was difficult for the twelve-year-old Molly Gibson, in *Wives and Daughters* (chapter 2), to manipulate:

> 'My lady, papa is come, and I am going away; and, my lady, I wish you goodnight, and thank you for your kindness. Your ladyship's kindness, I mean,' she said, correcting herself as she remembered Miss Browning's particular instructions as to the etiquette to be observed to earls and countesses, and their honourable progeny.

This third-person usage was strictly correct for the nobility from untitled people, because the class-system was further emphasized by a two-tier form of address. To quote *Manners and Tone of Good Society* (p. 50): 'An English Duke is addressed as "Duke" by the aristocracy and gentry, and never as "Your Grace" by members of those classes – all other classes would address him colloquially [*sic*] as "Your Grace".' In ranks below a duke, the two-tier system did not fully apply: no-one addressed a marquis as 'Marquis', but as 'Lord A.'. In Trollope's political novels there are dukes and duchesses in plenty, and the contrasting usage is fairly clear. True, Madame Goesler and Phineas Finn, as favoured friends, address the Duchess of Omnium as 'Duchess', but Mr Erle, a commoner, has 'your Grace' (*Phineas Redux*, chapter 63). Lord Chiltern addresses a letter without more ado as *Dear Duchess of Omnium* (chapter 31), and letters at this level are, of course, directly in the second person. A sagacious man like Phineas Finn would also choose the moment to revert to the more formal mode, to express his gratitude for help in his acquittal, for example. The Duchess playfully takes him up on the designation:

> 'Some people are your very excellent good friends. We, that is Marie and I, you know .... By the bye, you have hardly seen her, – have you?'
> 'Hardly, since I was upstairs with your Grace.'
> 'My Grace will manage better for you tomorrow.' (chapter 74)

Care was needed not to sound unctuous by introducing 'your Grace' too frequently. That unscrupulous adventurer, Ferdinand Lopez in *The Prime Minister* (chapter 42) shows that he is no gentleman by this means: a letter he writes to the Duke of Omnium, about a page and a half in length, contains the phrase 'your Grace' over twenty times. Lords, as we have seen, should not be addressed as 'my lord' too often. In this respect an American named Fisker in Trollope's *The Way We Live Now* (chapter 10) gives offence:

> Not one there had liked Fisker. His manners were not their manners... He said 'my lord' too often, and grated their prejudices equally whether he treated them with familiarity or deference.

The hero's wordly-wise mother, in *Ask Mamma* (chapter 40), gives him some advice about the casual use of titles which has the ring of authenticity: 'We all like talking of titles. Remember, all noblemen under the rank of dukes are lords in common conversation. No earls or marquises then.'[6] Certain titles are courtesy titles, of no legal validity, but observed as social custom and courtesy. Daughters of viscounts and barons, for example, bear the courtesy title of *Honourable*, which, according to *Manners and Rules of Good Society* (p. 51) should 'never be used colloquially'. Young Johnny

---

[6] A hundred years later, the point still held: 'It is non-U,' according to Ross (p. 25) 'to speak of an earl as *The Earl of P*—; he should be spoken of and to as *Lord P*—.'

Stanley considers that his *bête noire*, a certain Mrs Stuart, insists too much on this rather shaky title: 'No one could help knowing it, she keeps Honble before her name even now and was absurd enough to have it stuck on all her tin boxes' (*The Stanleys of Alderley*, p. 186). No doubt it required some knowledge of the fashionable world to get these things right: 'Countess of Kew, and her daughter; Countess of Canterton, and the Honourable Miss Fetlock – no, Lady Fetlock. A Countess's daughter is a lady, I'm dashed if she ain't' (*The Newcomes*, II, chapter 6). The daughter of an earl and countess was indeed a lady. An earl, a marquis or a duke was entitled to the strawberry leaf on his coronet: Lord Monmouth, Disraeli tells us, was 'a most distinguished nobleman ... who, if he carried the county and the manufacturing borough also, merited *the strawberry-leaf*' (*Coningsby*, V, chapter 33). A male commoner who married into the nobility did not, of course, acquire a title. Hence this anecdote from Thackeray's *The Book of Snobs* (chapter 8):

> Some old acquaintance who saw young Pump in the parlour at the bank in the City, said to him, familiarly, 'How's your wife, Pump my boy?'
> Mr Pump looked exceedingly puzzled and disgusted, and, after a pause, said, '*Lady Blanche Pump* is pretty well, I thank you.'
> 'Oh, I thought she was your wife!' said the familiar brute.

Further down the social scale, there are various forms of address for ladies. Let us consider, for example, Alice Vavasor, in Trollope's *Can You Forgive Her?* Alice has made a certain footing in society, Trollope tells us, but he adds, 'I am disposed to doubt her right to be considered as holding a place among the Upper Ten Thousand.' Yet any unmarried lady who, like Alice, can afford a personal maid, is entitled to be addressed as 'miss'; though perhaps it is a sign that Alice is past what Jane Austen would have called her bloom that her maid, Jane, refers to her also as 'ma'am': '"I shall feel so strange, *ma'am*, among all those people downstairs," said the girl. ... 'They're all like knowing each other, *miss*"' (chapter 22). *Miss* as an appellative was not unobjectionable. The anonymous member of the aristocracy who wrote *Manners and Tone of Good Society* (p. 55) comments as follows:

> It would be correct to address an unmarried young foreign lady as 'Mademoiselle' without the addition of her surname, even if she were the daughter of a vicomte or baron; but it would be extremely vulgar to address an English girl as 'Miss' without adding the surname. A foreigner addressing an English girl as 'Miss' would be excusable, as it is the rule on the continent to address young ladies as 'Mademoiselle', without adding the surname.

To Bertha Cross, heroine of Gissing's *Will Warburton* (1905), this use of *miss* was 'grocerly':

One thing Bertha noticed was that, though the grocer invariably addressed her mother as 'madam', in speaking to her he never used the grocerly 'miss'; and when, by chance, she heard him bestow this objectionable title upon a servant girl who was making purchases at the same time, Bertha not only felt grateful for the distinction, but saw in it a fresh proof of Mr Jollyman's good breeding. (chapter 19)

The anonymous author of *The Vulgarities of Speech Corrected* (1826) had objected to *ladyship* contracted to *la'ship* and also to the contraction of *madam* to *ma'am*, though he (or she) is disposed to allow that the latter may perhaps be used 'in speaking to females in the middle ranks of society.' *Madam*, incidentally, but not *ma'am*, could be used in reference as well as in address: 'She was struck with the change in "madam's" look' (*Wives and Daughters*, chapter 17). It is ironic that the two forms *madam* and *ma'am* have suffered something of a reversal in status: *madam* is now distinctly 'shoppy' (to use an epithet which the *OED* sometimes employs with advantage); while *ma'am* in these democratic times is reserved for the Queen. There is some continuity here, however. *Manners and Tone of Good Society* (p. 49) gives details of correct address to the monarch: *ma'am*, not *madam* from those of the rank of gentry and above; *your majesty*, from the rest of her subjects. Again the two-tier system applies.

At all events, in nineteenth-century England, *ma'am*, with its male counterpart *sir*, was the natural, the safe, and indeed the instinctive form of address used by the lower classes for those of a higher station. Hannah Cullwick, though eventually married to A. J. Munby, cannot forget her working-class habits of speech:

But she had made one 'dreadful mistake', as she called it. 'Do you know, I said "Goodbye ma'am" to Mrs Dusautoy. It came quite natural; it is so hard for me to speak to a lady, and not say "ma'am" to her! And I said "Goodbye sir", to Mr Dusautoy; because I thought I ought to show him respect as a clergyman.' (*Munby, Man of Two Worlds*, p. 373)

Long before the end of the century there was a further contraction of *ma'am* to *mum*. When Dorothea Brooke, at a notable point in the novel *Middlemarch* (chapter 77), pays a call on Rosamond Lydgate, and asks the maid if she is at home, the girl, Martha, replies: 'I'm not sure, my lady; I'll see, if you'll please walk in.' Martha is 'a little confused . . . but collected enough to be sure that "mum" was not the right title for this queenly young widow with a carriage and pair'. It is rather late for our purposes, but in 1907 M. E. Loane, nurse and district visitor in the East End, considers with professional shrewdness the differing forms of address to ladies, among the very poor:

The mode of address often affords a district nurse a roughly accurate measure of the society in which she finds herself. 'Missus' goes with unpolished but fairly respectable surroundings; 'ma'am' is usually a sign that the house-mother has been in regular service, while 'mum' marks the charwoman and her belongings; 'miss' is only heard in the upper circles of those we visit, while 'lady' gives pointed warning that we are among mendicants, actual or possible. (*The Next Street But One*, chapter 1)

With regard to the plural of *miss*, a problem arises: does one say 'The Miss Smiths' or 'The Misses Smith'? 'The Misses Lookaloft, as they call themselves' (*Barchester Towers*, chapter 35) were in no doubt; but the Misses Lookaloft were no models. This collocation is a Gallic importation. It is interesting that Jane Austen never has the usage, preferring to put the plural sign at the end in the native English way, as in 'The Miss Bertrams', 'The Lady Frasers'. On 12 June 1857, George Eliot wrote very forcefully to her publisher, John Blackwood, on just this point:

The printer's reader made a correction after I saw the proofs, and though he may sometimes do so with advantage, as I am very liable to overlook mistakes, I in this case particularly object to his alteration, and I mention it in order to request that it may not occur again. He has everywhere substituted the form 'The Misses So-and-So' for 'The Miss So-and-So's', a form which in England is confined to public announcements, to the backs of letters, and to the conversation of schoolmistresses. This is not the conversational English of good society, and causes the most disagreeable jolt in an easy style of narrative or description. (Mrs Oliphant, *William Blackwood and His Sons*, II, p. 441)

Sir is usually respectful, except when members of the upper classes are quarrelling together. It can even bring quite positive returns. When the brother of a publican expostulates with him, in Gissing's *Demos* (chapter 9), for addressing the parvenu Richard Mutimer as 'sir', he elicits 'the profound reply "D'you think he'd have 'ad that glass of whisky if I'd called him Dick?"' This monosyllable can be a formidable class barrier, as when Pip invites Joe Gargery to his new genteel apartments in London (*Great Expectations*, chapter 27): 'Whenever he subsided into affection, he called me Pip, and whenever he relapsed into politeness, he called me Sir.' Towards the end of the meeting, however, 'Our eyes met, and all the "Sir" melted out of that manly heart as he gave me his hand.'

One form of address whose fortunes began to fail somewhat as the century continued was *squire*. Probably the position of a *squire* was one of the first to be threatened by increased democracy. Yet it is interesting that in *Can You Forgive Her?* (chapter 17) a much respected master of hounds, a baronet, is given the courtesy title, as it were, of *the Squire*, without irony; and Squire Hamley of Hamley in *Wives and Daughters* and Squire Brown, father of Tom Brown, are portraits of men of standing and assurance who undoubtedly had their counterparts in reality. One can point to several contexts, however, where as an appellative *squire* is suspect. Already in *Hard*

Times (1854) Dickens reflects the town habit of using the word inappropriately and patronizingly, as when Sleary, master of the circus, troubled with asthma, addresses Gradgrind as 'Thquire' (I, chapter 8). In *Can You Forgive Her?* (chapter 41) George Vavasor feels uncomfortable when addressed by the electioneering agent Scruby: ' "Well, Squire," said Scruby, "how is it to be?" And Vavasor felt that he detected in the man's voice some diminution of that respect with which he had hitherto been treated.'

WITHIN THE FAMILY

As to modes of address within the family, there was little doubt as to the best usage for children in the early part of Queen Victoria's regin. *Papa* and *mamma* were used in the upper classes, and much favoured also by aspiring members of the middle classes. That social arbiter, Mrs General in *Little Dorrit* (II, chapter 5) lays down the law on the subject: ' "Papa' is a preferable mode of address," observed Mrs General. " 'Father' is rather vulgar, my dear. The word 'Papa', besides, gives a pretty form to the lips." ' Lower down the social scale words like *mammy* and *mummy, ma* and *pa* were possible. The recent *OED* Supplement puts the first quotation for *mummy* at 1784, whereas *mammy* and its abbreviation *mam*, and also *dad*, are sixteenth-century. Thackeray regularly began letters to his mother 'My dearest *mammy*', which must have been growing unfashionable; but this word had been common. Disraeli (*Vivian Grey*, I, chapter 3) has one schoolboy accuse another of being '*mammy*-sick'; and it is interesting that one of Savage's *Vulgarisms* (1833) is 'It's stewed to a *mammy*', for the quite different word *mummy* meaning 'a pulpy substance or mass'. *Mum* has also had from Middle English times the quite separate meaning of a command to silence (war-time security posters punned on this: 'Be like dad; keep mum'). However, as a pet name for *mother* and a shortening of *mummy, mum* seems to have been a nineteenth-century development, probably from dialect.

Both Dickens and Thackeray have a tendency to regard *papa* and *mamma* ironically. In *Little Dorrit* (I, chapter 2) Dickens writes of 'a majestic English mamma and papa of the patrician order'; and in *Vanity Fair* (chapter 49), Lord Steyne torments Lady Gaunt with: 'Pray madam, shall I tell you some little anecdotes about my Lady Bareacres, your *mamma*?' It is amusing to find a Manchester man, and one very much self-made, in Mrs Gaskell's short story 'The Manchester Marriage', reversing Mrs General's process:

> The pack of doctors could do no good to little Ailsie.... But her father (for so he insisted on being called, and also on Alice's no longer retaining the appellation of mamma, but becoming hence-forward mother)... infused a new element of... confidence into her life.

Pa and *ma*, which tend to sound rather vulgar in many Dickensian contexts, are to be found in the first half of the century among several families with claims to distinction. Of his projected marriage to Emily Tennyson, Arthur Hallam writes in 1832, 'Not a syllable have I spoken yet about my intentions to Pa or Ma' (R. B. Martin, *Tennyson: The Unquiet Heart*, p. 146). Henry Kingsley, whose novels are admittedly provincial, being so often set in Devon, has his heroines prefer *ma*, and also *grandma*, which has certainly prevailed over *grandmamma*: '"I say," she burst out, "that it is a wicked and shameful business from beginning to end, and I'll stop it! *Grandma*, how can you use your tact to find excuse? No, *ma*, I am not in the schoolroom"' (*Leighton Court*, chapter 18). The fate that overtook *mamma* and *papa* is noted by the *OED*: 'long considered genteel, but more and more left to children, and in the second half of the nineteenth century abandoned even by them'. *Mother* and *father* were, in any case, more usual appellatives with older children, and were generally used by novelists for serious effects. But the usage of the homely Mr Meagles, in *Little Dorrit* (I, chapter 2) of referring to his wife as 'mother', has never been heard in 'Society'. The way Dickens introduces the usage suggests that it was something of an innovation in 1854: 'Mother (my usual name for Mrs Meagles) began to cry.... "What's the matter, Mother?" said I.' Correspondingly, Mrs Meagles replies with 'Never mind, Father, never mind.' Lady Agnes Grove, in *The Social Fetich* (p. 39) deplores this usage: 'What is more terrible than when husbands call their wives "Mother" or worse still... "Wife". The first of these practices she so deplores continues today in unrefined circles; the second now seems to be restricted to giants in fairy tales! The haughty and provoking Mrs Gowan, who does not approve of her son's marriage with a daughter of the Meagles family, settles on an unusual and condescending hybrid vocative: 'And how do you both do, *Papa and Mama Meagles?*' (*Little Dorrit*, II, chapter 8).

Among the very best society, the distinction between reference and address dies hard. It is well exemplified in the Biblical: 'I will arise and go to *my Father*, and will say unto him *Father*, I have sinned.' The best people followed a similar practice in not omitting *my* for reference. When, in *Mansfield Park*, Sir Thomas Bertram arrives home suddenly from Antigua, Julia Bertram says, '*My father* is come! He is in the hall at this moment' (chapter 18). Lord Stanley writes to his wife in 1861, '*My Mother* is certainly weaker' (*The Stanleys of Alderley*, p. 265). To use *mother* and *father* here seemed, perhaps, too familiar, perhaps excessively emotional. An alternative expression for reference was imported, I believe, from France: '*The dear father* thought she was only two years older than him' (p. 55); 'I needn't be a charge upon *the old mother*' (*Pendennis*, I, chapter 32). Augustus Hare, in *The Story of My Life*, has a chapter heading (II, p. 367) 'Home Life with *the Mother*'. In the earlier part of the century aristocratic usage, even within the family, had sometimes been very stiff. Maria Josepha, first Lady Stanley, writing in the 1840s, refers to her husband in letters as 'My Lord'; but this does not survive in the later Stanley letters.

Not only boys, but even girls at the beginning of the century addressed their father as 'sir'. Elizabeth Bennet so addressed her not particularly venerable father (*Pride and Prejudice*, chapter 13); and so did Jos Sedley, when a grown man, address his elderly father, old Sedley (*Vanity Fair*, chapter 3). The practice seems to have been discontinued quite early in the century for girls, but boys continued till later. Clive Newcome uses *sir*, for instance, to his father the Colonel, who does not regret the fact that the excessive formality of his own youth has passed, when sons had addressed letters 'Honoured Father' or 'Honoured Sir' (*The Newcomes*, II, chapter 1). By the end of the century, it seems, boys had ceased to use *sir* to their fathers. Lady Grove, in *The Social Fetich* (p. 39) writes: 'I never knew anyone who addressed his father as "sir", and so why should a man be made to do so in books?' In Henry James's *The Portrait of a Lady* (chapter 5), a character is described whose mother 'was paternal, and even, according to the slang of the day, *gubernatorial*.' This is a characteristically oblique reference to the tendency for sons to replace the rather formal *sir* with *governor* or *guv'nor*, when addressing their fathers. When Frank Gresham is told by his father that he must pay a visit to nearby Courcy Castle, he protests: 'But you don't know how dull it is, *governor*' (*Dr Thorne*, chapter 14). The Latin pair *pater* and *mater*, anglicized in pronunciation to rhyme with *later*, were also schoolboy use.

The higher the rank, the more formal were the terms of address. Lady Lufton would have been pleased when her son called her 'my lady' occasionally, as well as 'mother' (*Framley Parsonage*, chapter 9); but there might be implications in formal address other than that of respect, as with old Bishop Grantly and his masterful son, the Archdeacon: "Why, my lord," he said, speaking to his father; and when he called his father "my lord" the good old bishop shook in his shoes, for he knew that an evil time was coming' (*The Warden*, chapter 9).

Various hypocoristic vocatives, while they may have been extant earlier, only gradually came into general use as the century proceeded. In a letter to an aspiring novelist written in 1864, Charlotte M. Yonge (born in 1823), writes of her childhood: 'I don't think such a familiarity as "Grannie" would have been dreamt of. I never saw it in any old book, and with neither of my grandmothers should any of us have attempted it, indeed my Grandmother Yonge was addressed as "ma'am" by all her sons and daughters' (Battiscombe, *Charlotte Mary Yonge*, p. 114). Much of Besant and Rice's *By Celia's Arbour* (1878) is set twenty-five years before, at the time of the Crimean war, and the difference in time is marked by such expressions as:

'"But, dear Aunt," – well-brought-up young people in those days did not venture on such a respectful endearment as "Auntie"' (chapter 46).

Addressing, and referring to, one's kith and kin (other than father and mother) as 'brother', 'sister' etc., is, as Jane Austen would say, 'only moderately genteel'. It is true that Mrs Bennet refers to 'my *sister* Philips' (*Pride and Prejudice*, chapter 49) and calls Mr Gardiner 'brother' (chapter 7), but this may not have been the best usage. The ill-bred Miss Brownings have *sister* in reference and address:

> 'I've not been able to sleep at all...' You know that was a little fancy of *sister's*, for she'd been snoring away as naturally as could be. So I... said in a low voice: '*Sister*, it's her ladyship and me.' (*Wives and Daughters*, chapter 14)

Sister with a surname is particularly characteristic of provincial usage. One thinks immediately of *The Mill on the Floss*, with 'sister Deane' and 'sister Pullet' (it is only gradually that we learn their Christian names of Sophy and Susan). There were possibilities here for the expression of a closer or a more distant sisterly relationship. Carry Brattle, in *The Vicar of Bullhampton* (chapter 6) is a 'fallen woman' and has left home:

> Carry was the last one that had left her; and now Fanny hardly dared to name the word sister above her breath. She could speak, indeed, of Sister Jay, the wife of the prosperous ironmonger at Warmington; but of sisters by their Christian names no mention was ever made.

In the same way (and again indicating provincial usage) cousins of a third person who are respectively adolescent and adult may be differentiated by surname and Christian name: "How old is *cousin Phillis*?" said I... but *cousin Holman* took no notice' (Mrs Gaskell, *Cousin Phillis*, chapter 1).

The familial use of the possessive adjective *our*, meaning 'of our family' is non-U, according to Ross (*Don't Say It*, p. 10), and so it was in the last century. It is true that the young Princess Victoria, taking pity on some gypsies one cold Christmas Day, writes 'Mamma has ordered broth... and several of *our* people have sent old flannel things for them' (*The Girlhood of Queen Victoria*, I, p. 181), but this means 'of our household', and is therefore different. But when Mrs Chivery (*Little Dorrit*, I, chapter 22) refers to her son as 'Our John', which Dickens prints with capitalised initial letters, it is clearly the marked idiom of someone of the rank of turnkey's wife: 'Miss Dorrit is the matter with *Our John*, sir; he's a-breaking his heart for her.'

There is a strong tendency in English to reduce *mistress* to a word whose pronunciation is usually rendered in print as 'missis' or 'missus'. This, of course, is the usual pronunciation of *Mrs* also, which is originally the same word. In Victorian novels, *missus* is both a non-U version of *mistress* in the sense of a female employer ('*Missus* is very kind, and there's plenty to eat and drink,' *Cranford*, chapter 4); and also the regular form of address and reference for a husband of the lower classes to use to his wife: 'Our reverend gent drops in and takes a glass, don't he *Missis!*' (*The Newcomes*, II, chapter 6); 'What with *the Missis* being laid up so, things have gone awk'arder nor usual' (*The Mill on the Floss*, I, chapter 8). The following quote suggests the origin of *Mr* also: 'It must not be forgotten that, whatever we may think of it, the cooking of "my missus" generally satisfies "my master"' (M. E. Loane, *The Next Street But One*, chapter 1).

LETTER-WRITING

Clearly, these varying forms of address suggest an almost bewildering variety of ways to begin for the letter-writer, who has time to think about it. Thus Josiah Crawley, in his bitter pride, debates within himself how he shall begin a letter to his former friend Arabin:

> He would fain, in his pride, have begun 'Sir'. The question was between that and 'My dear-Arabin'.[7] It had once between them always been 'Dear Frank' and 'Dear Joe'; but the occasion for 'Dear Frank' and 'Dear Joe' between them had long been past. (*The Last Chronicle of Barset*, chapter 62)

Others also hesitated over the right form of address:

> Jawleyford spoilt three sheets of cream-laid satin-wove note-paper (crested and ciphered) before he pleased himself with a beginning. First he had it 'Dear Sir', which he thought looked too stiff; then he had it 'My Dear Sir', which he thought looked too loving; next he had it 'Dear Spraggon', which he considered as too familiar; and then he tried 'Dear Mr Spraggon' which he thought would do. (*Mr Sponge's Sporting Tour*, chapter 25)

Errors in such matters pointed to a defective education. The Reverend Amos Barton, though a university man, shocked his parishioners the Miss Farquhars, whom he once 'addressed in a letter as Dear Mads., apparently an abbreviation for Madams' (George Eliot, *Scenes of Clerical Life*, I, chapter 2). For people of eminence, it might be difficult to find the right style of address. John Eames feels he ought to give his friend Lord de Guest a true account of the flogging of Crosbie, in order to contradict any falsifications by journalists on the subject, but how was he to begin the letter?

> He thought a good deal about the style in which he ought to address the peer, never having hitherto written to him. He began 'My dear Lord', on the sheet of paper, and then put it aside, thinking that it looked over-bold.

[7] According to R. W. Chapman (SPE Tract, no. 47, p. 240n.), 'At the beginning of a letter "My dear Sir, Smith, John" is more cordial, but not necessarily less formal, than "Dear Sir, Smith, John".'

In the end, he addressed Lord de Guest as 'My Lord'. In a letter in reply, Lord de Guest puts his favourite right in a postscript: 'When you write to me again – and don't be long, first begin your letter, "My dear Lord de Guest" – that is the proper way' (*The Small House at Allington*, chapter 36).

There was an official way of addressing a gentleman in writing. Originally a gentleman, if he was, according to the *OED* (*esquire*, sense 2),' a man belonging to the higher order of English gentry, ranking immediately below a knight', had a title accredited to him. This was *Esquire* written after the name. Social aspirants were warned by Savage in his *Vulgarisms* (1833) that 'Mr Smith Esquire' was wrong and 'Joseph Smith Esquire' was correct. The Christian name, as the *OED* points out (*esquire*, sense 3a), should not be abbreviated, so that 'T. Lookaloft Esquire' (p. 87) is incorrect. The *OED* also has a nice quotation from Miss Mulock's *Two Marriages* (1867) to show that the two titles of *Mr* and *Esquire* were considered as quite distinct, at least in some circles: 'Jane, wife of *Mr John Bowerbank* (he was not *Esquire* then).' Fifty years before this, in a letter to her nephew, Jane Austen had seen the title as appropriate to give to him on his reaching maturity as a member of the landed classes: 'One reason for my writing to you now, is that I may have the pleasure of directing to you Esq. – I give you joy of having left Winchester' (*Letters*, p. 467).

Those who were sticklers for rank and breeding did not accord the title of *Esquire* lightly. Of these pedants there is a splendid example in Trollope's *The Vicar of Bullhampton* (chapter 9):

> Miss Marrable was one of those ladies, – now few in number, – who within their heart of hearts conceive that money gives no title to social distinction, let the amount of money be ever so great.... Rank to her was a thing quite assured and ascertained, and she had no more doubt as to her own right to pass out of a room before the wife of a millionaire than she had of the right of a millionaire to spend his own guineas. She always addressed an attorney by letter as Mister, raising up her eyebrows when appealed to on the matter, and explaining that an attorney is not an esquire. She had an idea that the son of a gentleman, if he intended to maintain his rank as a gentleman, should earn his income as a clergyman, or as a barrister, or as a soldier, or as a sailor. These were the professions intended for gentlemen. She would not absolutely say that a physician was not a gentleman, or even a surgeon; but she would never allow to physic the same absolute privileges which, in her eyes, belonged to law and the church. There might also possibly be a doubt about the Civil Service and Civil Engineering; but she had no doubt whatever that when a man touched trade or commerce in any way he was doing that which was not the work of a gentleman. He might be very respectable, and it might be very necessary that he should do it; but brewers, bankers, and merchants were not gentlemen, and the world, according to Miss Marrable's theory, was going astray, because people were forgetting their landmarks.

But not everybody was as strict as Miss Marrable, and as the century continued the results of looser usage could even by anomalous. Gissing, in *Demos* (1886) chapter 8, savours the irony that a Socialist magazine entitled 'Fiery Cross' is addressed and sent out to subscribers who are designated 'Esquire':

> 'I believe father will take the paper if I ask him. One is better than nothing, isn't it, Alfred?'
>
> 'Good. We book Stephen Tew, Esquire.'
>
> 'But surely you mustn't call him Esquire?' suggested Adela.
>
> 'Oh, he is unregenerate; let him keep his baubles.'
>
> 'How are the regenerate designated?'
>
> 'Comrade, we prefer.'
>
> 'Also applied to women?'
>
> 'Well, I suppose not. As the word hasn't a feminine, call yourselves plain Letty Tew and Adela Waltham, without meaningless prefix.'
>
> 'What nonsense you are talking, Alfred!' remarked his mother. 'As if everybody in Wanley could address young ladies by their Christian names!'

Clearly the liberating process of Socialism was apt to encounter snags, but at least the designation *Esquire* was thrown open to democracy. Mr Goldspink, a banker in Surtees's *Plain or Ringlets?* (1860), receives a present of a haunch of venison from a duke, with 'a clean parchment label, with his own name regularly *esquired*, as we all are nowadays' (chapter 10). It followed from this that people addressed by letter as 'Mr' might feel very run-of-the-mill:

> Tennyson limps, his boots pinch – paid £2:12:6 for them; his bootmaker in the Burlington arcade, highly fashionable. 'Writes to me, "Mr Alfred Tennyson"'. I suggested, 'He feels he is doing you an honour, being plain *Mr.*, in consenting to make your boots.'
>
> T— 'One day while he was measuring me, I called attention to my corns, and said, "Have you any corns?" From that moment he threw off all respect!'
> (Allingham, *Diary*, p. 134)

But as an up-to-date title, *Mr*, too, was valued: 'Mr George, the farmer ... steps out from the rank.... You should not address him as Farmer George. Farmer as an affix is not the thing now; farmers are "Mr So-and-so" (*Hodge and his Masters*, chapter 8).

Vulgarity in letter-writing showed itself in various ways. Letters begun with the impersonal third person were apt to stray into the more personal grammatical construction. Mrs Goodenough, for example, in *Wives and Daughters* (chapter 31) writes as follows:

> Mrs Goodenough's respects to Mr Sheepshanks, and hopes he is in good health. She would be very glad if he would favour her with his company to tea on Monday. My daughter, in Combermere, has sent me a couple of guinea-fowls, and Mrs Goodenough hopes Mr Sheepshanks will stay and take a bit of supper.

Savage, in *Vulgarisms*, had warned that these third-person notes were a cause of 'great blundering', and had illustrated this point with two sentences: 'Mrs A hopes Mrs B will excuse my chaise not being sent'; 'Mr W's compliments to Mr S and I will be obliged if you will call tomorrow.'

As with single words, epistolary formulas were apt to decline in status. The habit of beginning a sentence with a noun clause subject and concluding with the formula 'is the wish of ... etc.' was doubtless originally an elegant inversion, but by the time of the writing of *The Small House at Allington* (1862), it is seen by Trollope as appropriate for the vulgar Joseph Cradell: 'That you may find in the kind smiles of L. D. consolation for any disappointment which this may occasion you, is the ardent wish of your true friend, Joseph Cradell' (chapter 59). According to M. E. Loane in *The Queen's Poor* (chapter 13) formulas had made the letters of the very poor monotonously alike: 'Epistles stiff and empty at the beginning, affectionate and incoherent at the end, and with little but the address to mark one from the other'.

5

Conclusion

For his article on *Linguistic Class-indicators in Present-day English* Ross read Mrs Henry Wood's Johnny Ludlow stories, which were eventually published in a six-volume edition in 1908. He justifies this seemingly eccentric choice of text (p. 30n) on the grounds that:

> The stories, which are narrated by Johnny Ludlow, are written in a colloquial style and contain many conversations. These portray the language of the squires of nearly a century ago, which is, essentially, the parent of the U-English of today . . . *Johnny Ludlow* is a valuable *Fundgrube* for the student of the subject.

In much the same way, I have looked to the English of Jane Austen and the Regency period for traces of conservatism in Victorian English. It is amongst the upper classes that observances and formalities are best preserved, and innovations and informalities most firmly resisted. Even the slang used is apt to be traditional. Elderly speakers, particularly, are liable to recall the language of their youth. Thus when Trollope has Lady Lufton say *country* for *county*, and gives to Mr Harding the phrase *great girl* for *big girl*, (pp. 16, 65), he is reminding us of the age of these characters, and that they were young during the time of the Regency. These are two people of impeccable gentility, and such expressions would come under Ross's denomination 'old-fashioned U'. A real-life character who is comparable is the first Lady Stanley (1771–1863), whose grammar would have appeared somewhat less than correct (though traditional) to a stricter age (p. 68).

Ross (p. 45) makes much of the U-tendency to be curt: to say 'What?' on not hearing a speaker properly, instead of 'I beg your pardon'; to say 'Sorry!' instead of making a fuller apology; and often to say nothing at all, after hiccuping or belching, for example. My observations of the Victorian period suggest that curtailment even extends to grammar. Pseudo-transitive verbs, with the object omitted but with a strong sense of omission, occur in such expressions as 'Did you find?' for 'Did you find the fox?' and 'I must show' for 'I must show myself'. A particularly significant, if small, example is the omission of the particle *to* after such verbs as *ought*, *mean* and *like*, where it now tends to be *de rigueur*. Thus, when Alice Vavasor, in *Can You Forgive*

Her? (chapter 21), demurs at the suggestion that Lady Glencora should go out of her way so that Alice shall see the town of Matching, Lady Glencora replies 'Ah, but I should like'. This brevity is made possible because of agreed and fixed circumstances, where much can be understood: everybody knows what is to be found on a hunt, for example. The same kind of fixed and ordered life favours the use of a dispositional present tense to describe future time. If the aristocracy could not quite control the operations of nature, they would have a good try: 'Lady Cork ... *goes* out of town next week to produce her seventh daughter at Marston' (*The Stanleys of Alderley*, p. 267). (Nancy Mitford's footnote informs us that this time she produced a son and heir.) Another grammatical point to note is that a distancing effect can sometimes be achieved with tenses: a past for a present infinitive, a pluperfect for a past tense; as in 'I quite expected *to have seen* Mr Thornton,' and 'I did not think it *had been* so late.'

As for distinctive kinds of pronunciation, these are something we can still observe, as U-speech becomes old-fashioned U-speech and then passes on into 'laughable archaism'. This last is the description, by the latest authority on pronunciation, of the old U pronunciation [ɔ:], in *lost*, *off*, etc. – a pronunciation still retained, however, by the Poet Laureate. Already, perhaps, the final [n] in *hunting* and *shooting* has gone the way of the vowels in *Rome* and *gold*, which were old-fashioned in Queen Victoria's childhood: 'Lord M. says *Room* and *goold*, for *Rome and gold*: but I pronounce it the latter way' (*The Girlhood of Queen Victoria*, II, p. 51). Despite a strong influence on elocution from the two authorities on pronunciation in the nineteenth century, Walker and Smart, there was much elision, even among the best speakers. Indeed a small but important marker was the treatment of unaccented syllables. Thus it was good to elide the middle syllable in *medicine and Waldegrave*, but not in *traveller* and *suddenly*. The present-day majority pronunciations of *often*, *poor*, *girl* and *hotel* were considered middle-class.

When, in 1880, Disraeli came to write *Endymion*, a novel set in the late 1820s, he was able to chronicle some of the major changes that had overtaken society since that time:

> The great world then, compared with the huge society of the present period, was limited in its proportions, and composed of elements more refined though less various. It consisted mainly of the great landed aristocracy, who had quite absorbed the nabobs of India, and had nearly appropriated the huge West Indian fortunes. Occasionally, an eminent banker or merchant invested a large portion of his accumulations in land. ... But those vast and successful invasions of society by new classes which have since occurred, though impending, had not commenced. The manufacturers, the railway kings, the colossal contractors, the discoverers of nuggets, had not yet found their place in society and in the senate. (chapter 5)

The acceptance of mercantile and manufacturing interests meant that the more traditional, landed elements in society had to listen to a great deal of the language of trade. To some extent they resisted. At retail trade the Lord Chamberlain drew the line, and words like *trade* and *shop*, never entirely in favour since Tudor times, took on a renewed opprobrium. The Court was believed to exert at least a distant influence on language. Thus it is interesting that when, in Meredith's short story 'The Case of General Ople and Lady Camper', Lady Camper pours scorn on the General's word *lady-friend*, the poor man's first reaction is 'What would the Queen say?' Mrs Trollope, in America, deplored the lack of a Court:

> which everywhere else is the glass wherein the higher orders dress themselves, and which again reflected from them to the classes below, goes far towards polishing, in some degree, a great majority of the population. (*Domestic Manners of the Americans*, chapter 14)

No doubt she would partly have ascribed to this deficiency the fact that she 'very seldom... heard a sentence elegantly turned... from the lips of an American' (chapter 5).

When the pressure from the newly rich entering the best society was at its height, perhaps from 1830 to 1865, there was a curious linguistic reflection of this with regard to the names and times of meals. When the hero of *Pelham* (1828) dined with a rustic clergyman friend, 'the dinner-hour was four' (chapter 63), a time that Jane Austen would have been accustomed to, but which would already have seemed antiquated to the sophisticated Pelham. In London, especially, the best people dined, often quite late, in the evening, and the later they dined, the more substantial their mid-day luncheon would have to be. But to make the mid-day meal into the main one, and above all to call it *dinner*, was a social solecism. The large number of references to hours of dining and names of meals shows how much attention was focused on this point in a society threatened by new invasions of their routine and privileges. Occasionally, the middle classes also beat their own boundaries, so to speak, by naming their meals.

As to the language of the middle and lower classes, it is possible to draw an analogy from clothing. In the 1888 edition of Mrs Beeton's *The Book of Household Management*, it is noticed (p. 1453) that 'the introduction of cheap silks and cottons, and, still more recently, those ambiguous "materials" and tweeds, have removed the landmarks between the mistress and her maid, between the master and his man.' To compare the rich collection of vulgarisms amassed by Savage in 1833 with later document-ation on the subject, is to be aware of an analogous process of landmark removal. For example, M. E. Loane, in *The Queen's Poor* (1905) observes from great experience of nursing amid the working classes of London the increasing pull of the standard language. She disavows (chapter 4) the 'orthographical orgies' by which novelists rendered the Cockney dialect. The letter 'h', for instance, is 'finding a home all over the country'. The poor 'begin to use freely the language that they see in print, while the rich carefully avoid a bookish tinge'. Rushing in where philologists would fear to tread, she enumerates the most stubborn grammatical errors still to be found: *as* for *that*, whether as relative pronoun or conjunction; a superabundance of negatives; faulty concord of subject and verb; and analogous forms such as *hisself, seed* (for *saw*), *comed* and *goed*. A strong preference for the object case, as in '*Me* and *him* went to see her' she represents as 'the unsatisfied craving of the language for disjunctive pronouns'. At any rate, she confidently asserts: 'These carried out in detail, exhaust the differences which mark the speech of the poor as I know them.' It is a foretaste of the situation today, when the indigenous language of these islands has never been more uniform.

An amusing piece of evidence for the toning down of class, and therefore of linguistic, distinctions, is provided by a review, in 1905, by Max Beerbohm of a play by R. C. Carton called *Mr Hopkinson*.[1] This is a farce turning on the embarrassment caused in high society by the parvenu son of a rate-collector who has come in for £40,000 year. Inevitably, Beerbohm thinks of Samuel Warren's novel of sixty years before, *Ten Thousand a Year*:

> Mr Hopkinson's father was a rate-collector, and by some means Mr Hopkinson has just come in for forty thousand a year. Ten thousand a year was the amount come in for by Mr Tittlebat Titmouse. Otherwise Mr Carton has not attempted to bring Samuel Warren up to date. In modern life we have compulsory education. Nor is there quite the old hard-and-fast division between the classes. The lower middle class picks up from 'society papers' a good smattering of the details of high life. The son of a latter-day rate-collector is no Hottentot. Yet, when the Duchess tells Mr Hopkinson that he must have a villa at Nice, 'Nice?' he says, 'that's somewhere beyond Ealing, isn't it?' After he has been moving for half a year in the highest circles, he is as uncouth as ever: ''arf a mo',' 'bit o' orl right', 'ever eat whelks?' 'My Lord,' and so on. Tittlebat Titmouse, if I remember rightly, acquired a veneer. But Mr Carton will have none of such subtleties. Mr Hopkinson starts as a full-blown 'snob' (in the old sense of the word: we are dealing with antiquities), and he continues in full bloom to the end.

Beerbohm wonders whether modern playwrights ever read contemporary books. 'Have they never dipped into the novels of George Gissing, or Mr H. G. Wells? .... Is Samuel Warren the final name on their syllabus?'

As to modes of address, Christian names were not the ubiquitous all-purpose appellatives they have since become. They were most typically used

---

[1] Max Beerbohm, *Last Theatres* (Rupert Hart-Davis, London, 1970), p. 129.

within the family, though they also marked a vital stage in upper-class courtship. Lower down the social scale, there was more informality; but here too it would be a mark of respect to address a woman one knew well, more formally. For a woman to address a married man, or a man a married woman, with the Christian name, could carry a suggestion of scandal. Designations of rank were greatly valued, though there were signs of some relaxation of formality as the century continued. Sons and daughters of noble households began to be addressed by their tutors and nurses with their Christian names. In 1844, etiquette was still rigid enough for people to notice that a young man and woman were in love by the fact that they shook hands each evening when the party separated (*The Ladies of Alderley*, p. 76). Yet paradoxically, along with a great respect for rank there went a desire to cut through some of the ceremony. Tennyson writes to the Duke of Argyll, addressing him as 'Dear Duke' and adding in a postscript: 'If you call me Mr Tennyson any longer I think I must your-grace you till the end of the chapter' (Hallam Tennyson, *Alfred Lord Tennyson: A Memoir*, p. 405). This fondness amongst men for the surname alone, which suggested bluff, manly friendship to the Victorians, somehow smacks of felony to us, since it so frequently occurs in newspaper reports of criminals. Wives referring to their husbands by surname alone is now very old-fashioned non-U (it was not good usage in the last century); while to refer to, or address, a woman by surname alone, as happened with female domestics and in girls' schools within living memory, is now generally thought repugnant. Lower class men were keener than their social superiors on retaining the humble designation of *Mr*.

Within the family, the aristocratic *mamma* and *papa* eventually lost ground, not to the older, and relatively classless, *mam* and *mammy* and *dad*, but to middle-class *mum* and *mummy* and *daddy*. It was not good usage, throughout the century, to use *mother* and *father* in reference; *my mother* and *my father* being preferred. Forms like *grannie*, *grandma* and *auntie*, unheard of at the beginning of the century, were evidence in themselves of increasing informality. It was also an indication of growing democracy that the title *Esquire* became a fairly meaningless designation widely used in addressing envelopes.

One may well wonder about the future of U speech. As Philip Larkin reminds us, 'Power of some sort or other will go on'; and, rather as he speculates on the last church-goers, we may wonder, perhaps, who will be 'the last, the very last' MP to speak of 'Government' without the article; or the last young lady to give offence by insisting too much on the courtesy title 'Honourable'. In what seem to have been his last observations on the subject, in a compilation *U and Non-U Revisited*, Ross is recorded in a dialogue with Richard Buckle, editor of the book, and others. The antitheses between U and non-U have not, he insists, changed, with one or two exceptions such as that *wireless* is no longer U but obsolescent, since everybody now says *radio*. But while asserting this continuity of U-usage in theory, Ross himself seems to spend more time in the dialogue recording the more egregious modern non-U-isms, such as 'You name it, we have it'; 'I saw him Monday; no, I tell a lie, it was Tuesday'; 'How silly can you get?' etc. Richard Buckle obviously feels that Ross's delimitation of U-speech is too extreme, and suggests the term 'Double-U', for words which the working-class and the upper-class have in common, such as *flog* for 'to sell': 'I've just flogged my Canalettos at Sotheby's', he says, is possible U-speech nowadays. Even in the last century the best people were not necessarily inhospitable to extreme colloquialisms, especially from America: 'The Ameer is what the Yankees call "a dead coon"' writes Disraeli (*Letters*, II, p. 195) – to anyone but Lady Bradford, he might have written the more usual phrase 'a gone coon'. Buckle's sense, also, that the linguistic forces of the upper and lower classes should combine against 'middle-class genteel-isms' is a latter-day version of a recurrent theme of Victoria's day. We find Lord Melborne discussing it in 1840:

> 'I don't like the middle classes,' Lord M. said, 'they say that the upper and lower classes are very much like each other in this country; the middle classes are bad, the higher and the lower classes there's some good in, but the middle classes are all affectation and conceit and pretence and concealment.' (*The Girlhood of Queen Victoria*, II, p. 305)

Whatever the fate of upper-class speech may be, there is no doubt that the subject of language and class is one that will continue to be absorbing. For as Gissing saw, the confusion and self-consciousness caused by the breakdown of class barriers only increases the interest of class as a subject of conversation. Writing in 1892, he notes:

> Classes are getting mixed, confused. Yes, but we are so conscious of the process that we talk of class distinctions more than of anything else – talk and think of them incessantly. (*Bore in Exile*, V, chapter 2)

There is no sign that this interest is abating.

Bibliography

FICTION

Austen, Jane, *Sense and Sensibility*, 1811
—— *Pride and Prejudice*, 1812
—— *Mansfield Park*, 1814
—— *Emma*, 1816
—— *Northanger Abbey*, 1818
—— *Persuasion*, 1818
—— *Minor Works* (ed. R. W. Chapman), 1954
Besant, Walter, *All Sorts and Conditions of Men*, 1882
Besant, Walter, and Rice, James, *The Golden Butterfly*, 1876
—— *By Celia's Arbour*, 1878
—— *The Seamy Side*, 1880
Braddon, Mary *Lady Audley's Secret*, 1862
Bronte, Anne, *Agnes Grey*, 1845
Collins, Wilkie, *Basil*, 1852
—— *The Woman in White*, 1860
Dickens, Charles, *Dombey and Son*, 1848
—— *David Copperfield*, 1849–50
—— *Bleak House*, 1852–3
—— *Hard Times*, 1854
—— *Little Dorrit*, 1857
—— *Great Expectations*, 1861
—— *Our Mutual Friend*, 1865
Disraeli, Benjamin, *Vivian Grey*, 1826–7
—— *Henrietta Temple*, 1836
—— *Coningsby*, 1844
—— *Sybil*, 1845
—— *Lothair*, 1870
—— *Endymion*, 1880
Eliot, George, *Scenes of Clerical Life*, 1858
—— *Adam Bede*, 1859
—— *The Mill on the Floss*, 1860
—— *Silas Marner*, 1861
—— *Felix Holt*, 1866

—— *Middlemarch*, 1872
—— *Daniel Deronda* 1876
Gaskell, Mrs, *Mary Barton*, 1848
—— *Cranford*, 1853
—— *North and South*, 1854
—— 'Mr Harrison's Confession', in *Round the Sofa*, 1859
—— *My Lady Ludlow*, 1859
—— *Cousin Phillis*, 1864
—— *Wives and Daughters*, 1865
Gissing, George, *Demos*, 1886
—— *Thyrza*, 1887
—— *New Grub Street*, 1891
—— *Born in Exile*, 1892
—— *The Odd Women*, 1893
—— *Will Warburton*, 1905
Hardy, Thomas, *A Pair of Blue Eyes*, 1873
—— *Two on a Tower*, 1882
—— *The Mayor of Casterbridge*, 1886
—— *Tess of the Durbervilles*, 1891
Hughes, Thomas, *Tom Brown's Schooldays*, 1857
—— *The Scouring of the White Horse*, 1859
—— *Tom Brown at Oxford*, 1861
James, Henry, *The Portrait of a Lady*, 1881
Jefferies, Richard, *Amaryllis at the Fair*, 1887
Kingsley, Charles, *Yeast*, 1848
—— *Alton Locke*, 1850
—— *Two Years Ago*, 1857
Kingsley, Henry, *Geoffrey Hamlyn*, 1859
—— *Ravenshoe*, 1862
—— *Leighton Court*, 1866
Lytton, Bulwer, *Pelham*, 1828
—— *Godolphin*, 1833
—— *Night and Morning*, 1841
—— *My Novel*, 1853
—— *A Strange Story*, 1862
Meredith, George, *The Ordeal of Richard Feverel*, 1859
—— *Evan Harrington*, 1861
—— *The Adventures of Harry Richmond*, 1871
—— 'The Case of General Ople and Lady Camper', 1877
Mitford, Mary Russell, *Our Village*, 1824–32
—— *Belford Regis*, 1835
Morrison, Arthur, *Tales of Mean Streets*, 1894
Oliphant, Mrs, *Salem Chapel*, 1863
—— *The Perpetual Curate*, 1864
Peacock, Thomas Love, *Crotchet Castle*, 1831
Quiller-Couch, Sir Arthur, *The Astonishing History of Troy Town*, 1888

Sala, G. A., *The Baddington Peerage*, 1860
Smith, Albert, *The Adventures of Mr Ledbury*, 1844
Surtees, Robert S., *Jorrocks's Jaunts and Jollities*, 1838
—— *Handley Cross*, 1843
—— *Mr Sponge's Sporting Tour*, 1853
—— *Ask Mamma*, 1858
—— *Plain or Ringlets?*, 1860
Thackeray, W. M., *The Book of Snobs*, 1848
—— *Vanity Fair*, 1848
—— *Pendennis*, 1849–50
—— *The Newcomes*, 1854–5
—— *Philip*, 1861–2
Trollope, Anthony, *The Warden*, 1855
—— *Barchester Towers*, 1857
—— *Dr Thorne*, 1858
—— *The Three Clerks*, 1858
—— *Framley Parsonage*, 1861
—— *Orley Farm*, 1862
—— *Rachel Ray*, 1863
—— *Can You Forgive Her?*, 1864
—— *The Small House at Allington*, 1864
—— *Miss Mackenzie*, 1865
—— *The Claverings*, 1867
—— *The Last Chronicle of Barset*, 1867
—— *The Vicar of Bullhampton*, 1870
—— *Ralph the Heir*, 1871
—— *Phineas Redux*, 1874
—— *The Way We Live Now*, 1875
—— *The Prime Minister*, 1876
—— *The American Senator*, 1877
—— *Mr Scarborough's Family*, 1883
Warren, Samuel, *Ten Thousand a Year*, 1841
Wells, H. G., *Kipps*, 1905

NON-FICTION AND OTHER REFERENCE WORKS

Alderley, The Ladies of, ed. Nancy Mitford, Hamish Hamilton, London, 1938.
Alderley, The Stanleys of, ed. Nancy Mitford, Hamish Hamilton, London, 1939.
Alford, H., *The Queen's English*, London, 1864, 3rd edn, 1870, 7th edn, 1889.
Allen, Walter, *The English Novel: A Short Critical History*, Phoenix House, London, 1954.
Allingham, William, *Diary*, introduction by Geoffrey Grigson, Centaur Press, Fontwell, 1967.
Amberley Papers, The, eds Bertrand and Patricia Russell, 2 vols, Allen and Unwin, London 1937.
Anon., *Habits of Good Society, The*, London, 1859.
—— *Hints on Etiquette*, London, 1836.

—— *How to Shine in Society*, Glasgow, 1860.

—— *Manners and Rules of Good Society*, by a Member of the Aristocracy, London, 1888.

—— *Manners and Tone of Good Society*, by a Member of the Aristocracy, London, 1879.

—— *Mixing in Society*, London, 1874

—— *Society Small Talk* or *What to Say and When to Say It*, by a Member of the Aristocracy, London, 1879.

—— *Vulgarities of Speech Corrected, The*, London, 1826.

Antrim, Louisa, Countess of, *Recollections*, The King's Stone Press, Shipston on Stour, 1937.

Arnold, Matthew, *Culture and Anarchy*, ed. J. Dover Wilson, Cambridge University Press, Cambridge, 1932.

Austen, Jane, *Letters to her Sister Cassandra and Others*, ed. R. W. Chapman, Oxford University Press, Oxford, 1932.

Elizabeth Barrett to Miss Mitford: Unpublished Letters, ed. Betty Miller, Murray, London, 1954.

Battiscombe, Georgina, *Charlotte Mary Yonge: The Story of an Uneventful Life*, Constable, London, 1943.

Beeton, Mrs Isabella, *The Book of Household Management*, London, 1888 edn.

Brook, G. L., *The Language of Dickens*, Deutsch, London, 1970.

Mrs Brookfield and her Circle, eds Charles and Frances Brookfield (2 vols), Pitman, London, 1905.

Carlyle, Jane Welsh, *A New Selection of her Letters*, arranged by Trudy Bliss, Gollancz, London, 1950.

Chapman, R. W., '"Oxford" English', Society for Pure English (SPE) Tract no. 37, 1932.

—— 'Names, Designations and Appellations', SPE Tract no. 47, 1936.

Clark, John, *The Language and Style of Anthony Trollope*, Deutsch, London, 1975.

Clough, A. H., *Poems*, 9th edn, London, 1882.

—— *The Correspondence of Arthur Hugh Clough*, 2 vols, ed. F. L. Mulhauser, Clarendon, Oxford, 1957.

Collinson, W. E., *Contemporary English: A Personal Speech Record*, Teubner, Leipzig and Berlin, 1927.

Creevey, Thomas, *The Creevey Papers*, ed. Sir Herbert Maxwell, 2 vols, Murray, London, 1903.

—— *The Creevey Papers*, ed. John Gore, Batsford, London, 1963.

Dana, R. H., *Hospitable England in the Seventies*, Murray, London, 1921.

Dickens: The Critical Heritage, ed. Philip Collins, Routledge and Kegan Paul, London, 1971.

Disraeli, B., *Letters to Lady Bradford and Lady Chesterfield*, ed. The Marquis of Zetland, 2 vols. Benn, London, 1929.

—— *Reminiscences*, eds Helen and Marvin Swartz, Hamilton, London, 1975.

Drinkwater, John, 'Martin Tupper' in *The Eighteen Eighties*, ed. Walter de la Mare, Cambridge University Press, Cambridge, 1930.

Eliot, George, *Essays of George Eliot*, ed. Thomas Pinney, Columbia University Press, Routledge and Kegan Paul, New York and London, 1963.

George Eliot: The Critical Heritage, ed. David Caroll, Routledge and Kegan Paul, London, 1971.

Elworthy, Frederick, *The West Somerset Word-Book*, London, 1888.

The Letters of Mrs Gaskell, eds J. A. V. Chapple and Arthur Pollard, Manchester University Press, Manchester, 1966.

Gerson, Stanley, *Sound and Symbol in the Dialogue of the Works of Charles Dickens*, Almqvist and Wiksell, Stockholm, 1967.

Gittings, Robert, *The Older Hardy*, Heinemann, London, 1978.

Grove, Lady Agnes, *The Social Fetich*, Smith, Elder, London, 1907.

Hall, Fitzedward, *Modern English*, London, 1873.

Hardy, Florence Emily, *The Life of Thomas Hardy*, Macmillan, London, 1930.

Hare, Augustus, *The Story of My Life*, 6 vols, London, 1896–1900.

Hole, S. Reynolds, *Then and Now*, Hutchinson, London, 1902.

Household Words (weekly journals conducted by Charles Dickens), 1850–9.

Hudson, Derek, *Munby, Man of Two Worlds*, Murray, London, 1972.

'Humphry, Mrs', *Manners for Men*, London, 1897.

James, Henry, *English Hours*, Heinemann, 1905.

James, M. R., *Eton and King's: Recollections Mostly Trivial*, Williams and Norgate, London, 1926.

Jefferies, Richard, *Hodge and his Masters*, London, 1880.

Jespersen, Otto, *A Modern English Grammar*, 7 vols, Allen and Unwin, Heidelberg, London and Copenhagen, 1922–49.

Kay-Shuttleworth, James, *Four Periods of Public Education as reviewed in 1832, 1839, 1846, 1862*, with an Introduction by Norman Morris, Harvester Press, Brighton, 1973.

Lewis, C. S., *Studies in Words*, Cambridge University Press, Cambridge, 1960.

Loane, M. E., *The Queen's Poor*, Arnold, London, 1905.

—— *The Next Street but One*, Arnold, London, 1907.

—— *From Their Point of View*, Arnold, London, 1908.

Lysons, Samuel, *Our Vulgar Tongue*, London, 1868.

Lytton, Bulwer, *England and the English*, 2nd edn, London, 1833.

Martin, R. B., *Tennyson: The Unquiet Heart*, Faber, London, 1980.

Mayhew, Henry, *London Labour and the London Poor*, 4 vols, Frank Cass, London, 1967.

Mitford, Nancy, (ed.), *Noblesse Oblige: An Enquiry into the Identifiable Characteristics of the English Aristocracy*, Hamish Hamilton, London, 1956.

Munster, Countless of, *My Memories and Miscellanies*, 2nd edn, Eveleigh Nash, London, 1904.

Oliphant, Laurence, *Piccadilly: A Fragment of Contemporary Biography*, London, 1870.

Oliphant, Mrs, *William Blackwood and His Sons: their Magazine and Friends*, 2 vols, London, 1897.

Orton, Harold, and Wright, Nathalia, *A Word Geography of England*, Seminar Press, London, 1974.

Page, Norman, *The Language of Jane Austen*, Blackwell, Oxford, 1972.

Phillipps, K. C., *Jane Austen's English*, Deutsch, London, 1970.

Ray, Gordon, N. *Thackeray: The Age of Wisdom*, Oxford University Press, London, 1958.

Richardson, Joanna, *The Pre-eminent Victorian: A Study of Tennyson*, Cape, London, 1962.

Roberts, W. J., *The Life and Friendships of Mary Russell Mitford*, Melrose, London, 1913.

Rogers, Samuel, *Recollections of the Table Talk of Samuel Rogers*, London, 1855.

Ross, A. S. C., 'Linguistic Class-indicators in Present-day English', *Neuphilologische Mitteilungen*, 55, 1954, pp. 20–56. (cited as 'Ross' above).

——*Don't Say It*, Hamish Hamilton, London, 1973.

Russell, G. W. E., *Collections and Recollections*, London, 1898.

Savage, W. H., *The Vulgarisms and Improprieties of the English Language*, London, 1833.

Smart, B. H., *Walker Remodelled: A New Critical Pronouncing Dictionary of the English Language*, London, 1836.

Smith, Logan Pearsall, *Reperusals and Recollections*, Constable, 1936.

Spencer, F. H., *An Inspector's Testament*, English Universities Press, London, 1938.

Stanley, Arthur Penrhyn, *The Life and Correspondence of Dr Arnold*, London, 1844.

Strang, Barbara, *Modern English Structure*, Arnold, London, 1962.

Tennyson, Hallam, *Alfred Lord Tennyson: A Memoir*, London, 1899.

Thompson, Flora, *Lark Rise to Candleford*, Oxford University Press, London, 1945.

Trollope, Anthony, *London Tradesmen*, reprinted from articles in the *Pall Mall Gazette* of 1880, Elkins, Mathews and Marott, London, 1927.

Trollope, Frances, *Domestic Manners of the Americans*, London, 1832.

Tucker, S. I., *Protean Shape: A Study in Eighteenth-century Vocabulary and Usage*, Athlone Press, London, 1967.

Victoria, Queen, *Leaves from the Journal of our Life in the Highlands*, London, 1868.

The Girlhood of Queen Victoria: A Selection from Her Majesty's Diaries, ed. Viscount Esher, 2 vols, Murray, London, 1912.

Walker, John, *A Critical Pronouncing Dictionary and Expositor of the English Language*, London, 1791.

Wells, J. C., *Accents of English*, 3 vols, Cambridge University Press, Cambridge, 1982.

Woodforde, James, *Diary of a Country Parson*, ed. John Beresford, Oxford University Press, London, 1935.

Wyld, H. C., *A History of Modern Colloquial English*, Blackwell, Oxford, 1936.

——*Studies in English Rhymes from Surrey to Pope*, Murray, London, 1923.

Young, G. M., *Victorian England: Portrait of an Age*, Oxford University Press, London, 1936.

Index of Words

General Index